NW 240

pages 173-188 missing

Wiltshire Record Society

(formerly the Records Branch of the Wiltshire
Archaeological and Natural History Society)

VOLUME 50

FOR THE YEAR 1994

Impression of 500 copies

THE LETTERS OF JOHN PENISTON,

SALISBURY ARCHITECT, CATHOLIC,

AND YEOMANRY OFFICER

1823 - 1830

EDITED BY

MICHAEL COWAN

TROWBRIDGE

1996

ISBN 0 901333 27 1

Produced for the Society by
Salisbury Printing Company Ltd, Salisbury
Printed in Great Britain

CONTENTS

PREFACE

Lt Col Cowan wishes to express his thanks to Mr Steven Hobbs, County and Diocesan Archivist, and the staff of the Wiltshire Record Office, with whom the Peniston archive is deposited on behalf of the Salisbury Diocesan Registry, for making the letter-books available, and for generous advice and assistance during the preparation of this edition. He would also like to acknowledge the kindness and help of Miss Suzanne Eward, Salisbury Cathedral Librarian; and Mr Bruce Purvis, Salisbury Local Studies Librarian, Wiltshire Libraries, Museums and Arts.

Members are asked to note that the International Standard Book Numbers printed in volumes 48 and 49 are incorrect. The correct numbers are: volume 48, ISBN 0 901333 25 5; volume 49, ISBN 0 901333 26 3.

Dr Jane Freeman retired in 1994 after six years' distinguished service as general editor of the Wiltshire Record Society series. Col Cowan and I both wish to express our appreciation of the skill with which she has guided this project, and I should like to add my personal gratitude for her kindness and advice upon my taking up the mantle of editor.

JOHN CHANDLER

ABBREVIATIONS

Boase: Boase, F., *Modern English Biography*, 3 vols., 1892

Brewer: *Brewer's dictionary of phrase and fable*, rev. I.H. Evans, 1970

CG: *The Clerical Guide*, 1829 ed.

Chambers: Chambers, Jill, *Wiltshire machine breakers*, 2 vols., 1993

DAB: Johnson, A., and Malone, D., *Dictionary of American Biography*, 1927-36

F: Foster, J., *Alumni Oxonienses, 1715-1886*, 1891

F-L: Fitzgerald-Lombard, Charles, *English and Welsh priests 1801-1914: a working list*, 1993

Graham: Graham, H., *The annals of the yeomanry cavalry of Wiltshire... from the time of its formation in 1794 to October 1884*, [vol.1], 1886

Hutchins: Hutchins, J., *The history and antiquities of the county of Dorset*, 3rd ed., 4 vols, 1861-70

Kelly: *Kelly's directory of Wiltshire*, 1848 and later eds.

LN: Horn, J.M. (ed.), *Le Neve, Fasti Ecclesiae Anglicanae, 1541-1857*, vol.6, [Salisbury Diocese], 1986

Newman and Pevsner: Newman, J., and Pevsner, N., *Dorset*, 1972 (The Buildings of England)

OED: *Oxford English dictionary*, 2nd ed., 1989

P: Pigot, J., *Pigot and Co's national commercial directory* [c.1830 editions used, unless stated; for Wiltshire see WRS vol.47]

RCH: Hoare, Sir Richard Colt, *The history of modern Wiltshire*, 6 vols, 1822-52

VCH: *Victoria history of the counties of England: Wiltshire* [in progress]

WAM: *Wiltshire Archaeological and Natural History Magazine* [in progress]

WRS: Wiltshire Record Society [in progress]

INTRODUCTION

THREE GENERATIONS OF LETTERS

John Peniston (c.1778-1848) founded a dynasty of Salisbury architects, which was continued by his son John Michael (1807-58), and grandson Henry (1832-1911).[1] Together they were responsible for more than 7,000 letters written between 1823 and 1858, which were copied into a series of letter-books now deposited in the Wiltshire Record Office (WRO 451/58-69). They form part of a much larger accumulation of Peniston business papers, which includes deeds, plans, printed and much miscellaneous material. Many of these items relate to letters included here. This volume presents in calendar form, with some full transcripts, nearly 1,700 letters written from October 1823, when the letter-books begin, until 31 December 1830. The latter date is arbitrary, chosen to produce a volume of manageable length and representative of the various facets of John Peniston's career. He was the writer of the majority of these letters, although during the course of 1829 and 1830 his son became increasingly involved in the more mundane aspects of the business, and a number of letters are his.

THE SCOPE OF THE LETTERS

Most of the letters are concerned with some aspect of the professional practice of John Peniston, by calling a surveyor and recorded on his gravestone as an architect. This work was wide-ranging in content and took place throughout Wiltshire, and to some extent in the adjacent counties. Within Wiltshire his additional responsibility as County Surveyor involved him in repairs and maintenance to bridges and prisons.

The business correspondence is interspersed with extensive and often detailed letters about the routine administration of the Wiltshire Yeomanry Cavalry, as well as the exceptional episode in November 1830 when the yeomanry suppressed the uprising of agricultural labourers referred to as the 'Swing' riots. These letters (**1625-41**, *passim*) provide important hitherto unpublished evidence about a well known and much studied local historical event.

His involvement as a prominent member of the local catholic community is reflected in a significant number of letters, in this sphere tending to chronicle the exceptional rather than routine events. There are occasional references also to a variety of business and private interests, including dealing in wine and whiting, estate management, and building cottages on speculation.

Peniston's letters are significant not just for what they say, but also for what they omit. He was a busy man, constantly travelling, who only wrote when it was necessary. The letters have little to say about building work in and immediately around Salisbury, which could easily be dealt with in person. There are only passing references to some matters which indicate substantial business. Conversely other projects, supervised from a distance, might generate a score or more letters. The rebuilding of Clarendon House and a dispute over work at Farnborough Place (Hants) result in more than fifty letters apiece.

The letters are a rich source of incidental information about the nature, extent and organization of a professional man's affairs in a relatively small provincial centre during the decade before the first impact of rail travel and the opening of the Victorian era. Some aspects of this career are discussed in greater detail below.

THE CORRESPONDENTS

The recipients of the letters form a fairly complete spectrum of society – aristocrats, gentry, clergy, professional colleagues, officials, tradesmen and artisans. A proportion lived in and around Salisbury, but Peniston's range of acquaintances extended throughout Wiltshire and neighbouring counties, particularly Hampshire and Dorset. More than 200 of the letters were sent to London addresses, and there were correspondents in Ireland and France.

Peers are noticeable because their houses were being refurbished or they were concerned with the Wiltshire Yeomanry. Some, such as Lord Palmerston, tended to be addressed directly; some feature in correspondence with their steward (Mr Webb for Lord Normanton) or their agent (Mr Baker in Dublin for the Earl of Enniskillen). Lord Arundell appears in both religious and yeomanry contexts.

Correspondence with Members of Parliament is a distinctive feature. Most letters are unrelated to parliamentary business, such as those to Charles Baring Wall, concerning work on his country house, Norman Court; or to John Benett, for whom Peniston was disposing of material from the ruins of Fonthill Abbey. When he needed to, however, Peniston drew on these useful contacts. Between February and April 1830 he canvassed opposition to a local bill which would have changed the basis of poor-rate assessment in Salisbury (**1253, 1311, 1314**). And in August 1830 he travelled to Essex to help in the successful election campaign for a parliamentary candidate, John Tyssen Tyrell (**1515**).

A further distinct group of correspondents is formed by his professional colleagues, architects and surveyors in neighbouring towns, such as Bath, Andover and Winchester. Peniston sometimes listed them when suggesting names for the selection of a referee (e.g. **556**). Some were clearly personal friends, such as Anthony Wingrove of Trowbridge, with whom he conducted a great deal of county business. Others were held in courteous respect, such as George Underwood of Bath (**1189**) or Mr Percy of Sherborne (**1611**). With William Garbett of Winchester, the most frequent correspondent in this category, his relationship fluctuated. Exasperation at his dilatory behaviour (e.g. **541, 598**) rapidly dissolved into satisfaction that he was appointed referee in a dispute (**566**). In 1830 Peniston rearranged the date of a meeting so that he and Garbett would be able to attend Salisbury race meeting (**1458**).

Relations between successful London architects and their provincial brethren are illustrated in various ways. Peniston appears to have had a close friendship with

Thomas Hopper (e.g. **755**), in whose office his son, John Michael, worked for a spell. He nevertheless wrote to him with deference, and seems happy to have regarded himself as Hopper's assistant (**704**). His relationship with a London engineer, Timothy Bramah, was similar. To a Catholic architect in London, Edward Foxhall, he offered to act as clerk of works (**1465**) but was rejected (**1483**). When a client replaced him with a Mr Tatham, he wrote that he did not have the vanity to compete with London architects (**1017**), but confronted by the overbearing William Hopperton he appears to have stood his ground (**1502**).

One professional colleague to whom Peniston may with some justification have felt superior was the young Richard Upjohn of Shaftesbury. Upjohn, through inexperience, had incurred the displeasure of the Shaftesbury Wesleyans (**799**), and facing bankruptcy decided to emigrate. He left for New York, with Peniston's good wishes (**793**) but with a debt unpaid (**852**); by 1840 he had established a successful practice, and became the first president of the American Institute of Architects. His Gothicizing influence on American architecture has been compared to that of Pugin in England, and he became, paradoxically, probably the most distinguished of Peniston's architectural correspondents.[2]

A majority of the business letters refer to the activities of tradesmen, their shortcomings greatly outnumbering their positive qualities. Peniston's chief complaints were of late delivery, shoddy workmanship, time-wasting, and failure to understand or follow plans. His most effective retaliation was to delay payment, a punishment which he often administered with relish, and occasionally with sarcasm (**451**). But it is in the nature of his business that letters about tradesmen were usually only required when matters had gone wrong, so that the collection as a whole places the building trade of the 1820s in an unrepresentively poor light. Accolades may be found among the brickbats (e.g. **696**), and by references and recommendations Peniston frequently strove to advance the careers of good workmen.

THE ARCHITECTURAL PRACTICE

In April 1824 a letter to Mr Watson (**39**) gives the first indication that Peniston was undertaking work for Lord Palmerston, the future prime minister, at his country home, Broadlands near Romsey. This particular letter concerns, typically, the coach-house and brewhouse. Most of his work on large and sometimes grand houses was mundane improvement. At Broadlands it continued throughout the period covered by this volume, concluding (**1432**) with a suggested solution to rising damp in the vestibule.

Peniston undertook other work for Lord Palmerston around his estate. A major project was Romsey National school, which permitted a rare excursion into style, with the observation that to use the Doric plan would be more costly (**200**). Six plans were enclosed, and it may be supposed that they were standards from a pattern book. Work on building the school was slow because there were litigious neighbours involved, and a committee. In all, some twenty letters relate to the work, including a request for prices for 'best memel inferior timber', from Richard Eldridge, a Southampton merchant, with whom Peniston regularly conducted business. That letter (**193**) also reveals another project to build some cottages, which in all other respects seems to have been progressing without the necessity for letters.

More modest than Broadlands, Langdown House at Hythe, beside Southampton Water, typifies Peniston's routine work. Dealings with the owner, Miss Mary Tate, started with a visit to her arranged in December 1825 (**358**), and the alterations were then outlined in March 1826 (**404**). Here as elsewhere they included the installation of water closets for the first time, and he wrote to her in London in April (**412**) about attaching one *en suite* to her bedroom. The closet proved troublesome, and in January 1827 Peniston discussed possible solutions with a Southampton plumber (**498**). Their suggestions presumably worked as there are no further letters on the subject.

The fullest, and somewhat unusual, description in these letters of work on a major property is that for Clarendon House, near Salisbury. In this case Peniston wrote frequently and in detail to the owner, Sir William Freemantle, often in London but sometimes in Brighton or Dorset, or to his steward Mr Webb. This is because, reluctantly, he was directing the work himself as principal contractor, and exposing himself to financial risk.

In May 1828 he wrote (**754**) that he would be pleased to direct the work, but had for some years declined the building business himself. By June he was sending specifications and estimates (**771**), and in August expressed a preference to engage tradesmen rather than contract for the work himself (**827**). By October he had been prevailed upon to offer to do the whole job of alteration, repair and building for £8,000 (**867**). This included a conservatory, which generated a complete correspondence in itself with Messrs Jones and Clark, metallic hot-house manufacturers of Birmingham, who had earlier supplied a conservatory for Norman Court at West Tytherley.

During the span of this volume nearly eighty letters were generated about the Clarendon work, covering a multitude of problems and arrangements. The furniture had to be moved and stored (**890**), a workman fell from the roof and was taken to Salisbury Infirmary (**954**); we learn how many coats of paint were to be applied to a door (**1332**), how the brewing machinery and billiard table were to be installed (e.g. **1210, 1273**), and about bells and clocks (**1252**).

Sir William Freemantle was not the easiest client, and had to be told firmly that it was too late to change the layout of the basement to the offices once the structure had reached the first floor (**988**). Much of the work, at Clarendon as elsewhere, involved 'offices', and after all the effort recorded it is rather sad to find it dismissed by Nikolaus Pevsner as a large nineteenth-century service wing, which may be demolished, and a disappointing interior, largely remodelled in the early nineteenth century.[3]

Apart from country houses, and smaller domestic projects, such as work on parsonage houses at Wylye, Hindon, and Great Wishford, and the terrace - De Vaux Place, Salisbury - in which the Peniston family themselves lived, the architectural practice embraced a great variety of building work. Peniston was involved, with Thomas Hopper, in work on remodelling Salisbury Council House (the present Guildhall), and his expertise was called upon when problems arose at Shaftesbury Town Hall (**480**), the Dorset County Asylum (**1586, 1594**), and Salisbury Infirmary (**97**). Tollhouses (**1208-9, 1687**), a Wesleyan chapel (**768**, etc), farm buildings (**244, 726**), an ice-house (**156**, etc), water-meadow hatches (**1111**), a public house (**3-4**, etc), and a malt house (**481**), were all premises which he planned or surveyed.

The period covered by the letters calendared in this volume, 1823-30, preceded the wholesale restoration and rebuilding of Anglican churches. Later, in 1831-2,

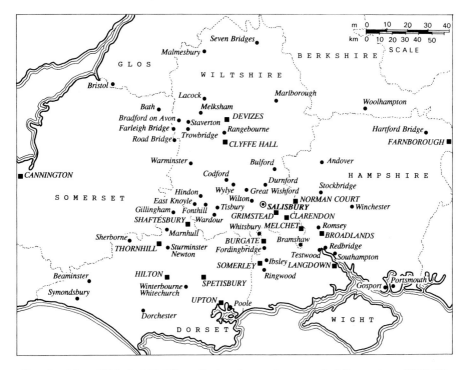

Location Map of Principal Buildings. Peniston's most important building projects, 1823-30,
are denoted by a square symbol and upper-case name. Other significant work or places
occurring frequently in the letters are denoted by a round symbol and lower-case name.

Peniston rebuilt in very creditable Gothic style St James Church, Devizes; but already
during the 1820s he was involved in work on three dilapidated village churches, at
Ibsley, Bramshaw and Alderbury. His Catholicism seems not to have disqualified him
from such work, and in other respects it was an advantage. Two Catholic
communities, at Spetisbury and Cannington, commissioned him to build chapels, and
his sometimes tempestuous dealings with their principals, Catherine Berrington and
Mary Knight, can be followed through the volume.

THE COUNTY SURVEYOR

Peniston's work as a surveyor becomes apparent as soon as the letter-books begin.
In November 1823 a letter to Rev Frederick Williams of Great Wishford (**5**)
introduces the subject of clerical dilapidations, without here actually using the term.
Assessing the amounts due for repairs from an outgoing to a new incumbent was a
routine task, and surveying Anglican parsonages was clearly useful bread-and-butter
work for the practice. In the letters Peniston often acknowledged being
recommended for such work, and almost all index entries to clergymen lead to
dilapidations. Most were dealt with rapidly, and occur in the letter-books only

because the agreed sum had to be reported to a distant client. In some instances, including Great Wishford, the commission led to further work, such as refurbishment of the rectory house.

Also in November 1823 we find four letters (**7–10**) which concern Peniston's formal appointment as Wiltshire County Surveyor, a post which he had held for eighteen months, and which he and his family continued to occupy until 1864. The County Surveyor was responsible to Quarter Sessions for the repair and maintenance of 'county' bridges (those on main roads), and short sections of road on either side leading up to them. The supervision of refractory and sometimes incompetent contractors employed on county bridges compelled Peniston to undertake considerable travel, and to pen some entertainingly exasperated correspondence (e.g. **1134, 1567**).

Apart from bridges the County Surveyor's other principal responsibility was towards the few buildings maintained by the county authority. In practice this meant the prisons at Fisherton (Salisbury), Marlborough and Devizes. Devizes new prison (also referred to as the gaol, house of correction, and penitentiary) had opened in 1817, five years before Peniston's appointment, and nearly forty letters relate to it, including a series devoted to the operation and ventilation of its notorious treadmill. A letter to Hopper in January 1830 (**1248**) about enlarging the prison wryly noted that 'the march of intellect' had produced 'more candidates for admission at the Devizes college than the present establishment can conveniently accommodate'. Peniston's experiences less than a year later might have made him less inclined to joke about the prison population.

THE WILTSHIRE YEOMANRY CAVALRY

In January 1825 occurs the first, somewhat oblique, reference to Peniston's role in the local yeomanry regiment (**187**). It is difficult to imagine in what other capacity he might have requested the loan of six carbines.

He had joined the Salisbury Troop of the regiment soon after its formation in 1794, was listed as a sergeant in 1797, when aged about twenty, and became Regimental Sergeant Major in 1809. He was to become a commissioned officer in 1825, and appears in practice to have performed many of the duties of the Adjutant. He was only appointed formally to that post in 1836 on the death of William Pettit. The first reference to the elderly Pettit, in June 1825 requesting extended leave of absence (**281**), is typical of a situation in which Peniston appears to have been overhauling the regimental administration for many years. Pettit's absences and shortcomings are more clearly indicated during 1829 and 1830.

Peniston must have been exceptionally knowledgeable about the actual conduct of affairs in a yeomanry regiment, and a great deal can be reconstructed from the individual letters. His involvement extended as far as ordering buttons from a London manufacturer (**1664**), and making complaint about a defect in the shakos supplied by a firm of army saddlers (**1660**). His letter of December 1830 to Berkeley Portman (**1665**), offering advice about establishing yeomanry troops in Dorset, is particularly illuminating about the actual, rather than the officially perceived, operation of the regiment.

The significant sequence of letters in November 1830 (**1625–9, 1634, 1636–41**, all transcribed in full) suggests that Peniston played an even stronger central role in the yeomanry at a time when there were well founded fears of popular uprising and revolution. Within the space of six days he was the person responding to information and taking the initiative in calling out his own Salisbury Troop, guiding his noble superiors, setting out a plan for the deployment of all the troops throughout the county, riding with his own troop for two days, commanding overnight a detached element at West Park, Rockbourne, as well as dealing with minutiae such as finding six pistols for the Hindon Troop - while all the time recording events in the lengthy fashion which reflected the delicacy of his position. However, he had been in a similar position before, precisely ten years earlier. This was during a riot in Salisbury in November 1820, provoked by the Earl of Liverpool's perceived leniency towards Queen Caroline.

That he was not always well disposed towards his military colleagues is revealed in an unguarded letter to an old friend (**866**). The letter also provides rare evidence of his physical state: aged about fifty, he wrote that he was becoming weighty, although the sixteen stone his horse had to carry presumably included his cavalry accoutrements. In later years occasional references to illness, generally gout, become more frequent, and this affliction was often given as the reason for delay.

ROMAN CATHOLICISM

Letters written during 1826 contain many of the references to Peniston's involvement with the affairs of his co-religionists. The correspondence was triggered by the illness and death of the Salisbury Catholic community's priest, Rev Nicholas Begin, a Frenchman who had ministered in the city since 1796.[4] The settlement of his estate and the financing of a successor found Peniston acting as the community's spokesman. During Begin's terminal illness, in March 1826, he dealt with relatives from France (**391**), and kept the Catholic hierarchy informed, while trying to calculate how the community might support an English priest to replace him (**398**). The succession had been resolved by January 1827, and Peniston wrote to thank Bishop Collingridge for appointing Rev O'Connor to the Salisbury mission (**497**).

Begin's estate was a more intractable problem. Incidental references (**443, 507**) reveal that in July 1826 and February 1827 Peniston paid visits to Paris. This was no light undertaking, especially the latter journey in winter, and the timing suggests that his main purpose was to try to resolve Begin's affairs. A letter to Begin's niece in France in August 1827 (**622**) reveals the extent of the problem - he had died owing nearly £500; and the debt had still not been settled when the matter passes out of the correspondence in November 1828 (**889**).

In France Peniston had several contacts, including an apparently close family friend, the wine exporter J.H. Gillo, from whom he made purchases for connoisseurs among the local gentry (**507**, etc). To Gillo he transmitted news of Catholic families in Salisbury, including the Harringtons. The death in 1828 (**850**) of his friend Thomas Harrington, landlord of the Black Horse Inn, committed Peniston to further vexatious financial business. Harrington died insolvent, as it transpired, and Peniston was executor of his estate, a task made more difficult by the profligate habits of his widow (**1558**, etc).

Occasional letters inform us of other Catholic contacts. There is a reference to the Jesuit college in Lancashire, Stonyhurst, where one of Peniston's sons boarded, and from which – as sons do – he failed to write (**667**). This was probably James William Peniston, his second son, then eighteen years old, who subsequently trained in Rome and entered the Jesuit priesthood in 1838.[5] Peniston maintained close links with the community at Wardour and its priest Richard Parker, helping where he could to solve problems (**619**), or advance individual careers (**825**). Controversy over the passage of the Catholic Relief Bill in March and April 1829 saw him organizing a counter-petition against Anti-Catholic propaganda in Wiltshire (**990–1**), and the pleasure felt in 'becoming really a free man' was expressed to John Benett the following year (**1253**).

TRANSPORT AND COMMUNICATION

Peniston travelled extensively about Wiltshire and beyond. He sent and received letters and packets, arranged and attended meetings, and ordered building materials and other goods, to be delivered by waggon, or by sea via Southampton or Poole.

He sometimes indicated when he himself intended to travel by stagecoach or hired chaise, but by implication more generally he travelled on horseback. In 1828 he wrote to a friend in Dorchester asking him to look out for a horse to replace his 'old charger' (**866**). A significant proportion of his letters deal with arrangements to meet clients, professional colleagues or tradesmen, and he usually stipulated that he would be in a particular village, house or inn on a specific day, rarely more precisely than in the morning or afternoon.

There was routine use of the postal system, which could generally be relied upon to deliver a prompt service. Sequences of dates on successive letters to particular individuals indicate exchanges within a day or two. 'Franks', or envelopes countersigned by an M.P. or other privileged person entitled to free use of the postal service, were obtained whenever possible; and packets 'too heavy for a frank' might be sent by coach or carrier. References to the postal system often reflect the sender's failure to pay postage (**586, 1382**), and in one instance Peniston refused to pay what he considered an exorbitant charge (**1358**).

Travel by stagecoach, for those accustomed to it, was straightforward and routine. Frustrations and delays occurred sporadically, but in general these resulted from the impossibility of communicating quickly a change of plan (**1025, 1544**) rather than from unreliability. As a seasoned passenger Peniston sometimes gave advice about stagecoach routes (**265, 1472**), although for a distant journey he sought advice himself (**893**).

Some of the new features to be installed in the larger houses, such as water closets, brewing machinery, and cast iron conservatories, together with specialist materials, including high quality plaster, mastic, roman cement and wallpaper, had to be conveyed from London or Birmingham. Timber was ordered from importers at Southampton, and mastic and other materials were also shipped to Southampton or Poole. The Kennet and Avon Canal was used to bring timber from Bath to Devizes (**1606**). Inevitably the carriage of materials occurs in letters most often when arrangements went wrong. The conservatory for Norman Court was delayed while on its way from Birmingham via Southampton (**348**, cf. **1046**). A Salisbury carrier refused to handle certain items (**354**). Inadequate packing or inept handling jeopardized the safety of window frames (**356**) and chimney pieces (**1199**). Conversely the routine carriage of local materials - brick, stone, timber - rarely generated correspondence, unless there was some exceptional circumstance, such as a queue of carts waiting at a brickworks (**1112**).

FAMILY AND PERSONAL

The Penistons were a prominent and what would today be called an upwardly mobile Catholic family in south Wiltshire during the last decades of the eighteenth century and for much of the nineteenth.[1] Thomas Peniston was 'director of the bricklayers' at New Wardour Castle, near Tisbury, during its construction between 1770 and 1776. His son John Peniston, the subject of this volume, practised as a professional man in the various spheres already described until his death in 1848 at the age of seventy.

John and his wife Sarah had five sons and five daughters between 1807 and 1822, but domestic matters intrude only slightly into the correspondence. To old colleagues there was the occasional expression of good wishes, and sometimes Mrs Peniston was associated in these. There is a more substantive reference to her when he congratulates a colleague's son on his marriage and hopes that it will be as happy as his own (**1364**). On a very few occasions she replied to letters in his absence or undertook errands (e.g. **990-1**).

Their eldest son, John Michael Peniston, is the only family member to figure prominently in the correspondence. He followed his father into the architectural practice, succeeded him as County Surveyor for Wiltshire, and became active in the Yeomanry. He died suddenly in May 1858, while officiating as Regimental Sergeant Major at the annual regimental camp, and while still fully in control of affairs. His eldest surviving son, Henry Peniston, appears to have inherited the business and, briefly, the public appointments; but the surviving letter-books end seven months later in December 1858.

John Michael was only seventeen years old when he first occurs in the letter-book in April 1824 (**40**), making sketches of doors for Great Wishford rectory. By December 1824 he was writing to a supplier, very briefly and correctly, on his father's behalf (**177**). Thereafter he occurs sporadically, assisting in the business, until May 1828 when he travelled to London to work as an assistant in Thomas Hopper's office (**755**). He appears to have been involved there in drawing up plans to alter Salisbury Council House, and acted as intermediary between Hopper and his father in Salisbury. His sojourn in London was brief, however (tension with his father over the matter is apparent in **778**), and by the end of the year he was back in Salisbury. Thereafter his role in the family business increased, and in the course of a frantically busy period through much of 1830 he was acting as his father's deputy during frequent absences and indispositions.

Other sons are less clearly visible in the letters. James William (born 1809), who entered the priesthood, was probably the son who failed to write home from Stonyhurst. George Augustus (born 1810) went with John Michael to London in

1828 and shared lodgings with him while working for a carpenter and joiner (**745**). He subsequently lost his chest during a journey to North Wales (**893-4, 909-10**), and was apparently working away from home during 1829 and 1830 (**918, 1585**). William Michael (born 1814) was studying in his father's office in 1829, while attending Henry Hatcher's school for mathematics (**951**). One undated letter, probably of October 1829 (**1178**), is signed by him, but may merely be a doodle. In May 1830 he was packed off to London to work for the Pimlico engineer, Timothy Bramah, with whom his father had a longstanding business connection and personal friendship (**1351, 1358-9**, etc.).

Peniston's daughters do not figure at all in the correspondence, apart from a single reference to 'Ellen' (Eleanora Arundell, born 1812). In this letter (**1025**) Ellen and other family members all seem to contribute to a confusing situation that provokes from Peniston a caustic but affectionate observation about the paucity of brains in his family.

The only other allusions to Peniston's family occur when he had to distance himself from cousins or other relatives working in Salisbury. In 1825 a matter relating to the 'late firm of Peniston and Co' was redirected to William or James Peniston (**293**). In 1828 a regular supplier was asked to distinguish him from his cousin James of the *City* of Salisbury, not the Close (**763**). And in 1830 a client was reminded to address letters to Peniston in the Close, so as not to be confused with a relative who was a builder (**1252**).

THE DOCUMENTS

When the letter-books begin Peniston had been in business for many years, but appears previously not to have recorded his correspondence in this way, as the title to the first gathering (see below) implies. With a few exceptions written from memory afterwards (e.g. **848**), the letter-books appear to consist of verbatim copies, by Peniston or assistants, made before the letters were sent. Several different hands may be identified, written with varying degrees of legibility and haste; and occasional mistakes in transcription are apparent (e.g. **798**).

The letters calendared here are contained in two paper volumes, bound in original nineteenth-century card covers. They are deposited in the Wiltshire Record Office, with call numbers WRO 451/58 and WRO 451/59, and are part of a collection transferred from Salisbury Diocesan Registry. How they, and other Peniston material, came to be in the registry is uncertain, but it is possible that they were once in the care of a solicitor's practice which also acted as diocesan registrar. The earlier volume (WRO 451/58) includes letters from October 1823 to 29 August 1827, here numbered **1-622**. The later volume (WRO 451/59) begins on 1 September 1827 (letter **623**), and continues beyond the span of this edition, to 9 September 1833.

WRO 451/58 is an ungainly volume, made up of five sections of differing length and page size, which prior to their binding together were regarded as separate letter-books, and numbered 1-5 accordingly. Dimensions (height before width), number of pages, dates and letter numbers (in this edition) are as follows: 1. 19.5 x 16cm, 52pp, Oct. 1823 to 25 March 1824, **1-36**; 2. 24 x 19cm, 52pp, 1 April 1824 to 26 Aug 1824, **37-95**; 3. 21 x 27cm, 94pp, 27 Aug 1824 to 7 Feb 1825, **96-197**; 4. 20 x 16.3cm,

336pp, 13 Feb 1825 to 11 Jan 1827, **200–484**; 5. 21 x 27cm, 94pp, 8 Dec 1826 to 29 Aug 1827, **485–622**. Neither pages nor letters are numbered. The longest book, number 4, is in fact made up of ten gatherings, some of which had previously been ruled and used for accounts, 1811-22. The letters are fitted in wherever space was available. The first page of book 2 is taken up with a mathematical calculation.

WRO 451/59 is more uniform in character, and seems to be made up of a further six letter-books, each of three gatherings, 43 x 27cm. The gatherings vary in length from about 18-40 pages each. Letters written between 6 Oct 1828 and 20 Nov 1828 (**869–904**), were copied into another, smaller gathering (18.5 x 24cm), which was probably regarded as a separate letter-book, and was subsequently bound with the others in its correct place. Thus these letter-books would have been numbered 6-12, but only the front cover of number 11 survives, and this is inscribed 'Letter Book no. 11 from May 11 1831 - May 11 1832'. During 1830 a tally was begun of the number of letters written, and from 30 Sept. 1830 (**1559**) the letters were numbered consecutively (see **1695**, note 1). This numbering had reached 393 by 11 May 1831, when book 10 ends, and was continued through subsequent books.

EDITORIAL NOTE

This edition offers a brief calendar of all the letters copied into WRO 451/58-9 until the end of 1830, with transcripts or partial transcripts of selected letters of particular interest. Significant place and personal names mentioned in the letters are included in the calendar, and are indexed. There is a separate index of selected subjects. Supplied matter, editorial or textual, has been introduced into the calendar in italics enclosed within square brackets, or as footnotes. Original spellings and (generally) titles of personal names have been retained, but most place names have been printed in their modern form. Unusual or aberrant spellings of identifiable place names have been printed, in round brackets, after the modern form of the name. The index frequently supplies additional information about persons and places, not given in the calendar.

Letters, except where noted, are presented in the order in which they appear in the document, and each has been given a separate entry. The form of entry is as follows: entry number, date of letter, name and address of recipient; summary of letter; footnotes. Where letters or portions of letters are transcribed in full this fact is signified by enclosing the transcript within single quotes. The punctuation within transcribed passages has been modernized. The character of letters not transcribed has been retained, where possible, in the summary by the retention of significant phrases and expressions. Many of the sources cited in footnotes have been abbreviated; a list of abbreviations precedes this introduction.

NOTES

1. For more biographical and other detail about John Peniston and his family see 'The Penistons: a Salisbury family of Catholic architects and yeomen 1770-1911', by Michael Cowan, in *Wiltshire Archaeological and Natural History Magazine*, vol. 80, 1986, pp.184-91

2. See 'Richard Upjohn' in *Dictionary of American Biography*, vol. 10, 1936, pp.125-6

3. Pevsner, N., and Cherry, B., *Wiltshire*, 2nd ed, 1975 (The Buildings of England), p.181

4. *Victoria History of Wiltshire*, vol.3, 1956, p.94

5. Fitzgerald-Lombard, Charles, *English and Welsh priests 1801-1914: a working list*, 1993, p.219

PENISTON LETTERS 1823–30

CALENDAR

1823

1 [*undated*[1]]. Mr Absalom, Portsea.
Suggests that a disputed account be referred to Mr Bramble.

1. Precedes **3–4**.

2 29 Oct. 1823. Bramah Esq, Pimlico.
Requests a survey of the tread mill at Devizes penitentiary built by Messrs G and H Stothert of Bath.

3 29 Oct. 1823. Mr Absalom, Portsea.
Has written to Mr Bramble about the Northumberland.[1]

1. Northumberland Arms, Gosport. See **24**.

4 29 Oct. 1823. Mr B Bramble.
Agrees to him handling the business of the repairs at the Northumberland.[1] Repeats that Mr Absalom may have a fair profit while doing justice to Mr Whitchurch.

1. Northumberland Arms, Gosport. See **24**.

5 4 Nov. 1823. Rev F D Williams.
Claim on the executors of the late Rev Mr Birch amounts to £8 1s. 6d. for the rickhouse yard and ground adjoining. Payment of £20 5s. is due for fixtures left in the Rectory House.[1]

1. Probably Great Wishford. See **40**.

6 7 Nov. 1823. W D Whitmarsh Esq.
Value of house, stable and garden in the Close[1] occupied by Miss Neave is £46. Miss Neave wishes the business settled soon.

1. Salisbury: P.

7 [*undated*[1]]. Mr Mark Hanks.
Repeats instruction to have the bridge[2] cased by Essington or some other workman. Materials to be preserved and the road made passable as soon as floods allow.

1. Written at the same time as **8**.
2. Cow Bridge or Holloway, Malmesbury. See **8**.

8 9 Nov. 1823. Mr Essington.
Notes that work done at Cow Bridge and Holloway [*Malmesbury*] has been destroyed by flood. Expects matters to be put right.

9 9 Nov. 1823. Mr Flower.
Had not visited Melksham Bridge as planned. Mr Jeffery had confirmed its safety. Had told Slater to drop a line over the bridge to check that sunken stone was still in position. Arranges meeting.

10 30 Nov. 1823. Mr Fleet.[1]
Discusses the confusion over his suggestion that Lady Pollen[2] appoint a surveyor to discuss a dispute with the county over river work that affected her wall.

1. Described in letter as Lady Pollen's steward.
2. Of Bulford Manor. See VCH15, p.66.

11 30 Nov. 1823. The Coal Brook Dale Company.
Requests them to inspect and repair flood damage to iron bridge at Bulford.

12 30 Nov. 1823. Mr G Stothert.
Cannot, with propriety, send a copy of Mr Bramah's report.[1] Promises to seek permission from the magistrates. Arranges meeting.

1. About Devizes Penitentiary. See **2**.

13 [*undated*]. Mr W Warren.
Declines to discuss Lady Pollen's business.[1] Had agreed to meet a respectable surveyor. Has already had a letter from Mr Fleet, who had paid the postage on it.

1. Probably at Bulford. See **10**.

14 30 Nov. 1823. B Wingrove Esq.
Confirms his intention to visit Studley bridge to order repairs.

15 [*undated*[1]]. Messrs G and H Stothert.
Reports success of experiments with their fly. Suggests various details concerning entry, ventilation and to stop rain penetration.[2]

1. Later than a meeting held on 4 Dec. 1823.
2. A small sketch is attached, which appears to refer to Devizes tread-mill. See **2** and **12**.

16 11 Dec. 1823. Dr Fisher.
Notes complaints about work at Burbage. Will investigate when Butler has finished the offices.

17 11 Dec. 1823. Grosett, Esq.
Intends to inspect Lacock Bridge. Thinks Ray Bridge in no immediate danger but had sent a person to see if it needed temporary support and will examine it again.

18 17 Dec. 1823. G Bucknall Estcourt, Esq.
Cannot find Mr Daniel's bill and will send for duplicate [*see* **20**]. Suggests meeting a few days before next sessions to facilitate payment of accounts.

19 17 Dec. 1823. Messrs Newman and Sons.
Has no knowledge of a claim on Mr Bennet. It would be passed to the latter's agents, Messrs Bowles and Chitty of Shaftesbury.

20 27 Dec. 1823. Mr Daniel, Surveyor, Warminster.
Asks for duplicate bill.

21 27 Dec. 1823. Mr Flooks.
Resigns from the Netton business. Has told Mr Skeats.

22 [*undated*]. G B Estcourt Esq.
Sends an abstract of bills from Mr Daniel. Will bring the bills himself because they are too heavy for a frank.[1]

1. A frank was an envelope bearing the superscribed signature of a person, such as an M.P., entitled to send letters post free: OED.

1824

23 18 Jan. 1824. Mr Darby, Coalbrookdale.
Reports that proposals to repair and re-erect the iron bridge at Bulford have been agreed by the magistrates. Work will start when the river level permits. A committee of magistrates will examine plans for the proposed new bridge at Woodford. Needs to know the weight of the castings to work out transport costs and type of abutment. Asks if bricks set in roman cement can be used as there is no stone quarry near.

24 18 Jan. 1824. Mr Absalom.
Regrets that attempts by Mr Bramble to settle the cost of repairs at the Northumberland Arms, Gosport have failed. Messrs Whitchurch offer a further £100 or arbitration [see **3-4**].

25 24 Jan. 1824. Mr Forder, Winchester.
Asks for information about a bill disputed by Mr Fisher [see **63**]. Some detail dates from mid-1820. Has little hope of success.

26 6 Feb. 1824. Mr Bramble.
Asks for help in arranging repairs at the late Rood's house in High Street, Gosport, for Mr Compigny. Will also meet Mr Absalom.

27 6 Feb. 1824. Mr Absalom.
Arranges meeting. Hopes to conclude the unpleasant business of the Northumberland [see **24**].

28 14 Feb. 1824. Miss Bowles, 7 Hanover Buildings.[1]
Encloses ultimatum from Messrs Roe. Suggests that it is paid on condition that bells and grates are included.

1. Probably Southampton, where Hanover Buildings was a fashionable address. Henry Roe and Son was a Southampton firm of builders: P.

29 4 March 1824. James Cull Esq, surveyor, Portsmouth.
Arranges meeting at Whitsbury (*Whitchbury*) or Rockbourne to assess clerical dilapidations. Agrees that there should be third party nominated and suggests someone from Winchester.

30 5 March 1824. Hon Coventry jun.
Intends to send plan of proposed alterations[1] to Mr Chalk by mail cart. Will arrange meeting.

1. To Burgate House. See **38**.

31 5 March 1824. Mr Flower.[1]
Presses for receipts and tradesmen's bills for work on Melksham Bridge and the connected roads. Needed immediately if they are to be passed at the next sessions.

1. Pencilled in later, in same hand.

32 6 March 1824. Mr Chalk.
Will send plans for addition to Mr Coventry's house.[1] Asks for estimate and specifications. Discusses passages, butler's pantry, servants' hall and housekeeper's room, which cannot be bigger without moving the coal shed.

1. Burgate House. See **38**.

33 6 March 1824. James Cull Esq, builder, Portsmouth.
Postpones meeting at Whitsbury.

34 15 March 1824. Mrs Moore, Close, Salisbury.
Estimates, with difficulty, cost of repairs to her dilapidated house at £285.

35 24 March 1824. Hon John Coventry jun, Burgate (*Burgat*) Cottage, Fordingbridge.
The stable building at Ibsley is to be pulled down by Mr Chalk immediately, and Mr Chalk may purchase bricks. Regarding the purchase of timber Mr Chalk must speak to a carpenter named Wells. Asks Coventry to show the letter to Chalk.

36 25 March 1824. H W Coles, slater, Southampton.
Asks for estimate for undertaking 'Countess'[1] slating at Melchet (*Melkshot*) Park, four miles from Romsey.

1. An intermediate size of roofing slate, 1ft 8in by 10in: OED.

37 1 April 1824. Earl of Malmesbury, Heron Court, Ringwood.
Awaits Dr Keate's letter. Has already heard from Mr Attwood and has surveyed buildings at Chilmark. Mr Lear will not claim dilapidations.

38 3 April 1824. Hon John Coventry jun., Burgate Cottage, Fordingbridge.
Will be visiting Burgate House to arrange work. Involves Mr Chalk. Queries form of
agreement Mr Coventry wants.

39 10 April 1824. Mr Watson.
Repeats long technical instructions, already given verbally to Pope, about placing a
cistern near the coachhouse and brewhouse at Broadlands. Details to be discussed
with Lord Palmerston when he is present.

40 16 April 1824.[1] Rev F D Williams, Wishford.
Refers to sketches of doors prepared by his son. Invites comment for their
improvement.

1. MS *Friday evening*, date not given.

41 16 April 1824. Rev Boucher, Hilton, Dorset.
Arranges to meet Mr Tulloch at Hilton in connection with work there.

42 [*undated*[1]]. [*addressee not stated*[2]].
Acknowledges letter received from Mr Coventry junior. Replies that the kitchen
window should be the same level as servants' hall and housekeeper's room.[3] Wells had
been told to re-use old bricks from Ibsley.

1. In response to a letter of 14 April, having been away four or five days.
2. Perhaps Mr Chalk. See **35, 38**.
3. Burgate House. See **35, 38**.

43 [*undated*]. Mr Cull, Portsmouth.
Technical instructions and seeking an opinion.

44 17 April 1824. Mr M Hanks.
Requests a receipt for monies paid for bridge works, including Cow Bridge
[*Malmesbury*].

45 [*undated*]. G B Estcourt Esq, Chairman of Committee of Accounts, County of
Wiltshire.
Encloses and explains book of accounts and abstract.

46 24 April 1824. Mr Lane, Eton College.
Arranges to meet at West Hale. [?*Hartley Wespall*].

47 24 April 1824. Rev H Boucher.
Changes an appointment.[1]

1. At Hilton. See **41**.

48 29 April 1824. Lord Malmesbury.
Has met Dr Keate's surveyor and inspected the dilapidations at Hartley Wespall (*Westpale*). Seeks instructions about the dilapidations at Chilmark.

49 1 May 1824. Lord Malmesbury.
Reports on dilapidations at Chilmark and Hartley Wespall, and arranges for the resolution of a discrepancy.

50 1 May 1824. Mr Lane.[1]
Has sent report on dilapidations at Hartley Wespall to Lord Malmesbury.

1. Pencilled in later in same hand.

51 2 May 1824. Messrs Grellier and Co.
Introduces Mr Dyke of Netton[1] who is building a bridge for the county. Orders 35 casks of cement for 'water work'.

1. Netton in Durnford, not Bishopstone. William Dyke, bricklayer of Netton, Durnford, is listed in Kelly, 1848 ed.

52 1 May 1824. Rev Dr Fisher,[1] Charter House, London.
Has the Poulshot account and will be in London.

1. Probably Dr John Fisher, Bishop of Salisbury, 1807-25, who was patron of Poulshot: LN, CG.

53 7 May 1824. W Cope, Stoneham Park.[1]
Explains that no-one can attend.

1. Letter written by J M Peniston in his father's absence.

54 7 May 1824. Messrs Green, Grillier, Morgan.[1]
Explains that Mr Dyke's cement should be sent to Netton[2] near Salisbury.

1. Letter written by J M Peniston in his father's absence. The company is listed in P as Grieve, Grellier and Morgan, but is variously spelled in the letters.
2. Netton in Durnford. See **51** note 1.

55 2 June 1824. Mr Strong.
Requests repairs to Ray, Lacock and Bulford Bridges. Asks about Boreham Bridge which has already been undertaken. Instructs preparation of 230[1] feet more coping for Mr Charles Wall,[2] to be sent to Devizes. General tone of dissatisfaction.

1. *sic*, cf. 62.
2. For Norman Court. See **62**.

56 3 June 1824. Mr Garbett, Winchester.
Sending memoranda with additions in red ink. Asks for early completion of the business.[1]

1. Rockbourne dilapidations. See **60**.

57 3 June 1824. J Bush Esq.
Cannot be at Bradford before 16 June. Will come then prepared to give orders for the immediate repair of the road mentioned.

58 19 June 1824. Mr Garbett.
Asks for valuation of the Whitsbury dilapidations.

59 19 June 1824. Mr Cull.
Seeks a discharge to pay to Rev Purvis £231 2s. 3d. estimated by Mr Garbett for the dilapidations at Whitsbury.

60 19 June 1824. Rev W Davis.
Pleased that action about the Whitsbury dilapidations meets with approval. Also received from the Mrs Longden's agent Bank Post Bills for £231 2s. 3d. Has written to Mr Cull about payment to Rev Purvis. Has also written to Mr Garbett about Rockbourne dilapidations [**56**]. Encloses valuation certificate estimating dilapidations of the rectorial buildings at £96 10s. 3d.

61 22 June 1824. Earl of Enniskillen.
Accepts commission to take charge of his Lordship's property at East Grimstead. Arranges to visit. Acknowledges Lord Pembroke's recommendation.

62 26 June 1824. Mr Strong, mason, Box near Bath.
Asks if the estimate for Bulford Bridge included both piers, as the estimate had used the singular form. Asks for delivery date for 320[1] feet of coping for Norman Court.

1. *sic*, cf. **55**.

63 26 June 1824. Mr Forder, surveyor, Winchester.
Has, with Mr Fisher, examined his account with the late Mr Morris [*see* **25**]. Asks why the bill of £2 11s 0d for workmen's beer is shown as £3 19s 0d.

64 27 June 1824. Mr Edwards, Crown Inn, Melksham.
Notes Dunford's proposals, which are fair. His wages are high but he is recommended by Mr Jeffreys. Not satisfied with carpenter but he can continue to be employed in the absence of anyone better and because only a small amount of carpentry involved. Mr Dunford can place orders and employ men he needs. Stone to be delivered to water's edge of Melksham Bridge.

65 27 June 1824. Mr Strong, mason.
Comments that estimate of stone is 900 feet, too much for one pier but not enough for both. To save time should immediately send enough stone for both piers. Will be charged for any delay. Encloses plan.

66 1 July 1824. Mr Strong, mason, Box.
Having had no replies about Bulford Bridge, has engaged Mr Beavis of Tisbury as mason.

67 2 July 1824. Mr Guthrie, Grange.
Queries construction method at Norman Court where a wall has settled affecting columns in the entrance hall. If he is going to Melchett Park to mark timber for the Grange, would he arrange a meeting at Norman Court to discuss the problem.

68 3 July 1824. Mr H P Burt, Devizes.
Complains that, by proposing additional support for a platform being removed from the tread-mill at Devizes Prison and re-erected at Marlborough Prison, the economy of re-using it will be lost. If it cannot be erected without additional castings, the work must wait until Peniston has visited Devizes.

69 5 July 1824. Mr Forder, surveyor, Winchester.
Has agreed with Mr Fisher to deduct £11 1s 0d from demand on Carter's estate. Enquires about disposal of papers.

70 5 July 1824. Rt Hon Lord Viscount Folkestone, Coleshill, Faringdon.
Discusses Fryars Bridge and West Mill Bridge, both on county boundary, and possible improvements before adoption as county bridges.

71 7 July 1824. Messrs Stevens and Blackmore, Chamberlains to the Mayor and Commonalty of the City of New Sarum.
Reports completion of work to the portico of the Council House according to statement delivered to the Royal Exchange Fire Office.

72 12 July 1824. Rt Hon Lord Viscount Palmerston.
Agrees a proposal for the kitchen entrance at Broadlands. Has found a veined marble fireplace for his Lordship's dressing room and ordered Marsh the mason to prepare Portland stone slab for hearth, assuming it will be covered by a rug. Plasterer had been delayed which in turn delayed the Salisbury carpenters. The domestic carpenters are making better progress but he had been sorry to find Pope alone at work in the laundry, the others being engaged in the park.

73 12 July 1824. [*addressee not stated*].
Arranges a meeting. Clarke and the county bricklayer can do the School House job but for anything of consequence he would employ Buckly.

74 17 July 1824. [*addressee not stated*].
Explains that an account has been sent to the Committee and is in the hands of Phipps.

75 17 July 1824. [*addressee not stated*[1]].
Has altered windows as suggested. Agrees changes to some walls.

1. Letter begins, 'My Lord'.

76 17 July 1824. Mr Darby, Coal Brook Dale.[1]
Work is to start on Bulford Bridge on 26 July and the assistance of their man is sought as soon as convenient. If he is authorized to give a receipt he can take payment for the survey.

1. Pencilled in later in same hand.

77 20 July 1824. Rt Hon Earl of Enniskillen.
Has received power of attorney. Has let Grimstead Manor to Mr Wall for £10 a year. The late Mr Wynch's accounts not yet prepared. Cannot yet ascertain Tubb's balance. Beauchamp has never paid rent for his garden, which was taken from the waste. His payment will be fixed and discussions held with other cottagers about their rents. Notes he has to be cautious about some quit rents.

78 20 July 1824. Mr Strong, stonemason, Box, near Bath.
Complains about no answers to letters, written from Devizes, about bridge repairs and coping stone for Mr Wall [*see* **55, 62, 65, 66**].

79 24 July 1824. Mr Strong, mason, Box.
Instructs him to write direct to C B Wall Esq, M.P., at Norman Court to arrange for their respective waggons to meet. Pleased to hear that Ray Bridge finished and enquires about Boreham Bridge. Will be at Lacock on Wednesday to examine the bridge which Mr Grossett wishes to have repaired.

80 26 July 1824. Rev C H Ridding.
Acknowledges request to value dilapidations.[1] Suggests representatives of late incumbent be informed. Understands from Mr Davis's office that there is faculty to remove barn. Thanks Mr Seagram for recommending him.

1. At Orcheston St Mary. See **185**.

81 31 July 1824. Mr Forder, Winchester.
Asks whether the Winchester Canal Company (as described to him) will hire out a screw pump for about a month, and at what rate.

82 31 July 1824. Mr B Bramble, builder, Portsmouth.
Messrs Whitchurch and Co. and Mr Paul and Co. will purchase the fountain. Construction of a wall is detailed. Plans requested. Asks for name of anyone who will hire out a screw pump.

83 2 Aug. 1824. C B Wall Esq, Grange, Hants.
Arranges for him to meet Guthrie at Norman Court to discuss the entrance hall columns.

84 4 Aug. 1824. Mr Bramble, builder, Portsmouth.
Acknowledges plan.[1] Copy needed by Mr Compigny or a reduced scale drawing could be put on the deed. Asks for remaining estimates, particularly for the 10 foot high party wall.

1. Probably relating to a house in High Street, Gosport. See **26**.

85 6 Aug. 1824. C B Wall Esq, Norman Court.
Would direct the masons as desired. On returning from a meeting with Lord Palmerston, seeks a bed on Saturday night in order to meet Guthrie the following day. Lord Enniskillen approves Wall having the manor of Grimstead for £10 a year with only the condition that he cannot grant any lease.

86 14 Aug. 1824.[1] George Underwood, Esq.
Arranges a meeting at Hilton.

1. Part of letter written the previous day.

87 17 Aug. 1824. W Salmon jun. Esq, Devizes.
Has forwarded a plan and estimate for an erection in 'our market'.

88 17 Aug. 1824. Lord Viscount Palmerston.
Confirms that it is feasible to have a bath sunk below the level of the closet flooring adjoining Lord Palmerston's bedroom.[1]

1. Presumably at Broadlands.

89 21 Aug. 1824. Mr Garbett, architect, Winchester.
Encloses cheque for £4 13s 9d, fee as referee on the subject of dilapidations at Whitsbury.

90 23 Aug. 1824. George Underwood Esq, architect, Bath.
Asks for confirmation of day they will meet at Hilton.

91 24 Aug. 1824. Mrs Heath, Park Cottage, Devizes.
Proposes to visit her next Monday afternoon.

92 24 Aug. 1824. Messrs Green, Grellier and Co.
Orders 15 more casks of roman cement for Mr Dyke. Also 5 casks for his own account.

93 24 Aug. 1824. Mr Strong, mason, Box near Bath.
Complains about delay to Boreham Bridge repairs. Other persons will be employed if repairs are not started before he has to report to the Committee of Magistrates at Devizes on Monday. Dr Fowler has repeated his enquiries about progress.

94 26 Aug. 1824. Mr Forder, architect, Winchester.
Agrees variations to a payment at Downton concerning fixtures and stock. Has reduced £5, giving up claim to flowers and shrubs. Added £1 for value of lead cistern in brewhouse. And 3s. 10d, the moiety of stamps.

95 [*undated*]. Mr B Bramble, builder, Portsmouth.
Has heard from Mr Blatch that repairs should proceed, except at the Phoenix. Urges a start to be made so that no complaints are received.

96 27 Aug. 1824. George Underwood Esq, architect, Bath.
Arranges to meet at Hilton on 2 Sept.

97 27 Aug. 1824. Rev Dr Nicholas, Chairman.
Responds to request to improve coolness at the [*Salisbury*] Infirmary chapel. Recommends ventilators at cost of £26 12s. Three window screens would cost £7 10s.

98 28 Aug. 1824. Mr Forder, surveyor, Winchester.
Argues about the detail of a garden [*see* **94**], requested by Mr Lear, and difference over charges. Query about a screw pump manufacturer [*see* **81**].

99 28 Aug. 1824. Mr Thomas Phippen, Queen Street, Bristol.
Asks agent of the Coalbrookdale Company (at request of Mr Darby) to advise about repairs to the footings of Bulford Bridge.

100 28 Aug. 1824. Rev Joah Furey, Fordingbridge.
Excuses Wells for leaving a job to work elsewhere on barns needed for this year's produce.

101 28 Aug. 1824. Mr Wells, Ibsley.
Explains that he has written to Mr Furey about the delay.

102 29 Aug. 1824. Mr B Bramble.
Complains about a most rascally transaction. Account of the disaster at Mr Crawford's has been sent to Messrs Whitchurch.

103 4 Sept. 1824. Mr Forder, surveyor, Winchester.
Discusses the argument with Mr Lear.

104 4 Sept. 1824. Mr John Tranter.
Explains a misunderstanding arising from his letter [**99**] to Mr Phippen about Bulford
Bridge.

105 9 Sept. 1824. Hon John Coventry.
Reports on Hicks' bill. Encloses his own account for work at Burgate House.

106 9 Sept. 1824. Mr Penn.
Discusses the shortcomings of the treadmill at Devizes gaol apparently caused by
accepting the cheapest tender. The Magistrates' Committee of Accounts are querying
expenses.

107 9 Sept. 1824. Mr Myers.
Encloses payment.

108 9 Sept. 1824. Mr Banks.
Issues instruction for work at Ray Bridge. Notes nothing seen of Mr Strong.

109 11 Sept. 1824. Hyde.
Reports measurement of the mud walling at the New Inn.[1] Should be happy to
explain calculations to Mr Gillingham.

1. Not located. Perhaps one of the two in Salisbury, since Samuel Gillingham and James Hyde
both traded in Milford Street, Salisbury: P.

110 11 Sept. 1824. Miss Heath, Park Cottage, Devizes.
Replies to observations about lead and other work being done.

111 15 Sept. 1824. Messrs Burt, Devizes.
Orders three locks for the new gaol. The keys to fit them will be sent by Gatehouse.
Also another lock, different from any other in use, with two keys.

112 18 Sept. 1824. Rev Berens.
Arranges a meeting at Fryars Mill Bridge to prepare a report for the magistrates.

113 24 Sept. 1824. Messrs Hartlands, Castle Green, Bristol.
Details faulty work for Miss Heath at Park Cottage. Lengthy technical detail about
lead work to the roof and gutters. Asks for matters to be put right before the winter.

114 26 Sept. 1824. Mr George Hollis.
Encloses cheque for £9 for use of screw pump.

115 27 Sept. 1824. Mr E Cocks, Governor.[1]
Encloses and explains accounts.

1. Of Devizes Penitentiary. See **139**.

116 28 Sept. 1824. Messrs Hartlands.
Acknowledges an unsatisfactory reply and threatens legal action to seek redress for the poor work at Park Cottage. Sends copy to Miss Heath [**117**].

117 28 Sept. 1824. Miss Heath.
Encloses a letter from Hartland and the reply he suggests [**116**].

118 4 Oct. 1824. Rev J Lear, Chilmark.
Replies to query about drains.[1]

1. With explanatory diagram.

119 4 Oct. 1824. G Bucknall Estcourt Esq.
Has arranged to send books and bills for the Committee of Accounts in Mr Dowding's box. Some bills, for Stanton St Quinton, Kington St Michael and Maiden Bradley Bridges, are not available. Mr Dudley at Mr Swayne's office thinks that they may be in Estcourt's box. Confines statement to accounts for 1822 and 1823, and encloses correspondence book showing payments made in the present year, including those for Bulford Bridge.

120 4 Oct. 1824. [*addressee not stated*[1]].
Reports on survey of premises in St Martins' Church Street [*Salisbury*]. House occupied by Mr Hodgson and two adjoining cottages and part of garden worth £1000. Chapel, house inhabited by Mr Begin and remainder of garden worth £900.

1. Letter begins 'My Lord'. It is clear from **134** that this letter was written to Lord Arundell.

121 4 Oct. 1824.[1] G Dew Esq.
Reports arbitrator's decision on fee to be paid to Mr Coventry for allowing Mr Pargetter to make bricks at Godshill.

1. MS *Monday evening*, undated.

122   5 Oct. 1824. [*addressee not stated*[1]].
Warns again that repairs being done will not be adequate or meet the terms of the lease. Offers further assistance.

1. Letter begins 'Dear Madam'.

123   7 Oct. 1824. Rt Hon the Earl of Enniskillen, Florence Court, Ireland.
Notes delay in getting hold of the accounts of the late Mr Wynch. Reports on several, generally unsatisfactory, aspects relating to accounts and tenancies at Grimstead.

124   7 Oct. 1824. Mr Wallis, plasterer, Southampton.
Will be at Southampton to see the timbers stripped of plastering.

125   7 Oct. 1824. J Benett Esq.
Has failed to place an apprentice with Mr Shorto or young Goddard. Suggests two other cutlers, Nash in Catharine Street and Botly in the Market Place,[1] who have shops but are working men and may not be suitable [*see* **133**]. Will hold the note from Mr Spring Rice until an answer is received.

1. All were Salisbury cutlers: P.

126   7 Oct. 1824. Thomas Flower Esq, Melksham.
Cannot yet pay a bill.

127   9 Oct. 1824. Messrs Hobbs and Hellyre, timber merchants, Redbridge.
Asks the cost of post and rail fencing to be erected adjoining Woodford Bridge.

128   [*undated*]. Mr Weaving, Emsworth, Hants.[1]
Will find a reed thatcher for Mr Hopper upon returning from sessions at Marlborough [*see* **146**].

1. Added in pencil.

129   21 Oct. 1824. Mr R Eldridge, Southampton.
Encloses delayed payment of £13 4s. 4d.

130   [*undated*]. Mr Hardy.
Order for sash windows from Mr Curley has been passed to Messrs Whitchurch.

131 25 Oct. 1824. Benjamin Wingrove Esq, Bath.
Encloses cheque for £38 13s 4d for repairs to bridges. Discusses responsibilities for various bridges and adjacent roads in the Trowbridge, Chippenham and Bradford areas.

132 25 Oct. 1824. George Underwood Esq, Bath.
Passes a request from Mr Boucher for a map connected with his purchase at Hilton and information about a right of way. Also a personal request: he is to ask for a salary increase as County Surveyor and wants to know what is paid in Berkshire and Devon.

133 24 Oct. 1824. John Benett Esq.
Unable to place an apprentice in the cutlery trade with Mr Botly, and Nash is probably unsuitable [see **125**]. Mrs Peniston expresses thanks for the gift of a brace of very fine birds.

134 25 Oct. 1824. Charles Bowles Esq, Shaftesbury.
Asks about settlement of the proposed division of property between the chapel and Mr Begin. Refers to correspondence on the subject with Lord Arundell.[1]

1. See **120**. The property was in Salisbury.

135 25 Oct. 1824. Thomas Flower Esq, Melksham.
Encloses cheque for £39 19s.

136 28 Oct. 1824. Mr Penn, engineer and millwright, Greenwich.
Asks, on behalf of the magistrates, for plan and estimate of cost for a new corn mill to be erected at Devizes, to be worked by the existing tread wheel machinery. Discusses arrangements for a visit if the existing equipment needs to be examined.

137 28 Oct. 1824. Mr Darby.
Asks for work to be continued at Bulford Bridge as soon as the masons finish the piers.

138 29 Oct. 1824. Mr Edwards, Melksham.
Encloses balance of payment for work on Melksham Bridge.

139 30 Oct. 1824. E Cocks Esq, Penitentiary, Devizes.
Encloses copies of letters to and from Mr Penn about arrangements to meet at Devizes.

140 31 Oct. 1824. J Penn Esq.
Arranges a meeting at Devizes.

141 1 Nov. 1824. Miss Heath.
Encloses letter from Mr Armstrong and suggests she accepts the offer concerning re-laying unsatisfactory lead work. His own charge up to date is five guineas. Future charges one guinea a visit if in Devizes on other business and four guineas for a special trip from Salisbury.

142 1 Nov. 1824. Rt Hon the Earl of Enniskillen.
Reports on an audit at Grimstead,[1] completed with difficulty. Lists rents received. Lists rents which he thinks are not to be collected. Encloses papers for signature.

1. See WRO 451/280-2.

143 2 Nov. 1824. Mr Myers.
Sends payment of £32 7s., balance due for work on Bradford Bridge and Trowle Bridge.

144 2 Nov. 1824. Mr Trotman.
Has valued property in Catherine Street,[1] taking into account the rent and Land Tax payable, at £1400. His charge is one guinea.

1. Salisbury, as Thomas Trotman was a Catherine Street butcher: P.

145 4 Nov. 1824. E Cocks Esq, Devizes.
Mr Penn has been thrown from his horse and cannot travel.

146 5 Nov. 1824. Mr Weaving, Emsworth, Hants.
Recommends Pearce of Shrewton as a reed thatcher [see **128**].

147 2 Nov. 1824. J Penn Esq.
Re-arranges meeting at Devizes.

148 13 Nov. 1824. William Armstrong Esq, architect, Bristol.
Explains that he has sent the recommendation to let some respectable plumber make the estimate and has passed on Messrs Hartland's request. Hopes to have nothing further to do with the business.

149 14 Nov. 1824. T G Bucknall Estcourt Esq.
Has sent separately a sheet of receipts and payments for the present year and asks if it is in the right form. Will send further papers by Gatehouse. Refers to payments concerning Bulford, Woodford, Melksham, Bradford, Harnham, Barford, Winterbourne Stoke, and Ray Bridges and for the road at Lacock Bridge.

150 16 Nov. 1824. T G Bucknall Estcourt Esq.
Further explanation about accounts. Bill for the screw pump is missing although paid.

151 16 Nov. 1824. Mr Strong.
Explains that Rev Mr Lear of Chilmark has laid an oak floor in the passage and does not want the stone ordered. Query about Boreham Bridge where the employees are a set of scamps. Expects Mr Edwards to have settled the account for Melksham Bridge. Mr Banks needs an account in order to present his own for Lacock.

152 16 Nov. 1824. Rev J Lear.
Apologizes for not cancelling the stone order earlier.

153 22 Nov. 1824. Benjamin Wingrove Esq, Bath.
Queries confusion about accounts for the road at Trowbridge Bridge and at Trowle Bridge. Refers to Stanton and Kington Bridges which the county has never before been called on to repair. The owners of Baldham Mill should maintain London Bridge.

154 22 Nov. 1824. T G Bucknall Estcourt Esq, 1 Brock Street, Bath.
Further lengthy explanation of accounts. Copy of the order made at Quarter Sessions to pay Peniston, as County Surveyor, £141 15s. 2d.

155 26 Nov. 1824. T G Bucknall Estcourt Esq, Chairman of the Committee of Accounts.
Will send account books and vouchers and memoranda the next day, by Gatehouse, to New Park.

156 26 Nov. 1824. T Bramah Esq.
Has surveyed an ice house[1] constructed to his plan and makes a long and detailed technical commentary.

1. At Burgate House. See **159**.

157 28 Nov. 1824. Messrs Hobbs and Hellyre.
Orders posts, rails and a wicket gate to be sent to Woodford Bridge.

158 3 Dec. 1824. [*addressee not stated*[1]].
Explains that valuation of property in Catherine Street reflects location. The same property elsewhere would be worth less.

1. Perhaps Mr Trotman. See **144**.

159 4 Dec. 1824. Hon John Coventry, Burgate House, Fordingbridge.
Had received reply [*see* **156**] about the ice house from Mr Bramah, who was much hurt at the inattention paid to his directions. Conveys further instructions to improve ventilation. Refers to the method of filling the house with ice.

160 4 Dec. 1824. E Cocks Esq, Governor, [*Devizes*] Penitentiary.
Arranges to check tradesmen's bills against their work.

161 4 Dec. 1824. John Purdue, Andover.
Has waited to get Lord Arundell to sign the annual certificate but has now signed it himself. Refers to Mr Hooper of the Salisbury Troop.

162 4 Dec. 1824. Mr Clarke, builder, Fordingbridge.
Queries account for plastering.

163 6 Dec. 1824. Rev John Owen Parr, Remenham Rectory, Henley upon Thames.
Reports survey of dilapidations at Durnford. The amount, including repairs to the chancel, is £165 13s.

164 6 Dec. 1824. Miss Heath.
Recommends accepting offer from Messrs Hartlands as better than legal proceedings.

165 6 Dec. 1824. Rt Rev Lord Bishop of Salisbury.
Apologises for delay in reporting on Durnford Church, examined in August at the same time as the survey of dilapidations at the vicarage house. Encloses report.

166 7 Dec. 1824. R White Esq, Solicitor, Essex[1] Street, London.
Reports examination of the dilapidations at Teffont Rectory. The present incumbent entitled to claim £113 14s 6d.

1. MS indistinctly written. White, Blake and Houseman, attorneys, are listed in P at 14 Essex Street, Strand.

167 8 Dec. 1824.[1] Rt Hon Lord Bridport.
Reports on the possibility that there may have been some deception on the part of
Mr C Brown.

1. MS *Wednesday evening*, undated.

168 10 Dec. 1824. Mr Banks, mason, Lacock.
Acknowledges a packet of bills and vigorously queries the amount of time said to
have been spent on the repairs.[1] Refers to Mr Strong. Meeting needed.

1. MS *at Ray Bridge*, struck through.

169 10 Dec. 1824. Mr Strong.
Sends copies of bills received from Mr Banks. Arranges meeting at Lacock.

170 12 Dec. 1824. E Cocks Esq.
Will inspect tradesmen's bills on next visit to Devizes. Has estimate from Mr Penn.
Asks for Buckley to be told of unsatisfactory work at Studley Bridge that will have
to be put right.

171 12 Dec. 1824. Messrs Hartland.
Arranges to meet at Devizes, at request of Miss Heath, to pay the balance of account.

172 12 Dec. 1824. Miss Heath.
Reports his arrangement to meet a gentleman from Messrs Hartland at Devizes.

173 12 Dec. 1824. G A Underwood Esq.
Makes further query about the plan of Hilton.

174 12 Dec. 1824. Mr Strong, mason, Box near Bath.
Arranges to meet at Lacock. Will have spent the night at Warminster.

175 12 Dec. 1824. Mr Banks, mason, Lacock.
Asks him to attend meeting with Mr Strong at Lacock.

176 13 Dec. 1824. Visiting magistrates, Penitentiary, Devizes.
Reports that Mr Bramah regards the estimate from Mr Penn to be much less than he
expected. Will be at Devizes on 17 [*Dec.*] to inspect work at the Penitentiary and the
Old Gaol. Mentions this in case the magistrates have any orders or personal
communications for him before the end of sessions.

177 17 Dec. 1824. Messrs Hobbs and Hellyre.[1]
Sends copy of letter of 28 Nov. [**157**], and requests the order be sent as soon as possible.

1. Written by J M Peniston, on father's behalf.

178 18 Dec. 1824. Hon John Coventry, Burgate House, Fordingbridge.
Will visit on 27 Dec. to examine work on the ice house specified by Mr Coventry, jun.

179 18 Dec. 1824. Mr R Fowler, Melksham.
Explains that the county is responsible for repairs to the road for one hundred yards from each end of the bridge. That the commissioners get their agents to estimate for repairs per mile and charge the County for their portion.

180 21 Dec. 1824. Miss Heath, Park Cottage, Devizes.
Thanks her for appreciation and generous payment. Agrees about the unworthiness of Mr Hartland.

181 21 Dec. 1824. Rev W J Younge, Rockbourne.
Arranges a meeting.

182 29 Dec. 1824. Rev F D Williams, Wishford.
Notes and returns Read's account. Comments on deduction for difference between copper and tin pipe. Mr Read should meet cost of glass in back door.

183 29 Dec. 1824. Hon John Coventry, Burgate House.
Returns Hicks's bills corrected after examination of the painting and glazing accounts. Will visit to meet Hicks and Chalk and to check quantities used.

184 30 Dec. 1824. Rt Hon Lord Bridport.
Has seen one chimneypiece. Brown may not be dishonest but is grossly deceptive.

185 30 Dec. 1824. Rev C Ridding, College, Winchester.
Has closed the survey of dilapidations at Orcheston[1] Rectory and seeks agreement. Late incumbent has agreed a sum of £162 9s.

1. Presumably Orcheston St Mary, since no change occurred at Orcheston St George between 1813 and 1830, and the rector (Rev C B P Lowther) was resident during the 1820s: Foster; Parish Registers.

1825

186 6 Jan. 1825. Messrs the Guardians of the Poor of the City of Salisbury.
Has valued a house in Culver Street at £6 10s.

187 20 Jan. 1825.[1] [*addressee not stated*[2]].
Asks to borrow half a dozen carbines as he can find neither these nor muskets. Offers
to pay any expenses.

1. MS *1824*, in error.
2. Letter begins, 'Dear Stent', so presumably James Stent of Dorchester. See **866**.

188 [*undated*]. Hon John Coventry, Burgate House.
Apologises for delay in returning tradesmen's bills. Chalk's charges are moderate but
time for the work seems excessive.

189 21 Jan. 1825. Edward Bates Esq, Secretary of the Tax Office, Somerset House.
Complains that a tax inspector, lately visiting the district, has denied a tax exemption
on his horse to Major Baker of the Wiltshire Yeomanry Cavalry on the grounds that
he performed no yeomanry duties in the year to 5 April 1824. Explains that the
regiment did not assemble for permanent duty in the year and that Major Baker,
formerly for many years in command of the Salisbury Troop, is now a staff officer and
prevented by etiquette from parading with any troop assembled in its own district.
Requests the Board to reconsider so that the regiment is not deprived of the services
of an effective and valuable officer.[1]

1. Peniston signs as 'Serg. Major W.Y.C.'

190 28 Jan. 1825. Messrs Jones and Clark, metallic hot house manufacturers, Lionell
Street, Birmingham.
Asks for specification and costs of a conservatory to be added to the dining room at
Norman Court.

191 28 Jan. 1825. Rt Hon Lord Viscount Palmerston, Broadlands.
Intends to call.

192 28 Jan. 1825. E Cocks Esq, Devizes.
Asks when visiting magistrates will meet. Will attend to get instructions about the
intended mill.

193 2 Feb. 1825. Mr Eldridge, timber merchant, Southampton.
Encloses payment for a bill. Is about to build some cottages and needs cheap material for floors and doors. Asks for price list. Also estimating for a National School eight miles from Southampton[1] and wants prices for best memel and inferior timbers. For the right terms may become a more extensive purchaser.

1. ?Romsey. See **196** note 2.

194 2 Feb. 1825. Mr Guthrie.
Arranges to meet at Norman Court to supervise removal of damaged columns.

195 2 Feb. 1825. Messrs Grieve, Grellier and Morgan.
Requested by Mr Dyke of Netton to remit £45 for cement. Will be paid by bank through their agents, Remington and Co.

196 8 Feb. 1825. [*addressee not stated*[1]].
Discusses plans, including choice of Doric for the school front,[2] bedrooms over the coach house, and moving a clock.

1. Letter begins, 'My Lord', thus Lord Palmerston. See **200**.
2. ?Romsey. See **462, 465**.

197 7 Feb. 1825. Charles Bowles Esq, Shaftesbury.
Concerning Mr Begin's business. Asks that Lord Arundell reconsider a decision not to pay interest on a mortgage on the chapel property.[1] Expresses the hope of the Salisbury congregation that they will not lose the patronage and protection of Lord Arundell. Will not tell Mr Begin until he hears again. Asks to be excused this approach because of strong effect expected on Mr Begin's feelings.[2]

1. At Salisbury. See **120, 134**.
2. Written from Norman Court.

198 10 Feb. 1825. J. Penn, Esq.
Requests a rough plan and section of the millhouse in time for a meeting of magistrates at Devizes.[1]

1. This and **199** are written upside down between **343** and **344** below.

199 10 Feb. 1825. [*addressee not stated*[1]].
Confirms a payment of £81 15s.9d. The deputation for Mr. Wall's keeper arrived safely.[2]

1. Letter begins, 'My Lord'.
2. This and **198** are written upside down between **343** and **344** below.

200 13 Feb. 1825. Lord Palmerston.
Sends six plans for the School and Schoolhouse.[1] Piles will be needed for the boggy ground. Discusses decorative details. The Doric plan will probably cost £750 in all, the alternative £50 cheaper.

1. ?Romsey. See **462, 465**.

201 13 Feb. 1825. Ernle Warriner Esq, Conock House, Devizes.
Arranges to call.

202 16 Feb. 1825. J Penn Esq, millwright, Greenwich.
Has been instructed to prepare for the intended mill house.[1] Repairs to the wheel will take a fortnight. Is obliged for the sketches. The Governor[2] is extremely ill.

1. At Devizes Penitentiary. See **198**.
2. Mr E Cocks. See **192, 225**.

203 16 Feb. 1825. Timothy Bramah Esq.
Discusses a construction.[1] Agrees girder should be cast in two.

1. For Norman Court. See **204**.

204 18 Feb. 1825. C Baring Wall Esq, New Norfolk Street, London.
Has safely taken down the column at Norman Court. Will repair with an iron core being brought from the Grange. To prevent a recurrence will put in a cast iron stressed girder to spread the weight. Has ordered this from Mr Bramah [**203**], not trusting country castings. Discusses work on the conservatory and the practicability of adding a closet to the bathroom.

205 19 Feb. 1825. Hon John Coventry, Burgate House.
Arranges to visit.

206 23 Feb. 1825. Hon John Coventry.
Has given various instructions to tradesmen.

207 1 March 1825. C Baring Wall Esq.
Has received plans, specification and estimate for the conservatory.[1] If approved, Jones can complete the building by July. Still awaiting the iron column from Guthrie.

1. For Norman Court. See **204**.

208 4 March 1825. T Bramah Esq.
As the beam will be weighty it should be sent by water to Southampton. Mr Wall will
be calling.

209 4 March 1825. C Baring Wall Esq.
Sends conservatory plans [*for Norman Court*].

210 5 March 1825. Rt Hon Earl of Enniskillen.
Corrects an error in previous statement of account.

211 7 March 1825.[1] Mr Warriner.
Has sketches of proposed alterations to the Manor House.[2]

1. MS *Monday*, presumably 7 March.
2. ?Conock. See **201**.

212 7 March 1825. C Baring Wall Esq.
[*Norman Court*]: Agrees that there should be folding glass doors. Discusses access to
the conservatory. Estimate of £348 for remaining work is based on brickwork coated
with roman cement for pilasters and cornice. Mr Bramah has prepared the cast iron
beam.

213 7 March 1825. Mr Guthrie.
Enquires about the iron column.

214 19 March 1825. Messrs Coade and Adams, 68 Strand, [*London*].
Asks that the person going to Burgate House calls on him on the way.

215 19 March 1825. Mr B Bramble, Portsmouth.
Accounts have been sent to Messrs Whitchurch.

216 25 March 1825. Mr Haywood, Governor, Penitentiary, Devizes.
Will complete correct account during next visit.

217 20 March 1825. Mr Crook, Keeper of the Marlborough Bridewell.
Will visit Marlborough to deal with accounts after magistrates meeting at Devizes.

218 27 March 1825.[1] Mr Crook.
Has a severe indisposition and is therefore sending bills by Mr Haywood at Devizes.

1. MS *Sunday morning*, undated.

219 27 March 1825.[1] [*addressee not stated*[2]].
Regrets that his medical attendant prohibits him leaving home, even in a post chaise.
Therefore sends bills. Has passed all bills except in one case which needs discussion
but £100 could be allowed. Encloses parcel for Crook at Marlborough.

1. MS *Sunday morning*, undated.
2. Presumably to Mr Haywood, see **218** above.

220 1 April 1825. Rt Hon Lord Bridport.
Confirms that Brown has undertaken to send the money.

221 1 April 1825. Mr R Hulbert, Pickwick, near Corsham.
Arranges to meet the committee at Lacock.

222 1 April 1825. Rev J Lear, Chilmark.
Wishes to delay a meeting as he has been indisposed.

223 2 April 1825. Messrs Jones and Clark.
Mr Wall prefers the last sketch[1] but hopes that there is an error in the cost. Asks for
an elevation drawing and explanation of the costs.

1. Norman Court conservatory. See **190**.

224 2 April 1825. C B Wall Esq.
Has made enquiries about an excise permit to move wine from Norman Court. Has
written to Messrs Jones and Clark [**223**].

225 8 April 1825. J Penn Esq.
Has been at [*Devizes*] Penitentiary to set out the Mill House. Refers to death of
Cocks. Is recovering slowly from a severe bilious attack.

226 9 April 1825. J Kelsey Esq.
Encloses tradesmen's bills with some explanation. Has made certain deductions.

227 11 April 1825. Rev C H Ridding, Winchester College.
Queries Mrs Austin's view of the dilapidations payment at Rollestone. She had appointed a regular surveyor who had agreed the sum. The law on clerical dilapidations has been applied and the sum is not excessive.

228 12 April 1825. C B Wall Esq.
Encloses copy of letter to Messrs Jones and Clark [**223**] and their drawing and lengthy explanation in reply.[1] Notes that this does not make it easy to see how much the cost might be reduced.

1. Norman Court conservatory. See **190**.

229 12 April 1825. Rt Hon Lord Viscount Palmerston.
Sends ground plan and elevation for a keeper's cottage. Attaches a scale useful for the workmen. Has not returned his Lordship's book in case alterations are needed.

230 13 April 1825. [*addressee not stated*].
The account for Melksham Bridge was too late for the present sessions. Mr Flower's bill for the road over and adjoining the bridge was too high compared to costs elsewhere. Quotes figures for various parts of the county. Will be at Melksham in a short time.

231 14 April 1825. Rev Joah Furey.
Regrets indisposition has delayed sending accounts.

232 17 April 1825. Messrs Jones and Clark.
[*Norman Court*]: The work is to be put in hand. Mr Wall has specified some modifications which will reduce the cost. Wishes to know when the footings will be set out so that workmen can be provided.

233 19 April 1825. Mr James Nicholas, carpenter, Upavon (*Uphaven*).
Asks if he will repair Upavon Bridge.

234 20 April 1825. Mr Bevis.
Asks him to estimate the cost of repairing the bridge just out of Amesbury on the Durrington road.

235 20 April 1825. Rev Lear, Chilmark.
Arranges to visit.

236 21 April 1825. Rt Hon Lord Viscount Palmerston.
Reports on work at Broadlands, including to the roof of the coach house. Will send sketch of range of rooms connected with the nursery.

237 21 April 1825. Mr Watson, Broadlands, Romsey.
Work on the coach house roof is to be delayed. Has written to Lord Palmerston on the subject [**236**].

238 22 April 1825. Wadham Locke Esq, Rowde Ford House, Devizes.
Has sent two plans for comparison.

239 25 April 1825. Mr Bickers.
Arranges meeting at Broadlands.[1]

1. Written by J M Peniston, on father's behalf.

240 25 April 1825. Rt Hon Lord Viscount Palmerston.
Sends sketch of the Nursery Wing, [*Broadlands*]. Discusses layout of bedrooms.

241 26 April 1825. Messrs Coade and Adams, paper manufacturers, 68 Strand, London.
Describes walls at Burgate House that are to be papered. Discusses mastic covering and some dampness that may not be injurious.

242 27 April 1825. Mr Bickers, Broadlands.
Has been unable to keep an appointment because of bad weather and unsound health. Is going by coach to Portsmouth and will call on return journey.

243 27 April 1825. [*addressee not stated*[1]].
Has filled in the returns in the way required. Encloses a further return to be signed, intended for the Lord Lieutenant's Office and connected with the ballot for the Militia.

1. Letter begins, 'My Lord'. Probably Lord Arundell. See **161**.

244 2 May 1825. Mr Bickers, Broadlands.
Encloses a valuation and an estimate of repairs needed to farm buildings.

245 2 May 1825. Mr Jones.
Arranges a meeting at Norman Court.

246 3 May 1825. Wadham Locke Esq.
Has made some alterations to the plans[1] and will discuss others. Has not added any
sum to the estimate of £900. Has recovered and will be at Devizes the following day.

1. For a house in Devizes. See **274, 276**.

247 6 May 1825. Mr Watson, Broadlands.
Sends drawings of the coach house roof and upstairs rooms.

248 7 May 1825. W Locke Esq.
Sends a specification with some explanation.[1]

1. For a house in Devizes. See **274, 276**.

249 9 May 1825. R Webb Esq.
Discusses the accounts for a painter who is more fool than knave.

250 [*undated*]. Mr Haywood, Governor.[1]
Has delayed visit because of Mr Locke's work. Asks for a few lines about progress to
be sent by George.[2]

1. Devizes Penitentiary. See **216**.
2. George George was a Marlborough carrier: WRS vol.40, p.xx.

251 14 May 1825.[1] Trinder Esq.[2]
Delays visit.

1. MS *Saturday morning*, undated.
2. Perhaps Charles Trinder, a Devizes surgeon: P.

252 14 May 1825. Mr H P Burt.
Has postponed his visit. Sends notes to be forwarded.

253 14 May 1825. Mrs Scott.
She had been deceived by Hill. The agreement was for him to be paid by the square
for labour and mortar, being paid extra for slates. Has written to Hill and will also see
him when in Devizes.

254 [*undated*]. Mr Hill.
Rebukes him for misinforming Mrs Scott about providing slates at Park Cottage. Asks for no further delay in doing the work.

255 21 May 1825. Rev J Lear, Chilmark.
Imagines that, with the precautions against damp taken, the proposed alterations will be effective.

256 24 May 1825. Trinder Esq.[1]
Sends tolerably correct drawing. Height should be from eight to nine feet. Will meet before the point needs to be settled.

1. See **251** note 2.

257 24 May 1825. Gen. Buller.
Has been asked by Mr Webb to report on Clarendon House, and intends to begin the next day.

258 24 May 1825.[1] Richard Cove Esq.
Cancels an engagement, having misunderstood a request to view land.

1. MS *Tues evening*, undated.

259 26 May 1825. Mr Floyd.
Walls of the keeper's cottage[1] above the footings need be no more than nine inches as they are intended to be rough cast.

1. Probably on the Broadlands estate. See **279**.

260 26 May 1825. Mr James Green.
Gives a reference for a builder, Mr J Towsey.

261 26 May 1825. Edward Davies Esq.
Discusses the new turnpike house which will adjoin Mr Wyndham's land.

262 27 May 1825. Messrs Elias Saph and Francis Brown, Sun Inn.[1]
Encloses an award concerning a dispute. Mr William Burroughs to pay £8 7s. 3d. to Mr James Fleming. Expenses to be shared.

1. Fisherton Anger: P.

263 31 May 1825. Thomas Webb Dyke Esq and Mrs Croome.
Estimates dilapidations to house, barn, stables, etc., lately occcupied by Mrs Croome at Bulford to be £20 7s. 6d.

264 31 May 1825. Edward Davies Esq.
Has measured the piece of Mr Wyndham's orchard on which the turnpike house will be built. The area is some 6 ft. x 30 ft. 9 in., valued at £1 10s.

265 3 June 1825. Mr Christopher Warren, mason, Southampton.
Wishes to meet at Lacock where work is to start on the bridge. Warren should take the Bristol Mail to Bath from where he may easily coach to Melksham, only three miles from Lacock. Will himself be at Devizes the previous night.

266 5 June 1825. William Wyndham Esq.
Confirms a remedy for tic douloureux which had successfully cured an acquaintance.

267 5 June 1825. [*addressee not stated*[1]].
[*Grimstead*]: Has delayed replying in expectation of receiving arrears from Tubb. Is loath to recommend extreme proceedings. Will have difficulty with bills for work done because Mr Wynch's accounts are no further forward.

1. Letter begins, 'My Lord', presumably the Earl of Enniskillen. See **305** below.

268 5 June 1825. Mr William Spraggs, chapman, Bristol.
Acknowledges request for payment of an account for £15 7s. from the late Mr Spraggs of Melksham, to be delivered to Mr Thomas Flower. Thinks it may already have been paid and will check with the Clerk of the Peace.

269 7 June 1825. W W Salmon Esq.
Encloses receipt for cheque for £14 14s. for superintending building work, 1821-4, at the house occupied by Mrs Beale in the Close, Salisbury.

270 8 June 1825. [*addressee not stated*[1]].
[*Broadlands*]: Sees no difficulty with the alterations proposed except for a bedroom fireplace. It may not be possible to cut back the chimney from the kitchen below, but this will be examined. Will attend to comments on plans for the keeper's cottage. Has fixed its position and will tell Floyd to start work.

1. Letter begins, 'My Lord', i.e. Lord Palmerston. See **272**.

271 8 June 1825. J Mirehouse, 20 Orchard St, London.
Has contacted Mr Boucher, who acts for Dr Burgess,[1] and will meet him at the Palace.

1. Dr Thomas Burgess, Bishop of Salisbury, 1825-37: LN.

272 10 June 1825. Mr Bickers, Broadlands, Romsey.
Encloses plan approved by Lord Palmerston. Height has been reduced and Floyd should not confuse two different scales. Work should start.

273 10 June 1825. William Hughes Esq, Devizes.
Suggests changes to plans for the dining room.

274 11 June 1825. Wadham Locke Esq.
Discusses alterations to plans for altering the house.[1] Changes are marked in red. Has told Wells to supervise the work occasionally and Mr White should be told of this.

1. In Devizes. See **276**.

275 11 June 1825. Mr B White, Devizes.
Asks to be sent a correct outline when the work has been set out. Will then frame working plans. The existing ones are neat but inaccurate.

276 11 June 1825. Mr Wells.
Has told Mr Locke that he will look in on the building work at Devizes once or twice a day. Gives detailed instructions about bricklaying and stresses the importance of mixing mortar to the correct specification.

277 12 June 1825. Mr Myles, Red Lion Inn, Lacock.
A cheque of £5 to Mr Warren.

278 15 June 1825. Mr Jefferey.
Discusses the costs and merits of earthen or lead pipes. Recommends lead in this case.

279 16 June 1825. Rt Hon Lord Viscount Palmerston.
Has corrected a mistake in the cottage plans. Will be at Broadlands to discuss alterations to the Nursery Wing. Will speak to Floyd. Has clarified some drawings.

280 18 June 1825. [*addressee not stated*[1]].
Has been at Redlynch and seen Barter who understands Mr Hopper's instructions and is preparing for the work. The portion to be covered will need 14 five-bushel casks of roman cement. Has previously ordered from Grieve, Grellier and Co, Bankside, Vauxhall. Better to order in quantity direct from the manufacturer. Has made many unsuccessful attempts to see Charles Brown and wishes to lend him the money to get out of a scrape.

1. Letter begins, 'My Lord', probably Lord Bridport. See **704**.

281 [*undated*]. Lt Col Baker.
Passes on Mr Pettit's request to extend leave of absence at Weymouth. Offers to act in his place if necessary.

282 20 June 1825. [*addressee not stated*[1]].
Encloses sketch and corrected plans. The narrowness of the doorway will be attended to and was an error by the transcriber of the plan. Carpenter and bricklayer will start as soon as the rooms are clear and the plasterer will follow.

1. Letter begins, 'My Lord'.

283 [*undated*]. [*addressee not stated*].
Apologises for delay and encloses plan for a larder.

284 25 June 1825. Rev F D Williams.
Conveys Read's estimate of £319 19s. 4d. for work on the stables, lofts, barn, brewhouse, and coach house, and to build a new barn.[1] And a further estimate of £430 8s. 4d. to build or rebuild wall, fences and railings. The latter to be reduced by £48 10s. if the garden hedge fence as far as the mud wall is not replaced by a brick wall.

1. Probably at Great Wishford. See **182**.

285 27 June 1825. [*addressee not stated*].
Encloses corrected timber bill. Cannot make out Buckley's bill, and visiting magistrates should allow fifty pounds on account to pay sawyer's workmen.

286 30 June 1825. William Hughes Esq, Devizes.
Will meet to discuss plan.

287 30 June 1825. J Mirehouse Esq, No 12 Paper Buildings, Temple, London.
Has agreed dilapidations at the Palace with Mr Fisher. Executors of the late Bishop of Salisbury are liable for £121 12s.

288 1 July 1825. J Penn Esq, engineer, Greenwich.
Awaits news at Devizes to make a report at the sessions. Shell of the building[1] is complete.

1. Mill house at Devizes Penitentiary. See **225**.

289 1 July 1825. Messrs Grieve, Grellier and Co.
Orders 12 casks of roman cement.

290 1 July 1825. B Wingrove Esq, Bath.
Asks him to repair the road adjoining Bradford Bridge. The former contractor is unsatisfactory and the Bradfordians are not to be trusted. Enquires about convenient source of best stone, which will be cheapest in the end.

291 5 July 1825. Mr Bamford, grocer, Southampton.
Regrets being unable yet to execute the order for whiting.

292 5 July 1825. Mr Cooksey, grocer, Southampton.
Regrets being unable yet to execute the order for whiting.

293 5 July 1825. Mr Hibbard.
An annual account to the late Mr Hibbard has never been settled. Has received bills of which nothing is known. If for the late firm of Peniston and Co they should be sent to Mr William or James Peniston.

294 5 July 1825. Peacock Esq, 41 Warwick St, Golders Green, London.
Asks for an account for the late Mr Cocks so that, as a trustee of his will, he can advise Mrs Cocks. She is distressed for money and wishes to borrow £20 to furnish a house to be taken from Mr Salmon.

295 5 July 1825. Mr Watson, Broadlands.
Introduces the bearer who is to put up the rustic railings on the bridge in the park.

296 9 July 1825. Mr Mizen.
Instruction to repair the road at Bradford Bridge until someone else can be found. But only sufficiently to prevent accidents.

297 16 July 1825. [*addressee not stated*[1]].
Should take advantage of fine weather to work on the conservatory at Norman Court. Discusses design of pilaster capital. Bricklayer is forward with the work and the mason with preparation.

1. To Messrs Clark and Jones. See **298**.

298 16 July 1825. C B Wall Esq.
Discusses costs and designs. Has written to Messrs Clark and Jones about the conservatory [**297**].

299 19 July 1825. Mr Woodman.
Queries dimensions of the new room.

300 19 July 1825. Rev George Edmonstone.[1]
Amount of mastic sent was half a hundredweight and will need half a gallon of linseed oil for a workable consistency. It should be mixed well with a shovel and trodden with naked feet. Instructs how the wall should be prepared and the mastic applied.

1. Vicar of Potterne: CG.

301 19 July 1825. Hon John Coventry, Burgate House.
Arranges to call.

302 20 July 1825. Benjamin Wingrove, Office for Roads, Bath.
Has been able to report to sessions at Warminster. Wishes to meet to discuss work at Bradford Bridge.

303 20 July 1825. Mr Knapp, surveyor, Bradford.
Has laid proposal for repair of Bradford Bridge before the court of sessions but they have directed another course.

304 20 July 1825. William Hughes Esq.
Complains about workmen not following the plans and asks for some defects to be corrected.

305 21 July 1825. Rt Hon Earl of Enniskillen, Florence Court, Ireland.
[*Grimstead*]: Reports that Tubb has paid some of his arrears and that the late Mr Wynch's accounts are still not made out. Has paid £150 to Messrs Drummonds.

306 26 July 1825. William Hughes Esq.
Arrangement to meet earlier than planned.[1]

1. Written by J M Peniston, on father's behalf.

307 26 July 1825. Mr Tulloch (*Tallock*), builder, Poole.
Asks for account of work done for Rev Mr Boucher who will not now build a new house as he has bought that at Hilton, lately occupied by Mr Fawkes.

308 26 July 1825. [*addressee not stated*[1]].
Sends report of repairs to be done at Christchurch. Will amend sketch of dairy and larder. Expects to discuss [*Burgate*] ice house with Mr Bramah when visiting London.

1. Probably Rt Hon John Coventry. See **310, 323**.

309 28 July 1825. Mr Warren.
Discusses work on Foot Bridge [*Lacock*], and other bridges.

310 1 Aug. 1825. Rt Hon John Coventry, Burgate House.
Sends sketch for an inexpensive dairy, with brick walls, a thatched roof and verandah supported by posts of rough knotted fir. Advises that any person can be prohibited from fishing the Avon where manorial property is on either side.

311 2 Aug. 1825. W Hughes Esq.
Agrees a minor change in the specification for some timber.

312 3 Aug. 1825. William Hughes Esq.
Discusses the position of a window.

313 3 Aug. 1825. Mr Watson, Broadlands.
Sorts out tasks for the carpenter, including re-laying the dressing room floor on which the warm bath is placed.

314 9 Aug. 1825. [*addressee not stated*[1]].
Discusses date for a visit to Broadlands. Note can reach him at the Bear at Devizes.

1. Letter begins, 'My Lord', thus to Lord Palmerston.

315   25 Aug. 1825. Rev Mr Ashe, Langley, Chippenham.
Acknowledges that the Clerk of Works at Lacock is not satisfied with preparations by the masons for work at Tytherton Kellaway Bridge. Will express an opinion without committing the county to any responsibility for the bridge. Offers advice, including that new stone should be attached to the existing piers by cramps secured with melted lead or roman cement. Clerk of Works may visit once or twice if expenses are met by the trustees.[1]

1. Written from Wardour. The trust is presumably Maud Heath's Charity.

316   25 Aug. 1825. Mr Warren.
Confirms that he may supervise at Tytherton provided there is no expense to the county.[1]

1. Written from Wardour.

317   25 Aug. 1825. Rev Henry Boucher, Clinton, Blandford.
Discusses alterations to the stable front. Will prepare plan for the water closet.[1]

1. Written from Wardour.

318   28 Aug. 1825. Miss Hughes, Devizes.
Agrees some changes, including a larger window and only one bookcase. The latter should be discussed with a cabinet maker in Devizes. Discusses other details. Despairs of Holloway understanding written instructions about the kitchen, which should wait until he visits Devizes on the way back from London.[1]

1. Written from Wardour.

319   12 Sept. 1825. Mr Hanks.
Asks for receipts for payments for work at Cow Bridge [*Malmesbury*].

320   13 Sept. 1825. Mr Strong, Pewsey.
Asks for bills for work on Pewsey Bridge. Has no order to work on the adjoining road and hopes that, although the county have adopted it, the commissioners will not be so morally unjust as to insist. If they do, the least amount of work is to be done until he can visit and settle matters.

321   17 Sept. 1825.[1] Mr Watson, Broadlands.
Will direct Lane to send a plasterer to Broadlands.

1. MS *27 Sept*, but letter seems to predate **327**, therefore 17 is probably intended.

322 17 Sept. 1825. Benjamin Wingrove Esq, Road Office, Bath.
Needs demands on the county by Michaelmas to include in accounts for current year.
Requests meeting at Bradford to arrange for work on the bridge.

323 17 Sept. 1825. Timothy Bramah Esq, Pimlico.
Discusses the ice house at Burgate. Considers the failure due to filling it with skimmings of the lightest frost which could not be expected to preserve itself. However he will examine the structure again as Mr Coventry asked. Encloses cheque which he had carried to London but had not had time to deliver.

324 17 Sept. 1825. Mr Wells.
Asks him to send George Golding to put in the floor joists at Fisherton.

325 [undated]. [addressee not stated].
Request for accounts.

326 17 Sept. 1825. Messrs Grieve, Grellier and Co., Waterloo Bridge Marble Wharf, Belvidere Road, London.
Orders twelve casks of cement via Southampton.

327 19 Sept. 1825. Mr Watson.
As Lane's brother has had an accident and cannot be sent to Broadlands, Floyd should apply the first coat.

328 19 Sept. 1825. [addressee not stated].
Advises that, although rather late in the season, Mr Coventry's garden walls [?at Burgate] could be pointed with a very well prepared mixture of one third cement, two thirds mortar and the cleanest sharp sand.

329 20 Sept. 1825. Mr Crook.
Request for bills.

330 23 Sept. 1825. Mr Beavis.
Rearrangement of an appointment.[1]

1. Written by J M Peniston, on father's behalf.

331 23 Sept. 1825. Mr M Hanks, Malmesbury.
Further request for a receipt.[1]

1. Written by J M Peniston, on father's behalf. The receipt was for Cow Bridge, Malmesbury. See **319**.

332 [undated[1]]. Hon John Coventry, Burgate House.
Forwards letter from Mrs Adams of Christchurch.

1. Mrs Adams's letter is dated 26 Sept., so this must be later.

333 [undated[1]]. [addressee not stated[2]].
Has sent her letter about removing the conservatory to Mr Coventry.

1. Mrs Adams's letter is dated 26 Sept., so this must be later.
2. To Mrs Adams, Christchurch. See **332**.

334 3 Oct. 1825. Rt Hon Lord Viscount Palmerston, Broadlands.
Revised estimate for the school[1] is not less than £750 to £800. Suggests that, as funds may be limited, it should be put to public tender.

1. At Romsey. See **462, 465**.

335 6 Oct. 1825. E Baker Esq, M.P.; H Biggs Esq, Stockton.
Has established that Messrs Tinney and Cobb are asking £950 for Mr Blatch's house. Considers this to be excessive [see **343**].

336 6 Oct. 1825. [addressee not stated[1]].
Forwards a reply from Mr Coventry about removing her conservatory.

1. To Mrs Adams, Christchurch. See **332, 333**.

337 8 Oct. 1825. Mr Meadows.
Gives formal notice, as County Surveyor, of a bill of indictment at the next Sessions about the unsafe state of the road at Coombe Bridge, as a result of neglect.

338 19 Oct. 1825. James Foot Esq, surveyor.
As Cornet of the Salisbury Troop, Wiltshire Yeomanry Cavalry, certifies attendance at the muster for six days in succession during the year to April 1825.

339 [*undated*]. J Penn Esq, engineer and millwright, Greenwich.
Acknowledges a letter which had abated comment at Quarter Sessions about the series of procrastinations. His own illness will cause absence from business for a time. Has replaced Buckley, the carpenter, who had been under restraint many months with little prospect of amendment. The new industrious and well disposed man will execute any work connected with the machinery[1] which does not come within Penn's contract.

1. At Devizes Penitentiary. See **225**.

340 19 Oct. 1825. Mr Henry King, Chilmark.
Acknowledges account of dilapidations to bridge at Fonthill Bishop. Expects that Quarter Sessions will order repairs.

341 [*undated*]. John Swayne Esq, Wilton.
Has met Mr Hopgood at Durrington. They agreed that the work by Mr William Warren was improperly or insufficiently executed and the contract sum should be reduced by £50 4s. 3d.

342 [*undated*]. Hon John Coventry jun, Burgate Cottage.
Thinks it unnecessary for Mr Bramah to inspect the ice house. The same problem had been found elsewhere. Care must be taken when packing the house to break the ice into small pieces, then compact it with wooden hammers.

343 23 Oct. 1825. John Blatch Esq, Sharland's Lodgings, High Street, Southampton.
Regrets that Mr Tinney has misunderstood offer [*see* **335**] on behalf of Mr Baker about fixtures. Has told Mr Cobb he would recommend £850, to include such fixtures as grates, coppers etc. If they are to be valued separately the offer is only £800.

344 [*undated*]. Mr J Hopgood, surveyor, Andover.
Arranges to survey a house at Durrington for Mr Swayne.

345 10 Nov. 1825. Mr Watson, Broadlands.
Will visit Broadlands, with his son, to check bills. Asks if Lord Palmerston wishes them to stay at the house or at an inn.

346 10 Nov. 1825. Benjamin Wingrove Esq, Road Office, Bath.
The account for work on bridge roads was too late for last year's settlement but will apply for money on account at the next sessions. The court had refused to raise the pathway of Bradford Bridge. Repairs should be made.

347   12 Nov. 1825. Mr Hughes, Devizes.
Asks for a large cart with two horses to collect window frames and other items.[1]

1. J M Peniston writes on behalf of his father, who is not yet quite well.

348   [*undated*]. Mr Jones.
Conveys Mr Wall's decision to have the conservatory erected[1] as soon as possible. Has written to Messrs Hobbs and Hellyre at Redbridge but they have no knowledge of the packages. Explanation may lie in their recent bankruptcy and derangement in the sailing of their vessel.

1. At Norman Court. See **297**.

349   21 Nov. 1825. Mr Watson.
Did not have time to analyse the bills while at Broadlands but has now done so. Comments on a mass of errors. Lead should not be moved in or out of Lord Palmerston's premises without being weighed. Makes several queries. Marsh not to be questioned and Lord Palmerston to be shown the letter.

350   21 Nov. 1825. Rev J Lear.
Has inventory of fixtures and furniture at Downton. Encloses valuation. Liability is £31 15s., the balance of £16 17s. being principally for paling and gates.

351   21 Nov. 1825. Mr Jones.
Has heard from Redbridge that some packages have arrived and the remainder expected. All will be sent to Norman Court.

352   22 Nov. 1825.[1] William Woodcock Esq.
Flue tiles are delayed as the drying has been very slow.

1. MS *Tuesday morn'*, undated.

353   22 Nov. 1825. Mr Collman, carpenter, Ringwood.
Arranges to meet to examine thatch work at Ellingham.

354   22 Nov. 1825. [*addressee not stated*[1]].
Explains delays. The cart had left the Plume of Feathers[2] at 12 o'clock but the carrier had refused some articles and another would be found. The order is finished except for the sash of the drawing room which awaits a metal bar from Bath.

1. Probably William Hughes. See **356**.
2. Probably Salisbury: P.

355 23 Nov. 1825. Mrs Hellyre, Redbridge.
Mr Wall will send his own teams for the packages for Norman Court.

356 27 Nov. 1825. William Hughes Esq.
The drawing room window cannot be sent because the metal bar has not arrived. Base mouldings for the dining and drawing rooms have been transposed. Fears that there is a disposition to mistakes. Packing boards had been returned damaged by nailing them together. The glass should be ready soon. Will be in Devizes shortly.

357 2 Dec. 1825. Charles Millet Esq.
Copies calculations for extensive repairs to the house at Ludgershall and the erection of a coach house, wash house and pantry. Can re-use some material. Cost will be £108 4s. Apologizes for delay but has been indisposed.

358 2 Dec. 1825. Miss Tate, Langdown, Southampton.
Arranges to visit.

359 3 Dec. 1825. Rev W J Young, Rockbourne.
Regrets delay and sends certificate of dilapidations at Rockbourne for £99 15s. 3d., dated 20 May 1824. Did not separate the chancel as this was unusual.

360 6 Dec. 1825. Rev W J Young, Rockbourne.
Dilapidations for the chancel amount to £8 2s. 6d.

361 6 Dec. 1825. Mr Robert Gambling, Whiteparish.
Willing to allow £6 10s. per acre for the tithes at Standfields Coppices.

362 12 Dec. 1825. Hon. D Pleydell Bouverie, Cliffe House.[1]
Proposes slight alteration to the stable building. The structure is not dangerous but work must be done with care. Reply is delayed because he has been unwell.

1. Clyffe Hall, Market Lavington: VCH 10, p.93.

363 12 Dec. 1825. Miss Tate, Langdown, Southampton.
Encloses sketch and report of the alterations proposed to the drawing room.

364 12 Dec. 1825. William Salmon jun, Brown Grove House, Devizes.
Encloses sketches of styles of double cottages marked A to D. One has a chamber floor, one a basement, one is the most effective and one the cheapest.

365 13 Dec. 1825. T Kelsey Esq.
Had volunteered his services to Lord Folkestone to superintend the bridge built at
Odstock. Is paid by the county but bridges are not recognised until complete.

366 [*undated*]. Mr Buckland.
Has been authorised by Mr Harris to sell the house for £450.

367 13 Dec. 1825. William Hughes Esq.
Is annoyed by the delay to the drawing room sash caused because the metal bar has
not arrived from Stillman of Bath, who may be haunted. The glass is ready. The delay
of the window linings is the fault of the carriers who ought to pay for them.

368 16 Dec. 1825. Mr Banks.
Is ready to pay £69 16s. 10d. for masonry, cartage and carpentry involved in the
repairs to Foot Bridge at Lacock. Blackham will be paid £8 5s. 6d. for digging clay
and £6 9s. for beer for workmen.

369 16 Dec. 1825. Mr R Hulbert, Pickwick, near Chippenham.
Informs the Commissioners of Corsham and Lacock Turnpike that he will survey
Lacock Bridge and report at the sessions.

370 19 Dec. 1825. [*addressee not stated*].
Considers that the county has the same rights under the Act to raise stone as the
Commissioners. Litigation is inadvisable and while doubts exist between the
Commissioners and landowners the county should not interfere. Would want to take
advantage of the judgement as road repair is heavy and obnoxious to the county.

371 22 Dec. 1825. [*addressee not stated*[1]].
The bar has arrived and the frames will be ready. The glass and glazier can follow.

1. William Hughes. See **367**.

372 24 Dec. 1825. [*addressee not stated*[1]].
Encloses cheque for £84 11s 4d. Intends inspecting the new bridge [*Lacock, Foot
Bridge*] and reporting to the sessions.

1. Mr Banks. See **368**.

373 31 Dec. 1825. J Penn Esq.
The men have not quite finished but the mill work appears extremely well done.
Does not know if the Court of Sessions will accept his judgement. Will be at Devizes.
Is slowly recovering from an indisposition which has lasted some months.

374 27 Dec. 1825. Mr Haywood, Governor of the Penitentiary, Devizes.
Cannot pay bills without a personal examination. Will be in Devizes to measure the
mill house, which should be closed as soon as possible. Will have Wells with him, and
Buckley had better attend and prepare two five foot measuring rods.

1826

375 24 Jan. 1826. Rev Yonge, Rockbourne.
Repairs to the house and offices would cost £64 11s 6d. Reference to Inwood's Tables (the best published) gives a life of 65 to be at 4% equalling 7¾ years' purchase.

376 24 Jan. 1826. Mr Watson.
[*Broadlands*]: Has inspected and returns the bills of Lord Palmerston. Lengthy comment including an overcharge for the use of heavy iron.

377 25 Jan. 1826. Cooper Esq, Staverton.
Has reported his letter at the last Sessions.

378 25 Jan. 1826. Rev J Mayo, Nibley House, Wotton under Edge, Gloucestershire.
Has met his son, also Rev Mayo, at Devizes and undertakes to inspect some buildings when work is ready.

379 2 Feb. 1826. Rt Hon Earl of Enniskillen.
Encloses account of receipts and payments for the Grimstead estate. Presses for acknowledgement of payments.

380 2 Feb. 1826. Hon J Coventry jun, Burgate Cottage.
Casts doubt on the reasons given by Gibbs for excessive charges and makes deduction. Sends sketch of proposed addition to cottage.

381 3 Feb. 1826. C Baring Wall Esq.
Sends sketches of cottages for approval.

382 6 Feb. 1826. [*addressee not stated*].
Encloses draft for recipient to send concerning safety inspection of Salisbury Theatre and the precautionary replacement of a roof brace, which Mr Penson[1] has promised to do.

1. John Penson was proprietor and manager of the Theatre, New Street, Salisbury: P.

383 7 Feb. 1826. Benjamin Wingrove Esq, Road Office, Bath.
Encloses cheque for £55 5s. 10d. for bridge repairs, including £8 9s. 6d. for work on Bradford Bridge road. Will inspect work on London Bridge [*?Trowbridge*] with Mr Swayne.

384 13 Feb. 1826. Rt Rev Dr Baines, Bath.
Reports that Rev Mr Begin has had serious apoplectic attack. Has asked for attendance of Rev Mr Parker.

385 13 Feb. 1826. Rev D Williams, Winchester College.
Agrees to survey dilapidations at Bradford Abbas. Thanks Rev Mr Ridding for recommending him.

386 17 Feb. 1826. T Bramah Esq, Pimlico, London.
Discusses the ice house[1] and says that it has not been properly tested by filling it this year.

1. Probably at Burgate House. See **323**.

387 20 Feb. 1826. Mr Ellis, builder, Sherborne.
Arranges to meet to survey at Bradford Abbas.

388 27 Feb. 1826. Rev Dr Williams, Winchester College.
Encloses account of Bradford Abbas dilapidations, excluding the chancel.

389 27 Feb. 1826. Hon D Pleydell Bouverie, Longford Castle.
Discusses details of the lean-to extension to the coach house which may have elm rafters. Will meet the carpenter to be employed at Clyffe Hall when next visiting Devizes. Regrets that offers for the mill do not match Mr Penn's valuation.

390 1 March 1826. Mr John Woodman.
Instruction to proceed with work for Mr Dyke, taking care not to infringe on neighbouring property.

391 2 March 1826. Rt Rev Dr Baines, Bathampton.
Reports that Mr Begin still lives. His relations from France have arrived and are anxious about their uncle's property. Suggests that debts will reduce the sum due. Expresses the anxiety of the congregation and asks about a successor.

392 2 March 1826. Rev Richard Parker, Wardour Castle.
Reports that Mr Begin will not live long. Notes Lord Arundell's wish not to interfere with the Salisbury congregation. Wishes to know whether they can be under the wing of Stonyhurst College. The congregation will do their best to pay for an English pastor.

393 [*undated*]. Mr Crouch, Spread Eagle.[1]
Requests settlement of an account for thatching straw used in repairs for Mr Wilson at Bemerton.

1. Not located. Probably the premises in New Canal, Salisbury.

394 13 March 1826. Miss Tate, Langdown House, Southampton.
Has appointed a person to superintend the alterations.

395 13 March 1826. Messrs Tanner and Sons, Castle Street.[1]
Provides valuation of Theatre.[2] Suggests appropriate annuity.

1. Salisbury, as J B S Tanner, attorney, had premises in Castle Street: P.
2. See **382**.

396 13 March 1826. Mr Bickers.
Approves some bills. Mr Eldridge's prices are for the best
timber.

397 13 March 1826. [*addressee not stated*].
Has bought a property. Encloses sketch and wishes to build houses similar to those in the environs of London. As many and as cheaply as possible. Discusses layout.

398 15 March 1826. Rt Rev Dr Baines, Bathampton.
The [*Salisbury*] congregation can collect about forty pounds a year. Doubts if that will be sufficient unless the presence of an English priest attracts more Catholic families to settle. There would also be rent on chapel property after meeting Mr Begin's claims and the £400 borrowed on the property. Mr Begin lingers on. Mr Parker had visited from Wardour and administered the sacrament to him.

399 16 March 1826. E R Butler Esq, Temple Chambers, Fleet Street, London.
Reports that Mr Begin has died. Claims will be settled by the trustees but matters will be delayed.

400 18 March 1826. [*addressee not stated*[1]].
Confirms that dilapidations at Bradford Abbas were only for the vicarage, and the gates and fences of the glebe land. Chancel repairs devolved on the Marquess of Anglesea as holder of the rectorial tithes. Had been employed for three days. Charge was £9 14s.

1. Rev Dr Williams. See **401**.

401 18 March 1826. Rev Ridding, Winchester College.
Encloses claim of £4 6s. 6d. for taking dilapidations at Orcheston.[1] Has also sent an apparently extravagant, but justified, account to Rev Dr Williams [**400**]. Grateful for recommendation.

1. Probably Orcheston St Mary. See **185** note 1.

402 24 March 1826. [*addressee not stated*].
Regrets parcel was too late to catch coach. Will meet the magistrates. Regrets the renewed failure of the head wheels.

403 25 March 1826. Mr Jones.
Re-arranges a meeting at Norman Court.

404 25 March 1826. Miss Tate, Langdown House, Southampton.
Discusses extensive repairs and alterations planned to china closet, butler's pantry, outhouses, yards, coal shed, pigsty, gentlemen's water closet, men's and women's outside privies, etc.

405 6 April 1826. Messrs Kepp, coppersmiths, Chandos Street, Covent Garden, London.
Arranges to meet their representative at Burgate House.

406 8 April 1826. Hon John Coventry, Burgate House.
Has arranged to meet Mr Kepp [**405**]. Confirms that woodwork requires painting.

407 11 April 1826. Rev F D Williams, Wishford.
Arranges to meet. Business involves Mr Lush and Mr Alfred.

408 11 April 1826. Rev Joseph Mayo, Ozleworth, Wootton under Edge.
Will meet Mr Mayo at Devizes to examine accounts.

409 11 April 1826. Rev J Mayo, Devizes.
Has written to Mr Mayo, his father, about meeting at Devizes [**408**].

410 12 April 1826. Mr Tulloch (*Tullock*), builder, Poole.
Encloses cheque for £15 on behalf of Mr Boucher, who mislaid account.[1]

1. Perhaps for work at Hilton. See **41**.

411 15 April 1826. Hon D Pleydell Bouverie, Clyffe Hall.
Encloses sketch for approval. Will discuss loose box adjoining saddle room when at
Lavington on way to Devizes. Proposal for drains appears unexceptionable.

412 24 April 1826. Miss Tate, Grosvenor (*Grovesnor*) Place, London.
Intends to visit Langdown House to inspect work. The glass door in the butler's
pantry can be changed. Had intended to use light iron bars for security. Will see if
water closet can be attached to her bedroom.

413 24 April 1826. Lord Palmerston.
Encloses plan to demonstrate understanding of alterations wanted. Problem of flues
can be overcome.

414 24 April 1826. Hon D Pleydell Bouverie, Clyffe Hall.
Will supervise work frequently when travelling to and from Devizes. Fears that
country workmen will take at least two months on the work. Pleased that intended
tour is possible because of this occasional supervision.

415 24 April 1826. Rev Joah Furey, Fordingbridge.
Seeks meeting to value dilapidations at Harbridge.

416 25 April 1826. Rev Joah Furey, Fordingbridge.
Reply to previous letter to be sent to Crown Inn, Ringwood.

417 29 April 1826. Hon D Pleydell Bouverie, Clyffe Hall.
Regrets that he now employs the man formerly at the Penitentiary as Clerk of Works
in Southampton. Will find someone else. Most of stable roof can be repaired rather
than replaced.

418   29 April 1826.   Rev Joseph Mayo, Ozleworth, Wootton under Edge, Gloucestershire.
Will travel from Bath on a Gloucester coach to meet the James's. Will bring a professional friend. This will not add to charges. May need to stay a night.

419   7 May 1826.   [*addressee not stated*].
Sends sketch of dining room skirtings at Norman Court. Discusses door and window design.

420   8 May 1826.   Cooper Esq, Staverton Mill, Bradford.
Sends cheque for £20 for repair of Staverton Bridge road.

421   9 May 1826.   Hon D Pleydell Bouverie, Clyffe Hall.
Sends plan. Taylor should add iron straps to strengthen roof. Roof should stay on until he visits.

422   9 May 1826.   Lt Col Baker, W.Y.C.[1]
Reports on disturbances at Trowbridge. Had been told that the Devizes, Melksham, Chippenham and Warminster Troops were on duty. Had warned the non-commissioned officers to be ready to summon the Troop but no intelligence had arrived by the Bristol mail. Riot had been suppressed and ringleaders secured. Enquires about his return. Pettit cannot do much but had gone to Devizes, assisted by Peniston's son. Offers to take Pettit's place when necessary. Has secured a piece of ground for exercise. Has received a dozen flintlocks since last duty and expects more.

1. Wiltshire Yeomanry Cavalry.

423   13 May 1826.   Lord Palmerston, Stanhope Street, London.
Excuses himself from business until his yeomanry duties, deputizing for the adjutant,[1] permit. Recommends a master carpenter.

1. Pettit. See **422**.

424   13 May 1826.   Rev S B Vince, Ruddells Hotel, St Martin's Lane, London.
Reports cost of dilapidations at Ringwood and Harbridge.

425   16 May 1826.   Messrs Kepp, coppersmiths, Chandos Street, Covent Garden, London.
Sends plan of part of Mr Coventry's roof[1] due to be covered in copper.

1. At Burgate House. See **405, 406**.

426 [*undated*[1]]. E R Butler Esq, Temple Chambers, Fleet Street, London.
Arranges to pay off loan to the late Mr Begin.

1. After 24 May, the date of Butler's letter, to which he refers.

427   29 May 1826.   Rev Mr De La Porte, Chaplain to the French Ambassador, London.
Explains that Mr Begin's property is being handled by Brodie and Dowding in Salisbury and Remington and Company in London. Miss Duchemin, the neice of Mr Begin, has left Salisbury.

428   29 May 1826. William Hughes Esq, Devizes.
Sends details of decoration for the drawing room.

429   29 May 1826.   Rev J Lear, Chilmark.
Sends plan for the flues and excuses delay due to military duties.

430   17 June 1826.   Lt Col Baker, W.Y.C.[1]
Reports discussions about who should take command of the Melksham Troop.

1. Wiltshire Yeomanry Cavalry.

431   18 June 1826.   Mr Floyd.
Instructs him to build strictly to the line and avoid dispute. Wells will prepare and drive the piles.

432   21 June 1826.   Rev Robert Ashe.
Reduces the charge for inspecting Kellaways (*Kelloway*) Bridge, as he had business in Devizes and the payment is to be from a charitable fund.[1]

1. Maud Heath's Causeway, of which Kellaways Bridge is part.

433   24 June 1826.   [*addressee not stated*[1]].
Has inspected a drain at Broadlands and given instructions for some remedial work. Barge boards have been put up. Work on the school building[2] is slow because of difficulties with neighbours. Some gentlemen of the committee for the proposed school feel that they have not been sufficiently consulted. Has an offer of timber at a good price if the committee's funds are available.

1. Letter begins, 'My Lord', i.e. Lord Palmerston.
2. At Romsey. See **462, 465**.

434 1 July 1826. Mrs Eyre.
Mrs Hodgson will keep her house[1] a year longer.

1. Perhaps in St Martin's Church Street, Salisbury. See **120**.

435 1 July 1826. Mrs Hodgson.
Regrets misunderstanding. The rent remains the same as when paid to Mr Begin.

436 1 July 1826. George Dew Esq, Canal [*Salisbury*].
Complains that Mr Coventry's instructions about a delivery of stone have been ignored.

437 8 July 1826. Mr Eldridge, timber merchant, Southampton.
Orders five loads of red pine in 30 or 45 foot lengths. Expects to pay Miss Tate's tradesmen soon.

438 11 July 1826. Mr Hudson.
Discussion of various bills for Mr Hale.

439 26 July 1826. Mr Hawkins.
Asks when plate glass can be delivered to Stockbridge for Mr Wall.[1]

1. Written by J M Peniston, on father's behalf.

440 1 Aug. 1826. Messrs Locke and Hughes, Devizes.
Introduces Mr James Taylor who is due to be paid £10 16s. 7d. for bricklaying at Clyffe Hall.

441 1 Aug. 1826. Mr Taylor, bricklayer.
Sends letter [**440**] about payment to Messrs Locke and Hughes of Devizes.

442 1 Aug. 1826. Lord Palmerston, Stanhope Street, London.
Returns plans showing alterations to the vestibule.

443 1 Aug. 1826. J Penn Esq, engineer, Greenwich.
Presented report[1] at the Warminster sessions but has not replied because of a visit to Paris. Encloses an order for £60. Requests a bill.

1. Probably relating to the mill machinery at Devizes Penitentiary. See **373, 509**.

444 1 Aug. 1826. Mr Eldridge, timber merchant, Southampton.
Sends cheque for £88 8s. 3d. Discusses other payments.

445 11 Aug. 1826. [*addressee not stated*].
Arranges meeting at Burgate Cottage.

446 16 Aug. 1826. [*addressee not stated*[1]].
Sends a list of charges of £235 1s. 4½d. in all for work at Langdown, and his
allowances totalling £228 8s. 0 ½d.

1. Letter begins, 'Madam', i.e. Miss Tate. See **412**.

447 19 Aug. 1826. Rev J Mayo.
Encloses sketch of alterations to cottage.

448 19 Aug. 1826. Mr Windsor.
Reports that he is due to be paid £1056 8s. 1d. for work at Norman Court. Has had
£500 on account and will be sending bills and receipts for the balance.

449 23 Aug. 1826. Rev Joah Furey.
Regrets to press for payment but has to meet heavy payments himself at Michaelmas.

450 24 Aug. 1826. Lord Palmerston.
Arranges to visit Broadlands.

451 25 Aug. 1826. Mr Ballister,[1] 62 High Street, Southampton.
'I cannot but regret the trouble you have had and the anxiety you must have
experienced for the safety of your account amounting to £1 18s. 8d. for drain pipes
delivered for Miss Tate in April last. And as unfortunately I only act as her surveyor
in this business I fear you must wait till the accounts are arranged for payment, when
should she honor me as the medium of settling with the tradesmen, I shall have great
pleasure in removing the anxiety you must so naturally feel. I am, Mr Ballister, your
most obedient and very humble servant.'

1. Perhaps John Labalestier, shopkeeper and dealer in sundries, High Street, Southampton: P.

452 24 Aug. 1826. Hon John Coventry.
Has estimated dilapidations at the farm[1] lately occupied by Mr Blachford as £71 15s.
Comments that most of the property needs rebuilding rather than repairing.

1. Criddlestile Farm. See **455**.

453 1 Sept. 1826. Mr Blackmore jun, Salisbury.
'Sir, It is of course difficult on so extensive a survey as the city of Salisbury presents to calculate what time will be employed; but I have no hesitation in stating that I am of opinion the expence cannot exceed two hundred pounds.'

454 1 Sept. 1826. Mr Eldridge, Southampton.
Confirms deduction from a bill for Miss Tate. Is surprised not to have had an order to pay it.

455 [undated]. [addressee not stated[1]].
Certifies dilapidations at Criddlestile Farm late in the occupation of Mr Blachford estimated at £71 15s [see **452**].

1. Letter headed, 'delivered to Mr Dew'.

456 6 Sept. 1826. Rt Hon Earl of Enniskillen, Florence Court, Ireland.
Explains delay in settling various estate problems.

457 11 Sept. 1826. Thos Hopper Esq, 35 Connaught Terrace, Edgeware Road, London.
Writes on behalf of Mr May to describe how an ice house is not draining properly. Asks for agreement to modifications.

458 21 Sept. 1826. Cooper Esq, Staverton Mill, Bradford.
Asks for the bill for repairs to the road at Staverton Mill Bridge before it is too late for approval at the forthcoming sessions.

459 21 Sept. 1826. Mr Wingrove jun, Trowbridge.
Asks for the bridge road accounts so that payment is not delayed until Michaelmas the following year. Also needs the bill if trifling repairs to the bridge at Trowbridge have been made.

460 [undated]. Mr Floyd.
Has been instructed by Lord Palmerston to proceed with work on the school.[1] Brickwork is to be started.

1. At Romsey. See **462, 465**.

461 21 Sept. 1826. Rev J O Parr, Henley.
Suggests repairs at Durnford should be delayed until the spring.

462 24 Sept. 1826. Mr Richard Coles, slater, Southampton.
Half of a roof is ready to be started. The School House at Romsey will soon be ready.

463 25 Sept. 1826. Mr Holmes.
Reports further boundary disputes with neighbours to right and left of [*Romsey*]
School Room [*see* **433**]. Has refused to pull down work and start again. Outlines
proposed agreement for ratification by Lord Palmerston.

464 27 Sept. 1826. Mr James Crook, keeper, Marlborough Bridewell.
Approves bills for the quarter.

465 29 Sept. 1826. Henry Holmes, Romsey.
Cannot meet his wishes by reporting to his noble employer that it is too late in the
year to comply with his directions respecting the schoolroom. However, by choice he
should prefer a postponement until spring. Regrets the actions of the Methodists, and
feels that he has incurred odium almost on every side. Suggests that Lord Palmerston
be told of the problem in the hope that he might postpone his intentions until spring.

466 4 Oct. 1826. Edward Stevens[1] Esq.
Encloses tradesmen's bills for work on Crane Bridge. [*Salisbury*]

1. Badly written, name uncertain.

467 8 Oct. 1826. Messrs Chinchen, Swanage.
Cannot yet pay for stone sent to Langdown House. Expects Miss Tate shortly to order
payment.

468 14 Oct. 1826. Hon John Coventry, Burgate House.
Sends bills for work at Burgate House and Burgate Cottage.

469 [*undated*]. Mr Hulbert, surveyor, Corsham.
Seeks payment from the Commissioners of the Lacock Trust for supervising the re-
erection of Lacock Bridge. Will pay for work to the roads over and adjoining Foot
and Ray Bridges. Will contract for the preservation of Lacock Bridge road when the
county recognises it.

470 20 Oct. 1826. Mr Sainsbury.
Gives instruction to repair Rangebourne Bridge so that it is secure for the winter.
May recommend the magistrates to build a new bridge.

471 22 Oct. 1826. C Baring Wall Esq, Norman Court.
Discusses meeting with Mr Jones.

472 24 Oct. 1826. Mr Jones, Messrs Jones and Clark.
Suggests that a letter to Mr Wall about disputed payment would be better than a meeting.

473 25 Oct. 1826. Charles Millett Esq, Hindon.
Sends delayed account for survey report and estimate at Ludgershall. Explains that travelling expenses were high.

474 25 Oct. 1826. E R Butler Esq.
Arranges to pay interest of £25 on the late Rev Begin's account.

475 26 Oct. 1826. Benjamin Wingrove Esq, Trowbridge.
Sends cheque for £87 14s. 4d. Asks for stamped receipt. Grateful for attention to bridge roads. Can he take charge of Staverton Mill Bridge without offence to Mr Cooper.

476 4 Nov. 1826. John Benett Esq, Pyt House.
Seeks confirmation of commission to value materials at Fonthill.[1] Mr Fisher of Salisbury has been appointed by the other party and wishes to proceed.

1. Fonthill Abbey collapsed on 21 Dec. 1825, and with part of the estate was purchased soon afterwards by Bennet for £130,000: WAM vol.49, p.512.

477 14 Nov. 1826. Rt Hon Earl of Enniskillen.
Reports correspondence with Messrs Tinney and Cobb about disputed tithes.

478 [undated]. [addressee not stated].
John [M Peniston] will send some plans by Cuff. The stone has not arrived. References to Père Howard and Père Begin, and to various aspects of chapel affairs. Asks recipient to inform Mr Jeffrey that he will call at Wardour on 28 Nov. after surveying dilapidations at Berwick St John, and before examining property at Tisbury.

479 27 Nov. 1826. Sir Charles Hulse, Breamore House.
Proposals will be approved by Mr Coventry. Will prepare the timber agreed with the carpenter in preparation for work in the meadows in the spring.

480 2 Dec. 1826. Charles Bowles Esq, Shaftesbury.
Reports on work in progress at the intended Town Hall at Shaftesbury. Explains why
a pier has given way and how it can be repaired. Has discussed estimates and conduct
of the work with Mr Down. The brickwork is safe but of poor appearance. The
building has been extended to include a water closet. The specification should be
amended to enable Earl Grosvenor's agent to measure and value the building when
completed. Mr Down should be allowed to proceed with the work. Prices need to
be checked. One of the two smiths has overcharged for work. Lead for cramping
stonework has been overcharged. Use of roman cement would save money. Masonry
should be offered to competition as custom sanctioned an abominable fraud in
calculating the perch at 15 instead of 16½ feet. All those concerned were accustomed
to employment by Lord Grosvenor and dependent on him. However costs should be
controlled.

481 2 Dec. 1826. Charles Bowles Esq, Shaftesbury.
Report on house and remains of a malthouse at Tisbury owned by Mrs Alford.

482 2 Dec. 1826. Messrs Tinney and Cobb.
Cannot value a charity property bounded by Milford and Culver Streets [*Salisbury*],
held by Messrs Whitchurch, as the occupants have no information about the other
boundaries.

483 5 Dec. 1826. Charles Bowles Esq.
Has delayed sending enclosed report [**480** or **481**] in hope of including account of
dilapidations at Berwick[1]. Has to arrange with Mr Fisher about the latter.

1. Berwick St John. See **478**.

484 11 Jan. 1827.[1] G Bosset Esq, Stratton, Cirencester.
Acknowledges estimate to repair Dauntsey Bridge. Will survey the bridge and contact
Mr Salway.

1. This letter is considerably out of sequence.

485 8 Dec. 1826. Henry Holmes Esq, Romsey.
Returns Mr Instone's bill as excessive. Cannot comment on the bell hanging and hot
air stove. Sum of £4 17s. 10d. to clean and repair the smoke jack was too much.

486 10 Dec. 1826. Lord Palmerston, Stanhope Street, London.
Reports the dining room floor at Broadlands to be decayed.

487 9 Dec. 1826. John Swayne Esq, Wilton.
Asks for settlement of account for timber purchased by Mr Dyke for Bulford Bridge.

488 16 Dec. 1826. Miss Tate, Langdown, Southampton.
Arranges to visit.

489 16 Dec. 1826. Mr John Cottman, builder, Ringwood.
Will visit to survey the work and stay at the Crown.

490 19 Dec. 1826. Mr John Cottman, Ringwood.
Changes day of visit.

491 20 Dec. 1826. Hon John Coventry, Burgate House.
Encloses accounts from tradesmen; from Sir Charles Hulse for timber; and his own professional accounts.

492 23 Dec. 1826. C Baring Wall Esq, MP, Norman Court.
Doubts the wisdom of paying Mr Jones for an alleged loss as it was their own fault.[1]
Charge for the folding doors was excessive as plate glass was not included.

1. See **471, 472**.

493 26 Dec. 1826. Mr Eldridge, timber merchant, Southampton.
Sends cheques totalling £186 14s. 6d. for various tradesmen. Has altered some of the accounts to Salisbury prices. Cannot conceive that deal is more valuable in Southampton. Enquires the lowest price for plastering laths.

494 28 Dec. 1826. Messrs Chinchen, Swanage.
Asks how they wish to be paid by Miss Tate. Offers to pay through his London bank.

1827

495 5 Jan. 1827. John Swayne Esq, Wilton.
Sends details of expenses for journeys made on behalf of the county to inspect work on bridges in 1824, 1825 and 1826.

496 13 Jan. 1827. Mr Wing, Burgate.
Vexed to learn that Mr Coventry was annoyed by that fellow Honeywell but it will be difficult to disprove the number of days for which he is charging. The bill should be paid and Honeywell dismissed from any further employment.

497 15 Jan. 1827. The Right Rev Dr Collingridge.
'My Lord. I feel somewhat ashamed in not having earlier offered the most grateful acknowledgements of our congregation to your Lordship for the appointment of the Revd Mr O'Connor to this mission. He is indeed my Lord everything we could have desired and more than we were entitled to expect. I sincerely hope we shall prove our gratitude by our conduct and become worthy of the blessing and advantages we at present enjoy.

'I begin to hope my Lord that though we cannot raise a fund adequate either to our wishes or the merits of Mr O'Connor it may by the aid of kind friends suffice for his support. The subscriptions of the resident congregation somewhat exceeds fifty pounds, Mr Bowles says that he is certain my Lord Arundell will continue his £20 and the Rev Mr Parker states that Stonyhurst will not withdraw its ten pounds a year. We have also been fortunate in receiving some donations and have reason to expect to add somewhat to the permanent income when poor Mr Begin's affairs are settled and the houses let – that which he last occupied is still unoccupied. It would be a very desirable situation for a catholic family if we could be so fortunate as to find one of respectability that would not only add to our numbers but contribute to the support of our pastor.

'We make monthly collections to meet the contingent expenses of the chapel and have reason to hope they will be sufficient to meet the demands.

'I do not know whether I should intrude upon your lordship by entering on the business of the chapel property as connected with the late Revd Mr Begin. I wait your permission to do so and remain with the highest respects, My Lord, Your Lordship's obedient servant, J Peniston.'

498 15 Jan. 1827. Mr Keeping, plumber, Southampton.
Regrets to learn that Mr Keeping has not discovered the cause of the stink from the water closet at Langdown. Miss Tate has written again about it. Discusses possible solutions. Asks that Keeping reads the letter to Mr Whitaker, who may have helpful observations.

499 15 Jan. 1827. Mr Eldridge, timber merchant, Southampton.
Orders deal laths.

500 18 Jan. 1827. Garbett Esq.
Has been referred to him as the person appointed by Mr Dampier on the subject of dilapidations at Wylye.

501 29 Jan. 1827. Timothy Bramah Esq, Pimlico, London.
Discusses a drainage problem on which Mr Bramah had advised Mr Coventry.

502 1 Feb. 1827. Mr Eldridge, timber merchant, Southampton.
Encloses cheque.

503 1 Feb. 1827. Hon John Coventry, Burgate House.
Agrees that a smith's bill is extravagant but does not know how to comment and will discuss it during a forthcoming visit.

504 7 Feb. 1827. Earl of Enniskillen.
[*Grimstead*]: Has been waiting for money from Tubb before it could be remitted to his lordship's bankers. Tubb promises well but does not always perform and he is loath to have recourse to severe measures.

505 7 Feb. 1827. C Baring Wall Esq M.P., Norman Court.
Arranges to visit.

506 7 Feb. 1827. Mr John Burn, wine merchant, 113 High Street, Southampton.
Encloses a cheque for £7 4s. 0d. The hampers and bottles will be returned in a few days.

507 9 Feb. 1827. [*addressee not stated*[1]].
'Dear Gillo, I am requested Col Baker, our *ci-devant* captain, to write to you on the subject of your St George wine. He has drunk some at Dr Fowler's and is anxious to have a hogshead of the same class, but trebly anxious to have it very very very good – but joking apart it may be worth your while to endeavour to please his palate he being considered a judge of wine of the first water, and if he pronounces it a fit beverage for persons *comme il faut* it may lead. You will conclude by seeing no more of me at Havre that I returned by another route. It was so, after spending a busy and very delighful week at Paris I returned via Boulogne. I very much regretted not having seen James Weeks. When you see him present my best regards and say when

next I visit France (which if I live a few years is not very impossible) it shall go hard but I shake him by the hand. Present my respectful regards to Mr Moss and your better half though unknown. Vide Hayden. The Weeks family are all well – Harrington's also. Poor Hyde who is still at Whitchurch is suffering from a periodical attack of erysipolas [*sic*], but we hope he is getting better. Mrs P. and family I thank God pretty well. They unite in best regards to you and yours. Dear Gillo, yours very sincerely, J Peniston.'

1. J H Gillo. See **591**.

508 13 Feb. 1827. Mr Hugh Bevan, furnishing ironmonger, 35, Marylebone Street, Piccadilly, London.
Has been requested by Mr Coventry to look at a grate at Burgate House with reference to the unreasonable bill. Discusses the work recorded and recommends that if the parts totalling £7 6s. 5d. are deducted he will recommend Mr Coventry to pay it, receiving the usual discount for prompt payment.

509 14 Feb. 1827. J Penn Esq, engineer and millwright, Greenwich.
Asks for details of accounts and travel expenses. Regrets having to ask but between the magistrates, the clerk to the peace and the late poor governor,[1] the originals are mislaid.

1. E Cocks, governor of Devizes Penitentiary, died 1825. See **225**.

510 14 Feb. 1827. J Fraser Esq, Duke Street, Westminster.
Arranges to correct some mistakes in bills for regimental expenses sent by Mr Pettit.

511 15 Feb. 1827. Mr Hugh Beavan, 35, Marylebone Street, Piccadilly, London.
Acknowledges an unsatisfactory reply about the bill for Burgate House but will not permit the bill to be paid.

512 17 Feb. 1827. [*addressee not stated*[1]].
Is not satisfied with a further letter and will recommend Mr Coventry to refer the correspondence to his solicitor.

1. Presumably to Mr Hugh Beavan. See **511**, **513**.

513 17 Feb. 1827. Hon John Coventry, Burgate House.
Will hold the letter to Mr Beavan until the post time on the following day in case Mr Coventry feels it to be too strong.

514 24 Feb. 1827. C Baring Wall Esq M.P., Berkeley Square, London.
Discusses a dispute with Messrs Harrisson over costs of building at Norman Court between 1821 and 1823.

515 25 Feb. 1827. C Baring Wall Esq M.P., Berkeley Square, London.
Remains assured in his opinion of the previous day that the cost of painting was considered included in the settlement of December 1822. Will refer to the papers connected with the claim when he returns home.

516 3 March 1827. Rev J Mayo, Devizes.
Encloses a working drawing that will enable the bricklayer to begin. The bricklayer should give his price for labour per rod and scaffolding. Mr Mayo should provide the materials. The carpenter should prepare an estimate.

517 3 March 1827. Mr Haywood, Penitentiary, Devizes.
Sends Mr Penn's account [*see* **509**]. Does not understand why journeys in 1823 and 1825 are charged in different ways. Corrects the account. Asks for the accompanying packet [**516**] to be delivered to Mr Mayo.

518 3 March 1827. Earl of Enniskillen, Florence Court, Ireland.
Encloses a receipt which had been accidentally omitted.

519 6 March 1827. C Baring Wall Esq M.P., Berkeley Square, London.
Discusses Mr Harrison's demand for painting at Norman Court, but this does not alter the impression that the final settlement was included in Mr Wall's payment of 28 December 1822.

520 6 March 1827. Edward Baker Esq M.P., House of Commons, London.
Has not heard from Mr Gillo but has now sent the letter [**507**] by a private hand via Southampton to cross by one of the packets. Has not heard from Mr Garbett but has written [**522**] taking for granted that the previous agreement would be the basis of his proposal.

521 6 March 1827. Mr Bellamy, Whitchurch, Dorset.
Discusses the Rev Mr Boucher's accounts.

522 6 March 1827. William Garbett Esq, architect, Winchester.
Presses for proposals for the erection of the new barn and what should be allowed to the Rev Mr Baker for rebuilding the house.[1]

1. At Wylye. See **500, 540**.

523 9 March 1827. C Baring Wall Esq M.P., Berkeley Square, London.
Discusses at length the claim for painting at Norman Court. Asks for a transcription of Mr Harrison's letter and receipt dated 28 December 1822.

524 10 March 1827.[1] Thomas Atkinson Esq.
Discusses payment arrangements for a survey in which they are joined and the need to refer to a third person if they cannot agree. Encloses a copy of his letter to the overseers [525].

1. MS *Saturday evening*, undated.

525 9 March 1827. Messrs the Churchwardens and Overseers of the City of Salisbury.
Circumstances prevent them from receiving the assessment for a new poor rate during their term of office. Asks for the appointment of a third person authorised to decide on any difference of opinion between Mr Atkinson and himself on the definitive arrangement of the business.

526 9 March 1827. William Wheeler Esq, Brown Street.
Asks for the enclosed [525] to be placed before the Committee.

527 11 March 1827. Mr James Mitchell, Burgate House.
Advises on timber needed for posts and rails.

528 13 March 1827. Rev Joseph Mayo, Devizes.
Sends elevation of garden front and perspective view of the two fronts. Discusses the roof supports.

529 26 March 1827. Edward Baker Esq M.P., House of Commons, London.
Has a reply from Mr Gillo that he will send the best sample of the St George wine the country can produce.[1] Can get no reply from Mr Garbett[2] and may request the Rev Mr Baker to write to the principal.

1. See **507**.
2. Wylye dilapidations. See **530, 540**.

530 26 March 1827. William Garbett Esq, architect, Winchester.
Regrets to trouble him about the Wylye dilapidation, but his principal cannot safely begin pulling down the old house until the business is settled.

531 30 March 1827. Rev Joah Furey.
Asks if the Rev Mr Evans still wishes to take Burgate Cottage.[1]

1. A page of Grimstead rentals, 1818-23, intervenes in the MS between this and the following letter.

532 2 April 1827. James Still Esq, [*East*] Knoyle.
Has surveyed the dilapidations occasioned by a fire at Mr Davenish's farm at Bulford and estimates the cost of repairs at £9 15s. 0d. Discusses other work required in great detail.[1]

1. It appears from **711** below that J M Peniston made a mistake in copying this letter to send to Still. It is corrected by **711**.

533 4 April 1827. Mr Bellamy, builder, Whitchurch, Dorset.
Arranges a meeting at Hilton to discuss the accounts.

534 4 April 1827. Thomas Fox Esq, Beaminster, Dorset.
Acknowledges a packet of bills and arranges to visit.

535 4 April 1827. Mr Stephen Gale, builder, Dorchester.
Will be at the Bull Inn, Bridport to discuss Mr Fox's disputed accounts.

536 4 April 1827. Rev Henry Boucher, Hilton, Dorset.
Confirms a meeting at Hilton in hope of finally arranging the tradesmen's accounts.

537 5 April 1827. William Garbett Esq, architect, Winchester.
Proposes meeting at Romsey to discuss the dilapidations at Wylye [*see* **541**].

538 5 April 1827. Edward Baker Esq M.P., House of Commons, London.
Has had difficulty in meeting Mr Garbett but has now arranged to do so [**537**]. Asks if a meeting of the regiment has been arranged, and refers to the gazetting of Mr Astley to the Everley [*Troop*].

539 5 April 1827. Mr Eldridge, timber merchant, Southampton.
Encloses a cheque. Asks about prices for memel timber and deal in the years from 1806 to 1810 to help with the examination of some accounts.

540 7 April 1827. Rev Francis Baker.
Annexes the valuation of dilapidations at Wylye which he has agreed with Mr Garbett. The total is £753 2s. 0d.

541 8 April 1827. Edward Baker Esq M.P.

'[*When*] I had the honor of last writing you [**538**] I mentioned that I had proposed meeting Mr Garbett at Romsey yesterday. Receiving no answer to my letter [**537**] requesting that meeting, anxious to conclude the business, and knowing that I should be engaged the whole of the ensuing week in Dorsetshire, I determined to seek the lion in his den. I therefore went yesterday to Winchester, concluding if he had been from home he would be likely to return the last day of the week. I was fortunate for after waiting a few hours I caught him on his return, and after a somewhat animated discussion, concluded with him at the sum of £753 2s. 0d. This if not quite equal to my wishes is fully equal to my expectations and I hope will prove satisfactory.'

542 8 April 1827. Mr Stephen Gale, builder, Dorchester.

Is about to set out for Dorsetshire, and discusses the confusion that has arisen about a meeting at Bridport to discuss Mr Fox's business. Asks for a reply to be sent to Milton Abbey.

543 14 April 1827. Rt Hon Earl of Enniskillen, 37 Duke Street, St James's, London.

Had conveyed His Lordship's letter to Messrs Tinney and Cobb but has not yet had a reply. Expects to see Tubb on Tuesday, the principal market day, and will then remit monies received to Messrs Drummonds.

544 16 April 1827. G Bissett Esq, Stratton, Cirencester.

Arranges to meet Mr Selway at Dauntsey Bridge to discuss repairs needed.

545 16 April 1827. R Webb Esq.

Forwards some tradesmen's accounts and will send others. Will collect Beauchamp's book when at Norman Court. Wishes to have some chat relative to his own account before presenting it, as Mr Wall offered some objection in a former instance.

546 18 April 1827.[1] [*addressee not stated*[2]].

Was unable to collect Beauchamp's book when at Norman Court but has arranged for it to be sent. Discusses some other bills.

1. 8 a.m.
2. To R Webb, since he refers to **545**, and presents Mrs Peniston's love and best wishes to Mrs Webb.

547 26 April 1827. William Garbett Esq, Winchester.

Suggests meeting at Newbury on Sunday night to enter on the business at Woolhampton early on Monday. A jury is to be empanelled at 12 o'clock and they may have to state the value of the dilapidations on the rectorial house.

548 [*undated*]. Rev J O Parr, Remenham Rectory, Henley on Thames, Oxfordshire. Work at Durnford has started. The workmen are resident in the neighbourhood. He has long employed the bricklayer, and the carpenter is the parish clerk. Agrees that the present tenants are anything but eligible but has heard that they intend leaving at Michaelmas. Expects no difficulty in finding a respectable tenant but needs to know what Mr Parr's views are about occasional residence before any offer is made. Explains that he acts as a general agent and will have great pleasure in being of service, but does not profess to have a knowledge of lands and is perfectly incompetent to ascertain the value of tithes.

549 28 April 1827. William Garbett Esq, architect, Winchester.
Proposes meeting at the Pelican Inn, Newbury. The business[1] cannot be postponed because the sheriff is coming from Wokingham (*Oakingham*), and the dilapidations have to be gone into, as their evidence will be required for the jury.[2]

1. At Woolhampton. See **547**.
2. Written by J M Peniston, on father's behalf.

550 4 May 1827. Earl of Enniskillen, 37 Duke Street, St James's, London.
Has directed his banker to pay £80 to his Lordship's account at Messrs Drummonds. Has only received £60 from Tubb and the remainder is for Mr Wall's two years rent of the Grimstead manor.

551 [*undated*]. Henry Holmes Esq, Romsey.
Arranges to meet relative to the examination of some accounts.

552 5 May 1827. Mr Allford.
Encloses demand on Rev Mr Baker for the Wylye dilapidations. Has charged extra for the journey to Winchester [*see* **541**]. Has gone once through the Woolhampton dilapidations and makes the amount about £180.

553 3 May 1827. E Baker Esq M.P., Limners Hotel, Conduit Street, London.
Encloses Captain Long's requisition for appointments. And has sent separately his last return, dated 1 Dec. 1826, listing clothing, arms, ammunition and appointments for men and horses.

554 6 May 1827. Lt Col Baker, W.Y.C.[1].
Has given Messrs Stevens and Blackmore the necessary instructions for Captain Long's cloaks. The meeting of the Hindon Troop was to measure the recruits for new cloaks. Queries whether Captain Wyndham should have sent to London for articles of saddlery for recruits. Hopes to meet the Rev Mr Baker at Wylye and arrange to make a start. Will consult Lord Arundell about troop arrangements. Asks if Mr Pettit should inform commandants of troops about the decision.

1. Wiltshire Yeomanry Cavalry.

555 8 May 1827. Thomas Fox Esq, Beaminster, Dorset.
Will get to Bridport by the mail and call on him before meeting Mr Gale at Symondsbury.

556 8 May 1827. Mr Gale, surveyor and builder, Dorchester.
Requests a meeting at Symondsbury. Nominates Mr Cornish of Exeter as his choice of the three gentlemen proposed. For his own part he names Mr Garbett of Winchester, Mr Foster of Bristol and Mr Bramble of Portsmouth.

557 9 May 1827. Mr Wing, Burgate Farm.
Thinks the annual rent for Burgate Cottage, garden and offices should be £30. The furniture should be valued and the land and homestead adjoining would be additional.

558 10 May 1827. William Garbett Esq, architect, Winchester.
The coincidence of their amounts is almost as extraordinary as the pacing and measurement. Makes £179 19s 2d on first going through. Has not heard from Mr Gale but has little expectation of settling without reference to a third party.

559 12 May 1827. Mr Penn, engineer, Greenwich.
Forwards part of the money due. Had reason to suppose that the visiting magistrates at Devizes would have settled the balance and suggests writing to the Governor.[1]

1. Mr Haywood. See **517**.

560 16 May 1827. Mr Selway, Chippenham.
'I fear I cannot give directions for filling up the road at Dauntsey Bridge as I apprehend the road has not been adopted by the county. I will however make application to the Clerk of the Peace and shall be happy if I can to meet the Rev Mr Bissett's wishes. The payment for the repairs will be ordered at the Michaelmas sessions and paid immediately after provided the work is finished sufficiently early for me to pass it to the Committee of Accounts, who meet about a month before the sessions.'

561 16 May 1827. Mr Bellamy, builder, Whitchurch, Dorset.
Regets delay but will forward the account to Mr Boucher during the present week.

562 16 May 1827. Mr Gale, surveyor, Dorchester.
Changes the time of meeting. Asks for agreement about the referee.

563 17 May 1827. Thomas Fox Esq, Green's Coffee House, Portugal Street, London. Has received an arbitration bond from Mr Harbin of Ringwood and thanks Mr Fox for the honour of naming him as referee between Mr Compton and Mr Joseph Dyett.[1] Suggests some changes to the arrangements for meeting.

1. For dilapidations at the Red Lion, Totton. See **594**.

564 17 May 1827. Rev Henry Boucher, Hilton, Dorset.
Has received a pressing letter about Bellamy' accounts. Has examined some of the bills and discusses payment.

565 17 May 1827. C Harbin Esq, Ringwood.
Will be happy to attend to the business if there can be an extension of the time.

566 21 May 1827. William Garbett Esq, architect, Winchester.
Has great satisfaction that Mr Garbett is appointed refereee between Mr Gale and himself in relation to the disputed account for Symondsbury rectory near Bridport. Discusses the arrangements with Mr Gale and warns that Mr Garbett's services are likely to be needed.

567 21 May 1827. Henry Holmes Esq, Romsey.
Will attend to Lord Palmerston's wishes relative to the school. Arranges to meet in Romsey to examine the bills.

568 21 May 1827. Mr Gale, builder, Dorchester.
Asks whether Mr Garbett should attend their meeting.

569 23 May 1827. Samuel Foot Esq.
Has proposed that the differences between Mr Brown and Mr Coombes be referred to Mr Swayne.

570 23[1] May 1827. C Harbin Esq, Ringwood.
Has heard from Mr Fox that the meeting with Mr Compton may be delayed.

1. MS *13*, but must post-date **565**, so 23 is presumably intended.

571 23 May 1827. William Garbett Esq, architect, Winchester.
Asks him to attend the meeting with Mr Gale at Bridport.

572 [*undated*[1]]. Hon John Coventry, 22 Baker Street, Portman Square, London.
Has had a series of applications for Burgate Cottage and has arranged to meet Captain
Lowe, of Lymington, who may wish to rent it and the two pieces of land. Proposes
thirty guineas a year for the cottage, furniture at a valuation or ten per cent a year for
its use, and three pounds per acre. Discusses arrangement for the present crops. Asks
for confirmation about work to be done at Burgate House.[1]

1. Probably 2 June 1827, since wording suggests that it was written on the same day as **573**.

573 2 June 1827. Captain Lowe, Pennington Cottage, near Lymington, Hants.
Arranges to meet at Burgate Cottage.

574 4 June 1827. George Underwood Esq, architect, Pierpoint Street, Bath.
Has an order to repair the Wiltshire moiety of Farley [*Farleigh Hungerford*] Bridge. Asks
if there is a corresponding direction for his county and if they can proceed
simultaneously.

575 7 June 1827. George Underwood Esq, architect, Pierpoint Street, Bath.
Agrees a meeting.

576 7 June 1827. Hon John Coventry, 22 Baker Street, Portman Square, London.
Has met Captain Lowe at Burgate. He is anxious to take only the cottage and only
for one year on condition that some more furniture is provided. Does not
recommend this and requests instructions.

577 9 June 1827. Thomas Fox Esq, Beaminster.
Awaits the award of the umpire on the Symondsbury business, but expects matters to
be satisfactory to Rev Mr Raymond.

578 [*undated*]. Messrs Moody and Son, plumbers, etc., Romsey.
Is happy to meet Mr Holmes's wishes to employ them for the work at the National
School at Romsey and will call to discuss this when next there.

579 9 June 1827. Captain Lowe, Pennington Cottage, Lymington.
Stated the proposals about Burgate Cottage to Mr Coventry who has declined to let
it on those conditions.

580 9 June 1827. J Hills Esq, 12 King Street, Portsea.
Informs him that Burgate Cottage is let.

581 14 June 1827. [*addressee not stated*[1]].
Had overslept in London and had barely time to save the coach. Describes estimates for the work at Wylye Rectory, and discusses their merits.

1. Perhaps Rev Francis Baker. See **554**.

582 15 June 1827. William Garbett Esq, architect, Winchester.
Copies a letter from his reverend employer[1] at Symondsbury discussing how the expenses should be divided.

1. Rev Raymond. See **577**.

583 15 June 1827. George Underwood Esq, architect, Pierrepoint Street, Bath.
Arranges to meet at Road.

584 15 June 1827. Mr Eldridge.
Orders 120 deals, half red and half white, to complete his floors. Needs them to be good, for immediate use and as cheap as possible because they are for his own use.

585 15 June 1827. Earl of Enniskillen, Florence Court, Ireland.
Has conveyed to Messrs Tinney and Cobb his Lordship's wishes for an early adjustment, with regard to Mr Wynch's account.

586 17 June 1827. W Kardd[1] Esq, Ryde, Isle of Wight.
Explains that Burgate Cottage is let. Regrets that no notice had been taken that the advertisement asked for letters to be post paid.

1. Name indistinctly written.

587 17 June 1827. C Harbin Esq, Ringwood.
Arranges to meet on Mr Fox's business at the Star Inn, Southampton.

588 22 June 1827. William Garbett Esq, Winchester.
Lists items in the bills said to have been paid by Mr Ware that have no vouchers. Expects that Mr Fox has been informed about how their expenses will be charged. Awaits the signed award.[1]

1. Symondsbury Rectory. See **593**.

589 24 June 1827. Rev Henry Boucher, Hilton, Dorset.
Identifies overcharging in the bills submitted.

590 24 June 1827. Philip Chitty Esq, Shaftesbury.
Has at last finished the measurement of materials at Fonthill Abbey with Mr Fisher [*see* **476**], but they have not yet finally arranged the price. As the articles at the abbey are entered to Mr Benett care should be taken to prevent further dilapidation or removal.

591 24 June 1827. J H Gillo, Havre de Grace, France.
'Dear Gillo, Dr Fowler has requested me to desire you will forward a hogshead of the genuine St George for Mr McAdam a descendant of the Collosus of Roads.[1] I will also thank you at the same time to send the same measure for myself. I have got another order from an old acquaintance of yours, the Revd Henry Boucher who wishes you to send him. I have, to guard against mistakes, transcribed that part of Mr Boucher's letter referring to the wines and hope it may lead to more extensive orders the Dorsetshire gentry being rather bon vivants. I shall feel obliged if you will tell me how best to manage the wine (when I get it), whether it may be drank from the wood or how long it should remain in bottle. I have little news to send you. The Weeks's, Harringtons and my own family are, I thank God, well. With best respects to your better half, I remain my dear Gillo very faithfully yours.'

1. MS *Roads*, underlined.

592 27 June 1827. Mr Haywood, Penitentiary, Devizes.
Has examined the two bills and has queried the allowance given by Mr Burt for the old shaft. Presumes it to be cast iron but if it is wrought there is insufficient allowance.

593 29 June 1827. William Garbett Esq, architect, Winchester.
Reminds him that the following day is the last one for signing the Symondsbury award. Asks how long they will be involved with the Stockbridge trustees and their *ci-devant* surveyor.

594 1 July 1827. Thomas Fox Esq.
Reports that Mr Compton's demand on Mr Dyett for dilapidations at the Red Lion, Totton, was excessive [*see* **563**], but the man calling himself a surveyor had been deceived only by his own egregious stupidity. His own expenses should be divided equally between Mr Compton and Mr Dyett.[1]

1. See WRO 451/229 for evidence presented in this case.

595 1 July 1827. C Harbin Esq, Ringwood.
Copies extracts from his letter [**594**] to Mr Fox about dilapidations at the Red Lion, Totton.

596 1 July 1827. J Penn Esq, engineer, Greenwich.
Asks advice about disposing of the property of a friend[1] at Bromley at Bow near London. This is a steam engine of thirty horse power driving seven pairs of stones for corn and one for grinding colors [*sic*], extensive warehouses and comfortable dwelling house with large garden lately occupied by Mr Thomas, and navigable canal close by. Hopes the visiting magistrates at Devizes have settled his account.

1. Thomas Fox. See **598**.

597 1 July 1827. William Garbett Esq.
Asks for a copy of the award by return of post.

598 4 July 1827. Thomas Fox Esq, Beaminster, Dorset.
'Dear Sir, I regret but am not surprized at your uneasiness relative to Raymond and Warr. I wrote to Mr Garbett on Friday last [**593**] reminding him that Saturday was the last day on which his award would be legal. By return I received a letter dated the 29th overkept the post reopened to notice the receipt of mine in which he says, "copy Mr Garbett's letter". The foregoing is the whole of his letter on the subject. I immediately wrote him requesting most urgently that he would by return of post send me a copy of his award, stating that if he felt it necessary he might send it on a stamp; also observing that I thought it probable you would require a stamped copy on the part of Mr Raymond, which I considered the terms of the award empowered you to demand.

'Two posts have now elapsed and I have received no answer what the Devil it may I know not - I do know his intolerable habit of procrastination and guess it proceeds from it.

'I have not forgotten Bromley. I wrote to Penn by last Sunday night's posts [**596**] and have little doubt but that if he can he will give his assistance.

'I am very respectfully Dear Sir, your obedient servant, J Peniston.'

599 7 July 1827. C B Wall Esq, Berkeley Square, London.
Has, with Mr Webb, examined accounts for painting at Norman Court, which did not appear to have been paid contrary to his previous wrong conclusion. A sum of £88 15s. was due to Mr Harrisson, but thinks it odd that the matter has slumbered so long. Apologizes for the annoyance that Mr Wall must experience.

600 7 July 1827. Thomas Fox Esq, Beaminster, Dorset.
Sends a copy of Mr Garbett's letter and asks if a copy of the award is needed.

601 7 July 1827. James Still Esq, [*East*] Knoyle.
Will examine the carpentry work at Bulford.

602 8 July 1827. T Hopper Esq, Connaught Terrace, [*London*].
Acknowledges that packet arrived during his absence. John [*M Peniston*] has waited on Mr Atkinson with the drawings and he will set seriously to work with the specification on return from the sessions. Is honoured by the reference from Mr Hopper and Colonel Baker but needs to have a little chat with them before he can determine.[1]

1. Probably relates to Salisbury Council House. See **769**.

603 [*undated*]. Thomas Fox Esq, Beaminster, Dorset.
Forwards a letter dated 7 July from Mr Penn at Greenwich, who offers to survey and value the mills.[1]

1. At Bromley by Bow. See **596**.

604 8 July 1827. Edward Baker Esq, Limners Hotel, Conduit Street, London.
Urges that the Wylye contract should be signed, as Mr Fleming's work is going on rapidly and merits his approval.

605 9 July 1827. Hon John Coventry, Burgate House, Fordingbridge.
Sends a general statement of account and will make an analysis of expenditure under its respective heads.

606 14 July 1827. [*addressee not stated*[1]].
Responds to a request to set out his charges on Mr Raymond. These are time and tavern expenses for ten days at three guineas a day. For coach and chaise hire £6 14s. 6d. For postage and incidentals 5s 6d. And five guineas for a week at home abstracting and examining the accounts with his son.[2]

1. Presumably Thomas Fox. See **613**.
2. Symondsbury Rectory award. See **577**.

607 14 July 1827. James Still Esq, [*East*] Knoyle.
Arranges to meet at Bulford to examine the work.

608 14 July 1827. Moody Esq, Bathampton House.
Has arranged with Mr Maitland's surveyor that the dilapidations at Little Langford are £41 15s. 1d.

609 14 July 1827. Rev Mr Mayo, Devizes.
Agrees that some measurements could be changed.

610 16 July 1827. Lord Palmerston, Stanhope Street, London.
Discusses details of work at Broadlands. Will instruct Pope to ease the top of the hall door and hopes that there will be no further settlement.

611 [*undated*]. [*addressee not stated*].
Charge for taking dilapidations at Little Langford was £3 11s. 6d. including expenses and the moiety of the stamp.

612 22 July 1827. James Still Esq, [*East*] Knoyle.
Encloses bills for the carpenter and bricklayer at Bulford and has made some deductions from the latter.

613 23 July 1827. Thomas Fox Esq, Beaminster, Dorset.
Has received the favour[1] containing the half-notes for £48, which is more than the amount of his claim. Will return the difference when they next meet. Is grateful for nomination to an appointment. Refers to Penn's letter about the mill property.

1. Letter: OED.

614 26 July 1827. Mr W J Le Feuvre, Southampton.
Gives instructions concerning two hogsheads and three cases of wine sent by Mr Gillo to Southampton for himself, Rev Mr Boucher of Hilton in Dorsetshire and Mr McAdam at Barford.

615 31 July 1827. MacAdam Esq, Burcombe.
Discusses payment for and delivery of the wine consigned to Southampton.

616 31 July 1827. Rev Henry Boucher, Hilton, Dorset.
Discusses payment for and delivery of the wine consigned to Southampton.

617 1 Aug. 1827. Mr Le Feuvre, Southampton.
Encloses a cheque made up of £19 3s. 11d. duty on the hogshead marked P, and Mr Gillo's charge of 200 francs presumed to the sum English £8 6s. 8d. The hogshead should be forwarded to Mr Charles Stokes, grocer, Silver Street, Salisbury. Had asked the other two gentlemen to send their payments and forwarding directions.

618 6 Aug. 1827. William Garbett Esq, architect, Winchester.
Comments that a meeting would be premature as the bond had not yet been signed. Has settled satisfactorily with his Dorsetshire employers.

619 6 Aug. 1827. Rev R Parker, Wardour Castle, Wilts.
Has discussed the unfortunate subject with Mr Coates who recommends trying the plan for a week or two previous to consigning Anne to an asylum. Has secured for her a situation with a person named Wells living in Milford Street nearly opposite Mr Whitchurch's brewery. If they go directly there and let him know when they arrive he will see that Wells is sent to receive her.[1]

1. A marginal note against this letter details Dr Lambert's fish bill for 13½ lb of salmon and 2½ lb of lobster, totalling £1 5s. 10d.

620 8 Aug. 1827. W J Le Feuvre Esq, Southampton.
Encloses a remittance received from Mr McAdam for the hogshead of wine. This is to be sent by Ratty to Salisbury, sending a line by the previous evening's mail to Mr McAdam, Burcombe House, Salisbury, who would send a cart to receive it.

621 25 Aug. 1827. Rev H Boucher.
Has just been able to examine the accounts for Daw's work at Hilton, as exhibited by the Messrs Bellamy, father versus son. There are discrepancies in prices and quantities. Explains briefly and will do so more fully when they next meet.

622 29 Aug. 1827. Miss Duchemin.
Writes at the request of Miss Weeks with the information available about the affairs of her late respected uncle, the Rev Mr Begin. There is an overall debt of £488 11s. 3d. If at the ensuing Michaelmas there should be any balance of rents after the interest on monies, taxes and repairs are paid, he will have pleasure in forwarding it. Regrets that the absence of the Rev Dr Baines and Lord Arundell on the continent prevents the arrangement finally of the very unpleasant business.

623 1 Sept. 1827. Rev J O Parr, Henley on Thames, Oxfordshire.
Asks on behalf of Mr Conduit of Durnford about renting the vicarage house at Durnford, and part of the arable land. Copies Conduit's letter.

624 1 Sept. 1827. Mr Hopgood, surveyor, Andover.
Arranges meeting to supervise putting in party gutters.

625 8 Sept. 1827. Rt Hon Lord Viscount Palmerston.
Arranges meeting.

626 9 Sept. 1827. Philip Chitty Esq, Shaftesbury.
'Dear Sir, I have been from home the whole of the last week or you would sooner have received the accompanying valuation. I think it necessary, on the part of Mr

Benett, to observe that unless he gets prompt possession of the Abbey [*Fonthill*], judging of the future by the past, he will require an abatement for injury done to the property, much of the glass and some portions of it the most valuable having been destroyed between our first survey and final valuation.'

627 9 Sept. 1827.   Lieutenant General Buller, Clarendon Park.
Discusses a recent shooting party and damaged fences. Acknowledges a gift of game.

628 8 Sept. 1827.   Rev Charles T Longley, Christ Church, Oxford.
Acknowledges appointment to survey dilapidations at Tytherley.

629 11 Sept. 1827.   William Garbett Esq, architect, Winchester.
Has heard nothing about the Stockbridge Trust business. Will take the Little Salisbury [*Coach*] via Andover and Whitchurch for a meeting at Woolhampton where Mr Alford has secured beds for them.

630 11 Sept. 1827.   Messrs Gaden and Adey, Poole.
Requests a delivery of coal for Burgate ordered two months previously.

631 12 Sept. 1827.   [*addressee not stated*].
Regrets cannot comply with request from churchwardens and overseers,[1] conveyed by their chairman Mr Wheeler, to have his private books for examination. But repeats offer to provide any information about the assessed property.

1. Of Salisbury. See **525, 526**.

632 12 Sept. 1827. James Lacey Esq.
Negotiates about an exchange for his old chimney piece. A bargain and perfect of its kind.

633 21 Sept. 1827.   Mr Hale, George Inn, Trowbridge.
Enquires about his travelling bag which should have been delivered by the coachman to the Bear Inn, Devizes.

634 21 Sept. 1827. James Still Esq.
Acknowledges that Mr Taylor has convicted him of error in an account and corrects figures.

635 25 Sept. 1827. Churchwardens and Overseers of the City of Salisbury.
Agrees to pay one shilling per book [*sic*] for each cottage he possesses provided such payment is general by other owners of cottages in Salisbury.

636 29 Sept. 1827. H Cooper Esq, Staverton Mill, Bradford.
Asks for account of expenditure on the road over and adjoining Staverton Bridge.

637 29 Sept. 1827. Rt Hon Lord Viscount Palmerston, Broadlands.
Arranges to visit.

638 29 Sept. 1827. William Garbett Esq.
Proposes meeting in Southampton on 23 Oct. about the Stockbridge road business. Should nominate an umpire not connected with either party.

639 30 Sept. 1827. Mr Mark Hanks, Malmesbury.
Points out omission in the accounts for work on St Johns Bridge and the bridge road at Cow Bridge [*both Malmesbury*], which, if not presented, must stand over for another year.

640 [*undated*]. Mr Beavis.
Asks for a regular bill for work on Chitterne Bridge.

641 5 Oct. 1827. Philip Chitty Esq.
Encloses bill and that of Mr Fisher for Fonthill valuation.[1]

1. The sum of £51 2s. 0d. is written, which is presumably just Peniston's bill.

642 6 Oct. 1827. Mr Webb, Melchet Park.
Sends four plans and an elevation for the east front with a portico added. Forthcoming county sessions at Marlborough will mean the rest will be delayed.[1]

1. MS headed *Clarendon House*.

643 7 Oct. 1827. Rt Hon Lord Viscount Palmerston, Stanhope Street, London.
Encloses sketch of proposed alteration of the vestibule at Broadlands, but the skylight may be too petit [*sic*] to be effective. A damp wall should be dried with charcoal braziers and coated with mastic.

644 9 Oct. 1827. William Garbett Esq, architect, Winchester.
Understands arbitration bonds have been prepared.[1] Discusses appointment of an independent arbitrator and suggests either Mr Cubit or Mr Bramah, with little to choose between cost of coming from Bath or London. Does not know Mr Cockerell but thinks that his having been employed locally on the Andover Canal would mean fearing local connection. Mr Gale of Dorchester is another suggestion.

1. For the Stockbridge Road business. See **638**.

645 9 Oct. 1827. Rev J O Parr, Remenham Rectory, Henley on Thames, Oxfordshire.
Unable to complete enquiries about rectorial possessions at Durnford. Glebe land is occupied by Mrs Dear who rents it from Lord Malmsbury. Mr Conduit declined to take possession. Discusses other possible tenants. Repairs to both church and chancel, previously surveyed and reported to Bishop Fisher, are still defective. Lord Malmsbury is responsible for the chancel but not the church.

646 11 Oct. 1827. Hon John Coventry, Burgate House.
Will inspect the work needed to repair the hatches and banks at Burgate Farm after the sessions. It is clear that Mr Jerrard will not do the work.

647 19 Oct. 1827. Mr Floyd.
Suggests Mr Marsh has been accustomed to do Lord Palmerston's work and had better be applied to about the pavement.

648 16 Oct. 1827.[1] William Garbett Esq, architect, Winchester.
Agrees that they should manage without the expense of a barrister. Discusses problems of choosing an umpire and whether the umpire should attend examination of witnesses.[2] Meeting is rearranged to 25 Oct. Regrets Southampton is not acceptable as a meeting place, objects to meeting at Stockbridge, and suggests Romsey.

1. Corrected from 17 Oct.
2. Stockbridge Road business. See **638**.

649 20 Oct. 1827. Mr Eldridge, timber merchant, Southampton.
Encloses cheque which has been delayed in expectation of needing more deals.

650 20 Oct. 1827. Mr Mark Hanks, Malmesbury, Wilts.
Encloses cheque to pay three tradesmen and asks for stamped receipts.

651 20 Oct. 1827. Mr Wingrove, surveyor, Trowbridge.
Sends the amount due for the bridge roads, but asks him to speak to Mr Cooper about the Staverton Mill Bridge as an uncertain sum sadly deranges the accounts.

652 20 Oct. 1827. Mr Hulbert, surveyor, Corsham.
Sends cheque for the annual repairs to the three Lacock bridges.

653 20 Oct. 1827. Mr G Salway (*Solway*), builder, Chippenham.
Sends cheque for repairs to Dauntsey Bridge.

654 23 Oct. 1827. Richard Nightingale Esq. Lyndhurst.
Accepts joint nomination with Mr W H Roe and will be at the Angel Inn, Lymington, on Friday to meet them.

655 23 Oct. 1827. Mr W H Roe, surveyor, Southampton.
Confirms the arrangement with Mr Nightingale.

656 23 Oct. 1827. [*addressee not stated*].
Estimates dilapidations at rectorial house at Tytherly at £94 9s. 2d., including repair to the chancel.

657 23 Oct. 1827. Rev Charles T Longley, Christ Church, Oxford.
Hopes the amount of dilapidations at Tytherly will meet approval of the party that has to pay. But the *ex parte* way in which they had been taken is seldom so successful.

658 29 Oct. 1827. Earl of Enniskillen, Florence Court, Ireland.
Will meet Tubb to receive quit rents at Grimstead. Messrs Tinney and Cobb have sent statement of the late Mr Wynch's accounts which would be examined.

659 29 Oct. 1827. R Butler Esq, solicitor, Lincoln's Inn,[1] London.
Has asked Messrs Remington to pay £25 as interest of mortgagee and £2 7s. 8d. private demand on the late Rev Mr Begin.

1. Lincoln's Inn struck through in pencil, and Temple Chambers substituted.

660 30 Oct. 1827. Rev John Owen Parr, Henley on Thames, Remenham Rectory.
Reports that Mr Smith has quitted the house at Durnford, but refused to pay the full rent because of being inconvenienced by the repairs, and wanted to refer the question of abatement to arbitrators. Suggests that this is agreed as Mr Smith is a troublesome man.

661 8 Nov. 1827. Rev J O Parr.
Acknowledges wishes about Mr Smith. The expected new tenant would not now take possession and he has suggested that Mrs Dear takes the house, provided that only respectable parties occupy it. Suggests annual rent of £18.

662 10 Nov. 1827. J Benett Esq M.P., Pyt House.
Arranges to call the following day.

663 10 Nov. 1827.[1] T Lane Wood Esq, Leighton Buzzard, Bedfordshire.
Reports on inspection at Burgate Farm and discussion with Mr Coventry. Unless legally compelled Mr Jerrard will not do the work and it will be better to charge dilapidations of some £200 [*see* **664**].

1. MS *Saturday evening*, no date given.

664 15 Nov. 1827. T Lane Wood Esq, Leighton Buzzard, Bedfordshire.
Reports that Mr Wing has given notice to quit, having used offensive language in conversation with Mr Coventry. Mr Jerrard should pay Mr Coventry dilapidations of £210 4s. 10d. and also provide thatching straw and the carriage of material to repair the meadows.

665 15 Nov. 1827. Mr Wing, Burgate.
Instructs him to use a handy ditch for the rubbish. Should hire extra labourers for the digging.

666 17 Nov. 1827. W H Roe, surveyor, Southampton.
Acknowledges a cheque for £14 17s. 6d. and the compliment on his recent appointment. Will forward the parliamentary enquiry referred to in their theological discussion at Lymington.

667 20 Nov. 1827. Rev Richard Norris, Stonyhurst College, Blackburn, Lancashire.
Sends arrears of fees for his son.[1] Will support Mr Tristram's education till he is qualified to make himself useful, he hopes within two years. Is obliged to have received acknowledgement that his son should write.

1. Probably James Peniston. See **1521**.

668 5 Dec. 1827. Rev Henry Boucher, Hilton.
Encloses an abstract and details of various bills. Also his own account which is high because of the travelling involved.

669 16 Dec. 1827. Beddome Esq, Romsey.
Agrees to oblige a friend of Mr Alexander on a future visit to Broadlands.

670 20 Dec. 1827. G Underwood Esq, architect, Pierrepoint Street, Bath.
Arranges to inspect Farley [*Farleigh Hungerford*] bridge during forthcoming visit to Bath.

671 20 Dec. 1827. William Woodcock Esq.
Agrees to extra payment for difficult work in the water at two bridges.

672 24 Dec. 1827. John Benett Esq M.P.
[*Fonthill Abbey*]: 'Sir, I regret that my absence prevented my answering your favour of the 21st earlier. I am completely at a loss to say what price should be fixed for the mettallic contents of the fallen tower. It is I take it a species of lottery and I think you had better decline taking any specific sum - but say I am open to receive any tender they may be disposed to offer. But let their proposals be specific as to what they included for their bidding.

'I understand there was the remains of a lead cistern, pipes, etc in the Fountain Court. Is it intended this is to form a portion of the property to be bid for? The extent of the sum offered will guide my recommendation. Waiting your answer, I am most respectfully your faithful and obedient servant, J Peniston.'

673 27 Dec. 1827. John Bennett Esq M.P., Lyme Regis, Dorset.
'Sir, Though I expected a treasure in the ruins of the tower I was not prepared for its extent, and though no doubt the party willing to give the sum you state must be well acquainted with its value, I think it too eligible an offer to be refused.

'I will go over to the abbey [*Fonthill*] on Wednesday next. In the mean time I will thank you to obtain what information you can and tell me with whom I may confer on the subject. I was in Bath last week and being acquainted with Mr G Underwood the architect I have desired him to notify to the builders with whom he is engaged the articles we have to dispose of. In the spring I trust we shall find desirable market. I am, sir, most respectfully your faithful and obedient servant, J Peniston.'

1828

674 11 Jan. 1828. Hon J Coventry, 38 Albermarle Street, London.
Has visited Burgate to give instruction about filling the ice house.

675 16 Jan. 1828. J K Beddome Esq, Romsey.
Discusses a disputed wall.[1] Fears that no compromise can be reached with Mr Sleat and suggests that the matter should be referred to Mr Garbett.

1. In Romsey. See **678**.

676 15 Jan. 1828. [*addressee not stated*].
Arranges a visit to Shaftesbury. Comments on the uncertain movements of Don Miguel. Explains that the letter was written at Devizes but missed the post, and that Mr S Chitty has agreed to the date of the meeting.

677 [*undated*]. [*addressee not stated*].
Encloses accounts. Has not seen Sir William Freemantle in the suite of Don Miguel. Is pleased that the visit went well.

678 9 Jan. 1828.[1] William Garbett Esq, architect, Winchester.
Asks him to meet at the White Horse Inn [*?Romsey*], as umpire to the dispute between Peniston and Mr Sleate of Salisbury about a wall in Romsey.

1. Perhaps a mistake for 19 Jan. 1828, as letter must post-date **675**.

679 23 Jan. 1828. Mr Richard Upjohn, builder, Shaftesbury.
Regrets to learn that Mr Short is dissatisfied with the account. The work had been properly measured and Mr Upjohn might not have to bear the cost of a further inspection.

680 [*undated*]. [*addressee not stated*].
Reviews a number of rating assessments for the collecting overseer of St Edmunds [*Salisbury*].

681 27 Jan. 1828. Mr Richard Upjohn, builder, Shaftesbury.
Arranges a visit.

682 28 Jan. 1828. George Bright Footner Esq, solicitor, Romsey.
Cannot yet meet Mr Moodey's wishes to send the award but will do so soon.[1]
Declines to prepare the acknowledgement to be signed by Mr Humby, but suggests
it is limited to a retraction of statements made rather than an admission of
misconduct.

1. Presumably relates to a dispute over payment during the building of Romsey National
School. Moodey was employed as plumber [**578**] and Humby as carpenter [**736**].

683 28 Jan. 1828. Mr Henry Lambert, Mr Knapp's, Bath.
Cannot give the information asked for but confirms details about Mr Charles Baker,
timber merchant of Southampton, who has erected a sawmill, and has supplied deals
to one of his builder.

684 29 Jan. 1828. Mr Haywood, Penitentiary, Devizes.
Encloses the painting account which had been mislaid. Sends message to Mr H P
Burt that unless the bells are hung there will be a pretty peal rung about his ears. Or,
more seriously, there will be great inconvenience.

685 29 Jan. 1828. George Bright Footner Esq, solicitor, Romsey.
Will send the award by the night mail. Has included his own expenses in the amount
to be paid by Mr Humby.[1]

1. See **682** and note.

686 30 Jan. 1828. Mr Joseph Humby, builder, Romsey.
Has learnt that Mr Moodey is satisfied with the admission made, and therefore sends
the key to the carpet bag. On presenting the letter and key to Mr Bell the bag would
be opened and his books returned. The bag and key then to be delivered to Mr
Moodey.[1]

1. See **682** and note.

687 31 Jan. 1828. Hon J Coventry, 38 Albermarle Street, London.
Reports on flood damage to the riverbank at Burgate.

688 1 Feb. 1828. Mr Wingrove jun, surveyor, Trowbridge.
Asks for inspection of work needed at Staverton Mill Bridge, and the road connected
with it.

689 3 Feb. 1828. Rt Hon Lord Viscount Palmerston, Stanhope Street, London.
Arranges visit to servants' hall at Broadlands. Acknowledges a present of game.

690 5 Feb. 1828. William Garbett Esq, architect, Winchester.
Discusses witnesses and costs in respect of the disputed wall at Romsey.

691 12 Feb. 1828. Rt Hon Lord Viscount Palmerston, Stanhope Street, London.
Discusses work at Broadlands at great length, particularly drainage and control of damp.

692 12 Feb. 1828. Rt Hon John Coventry, 38 Albermarle Street, London.
Acknowledges wishes about Burgate House.

693 14 Feb. 1828. Mr Kent, bricklayer, 'Whitechurch', Dorset.
Will check a bill if it is sent by hand of Rev Mr Boucher.

694 12 Feb. 1828. Mr G Sharp, Romsey.
Estimates that Mr Humby's account will be between £120 and £130.

695 13 Feb. 1828. Rt Hon Lord Viscount Palmerston, Stanhope St, London.
[*Broadlands*]: Encloses plan and sections of the closet and coal cellar. The new passage will mean underpinning the footings of the servants' room.

696 13 Feb. 1828. G A Underwood Esq, architect, Pierrepoint Street, Bath.
Suggests choosing a mason called Mizen of Bradford who is a tolerable honest fellow as times go.

697 14 Feb. 1828. Rt Hon Lord Viscount Palmerston, Stanhope Street, London.
[*Broadlands*]: Encloses a sketch changing the closet entrance to the coal cellar.

698 15 Feb. 1828. Thomas Hopper Esq, architect, Sovereign Street, Connaught Terrace, Edgeware Road, London.
Suggests minor changes to plans for the proposed alterations to the Council House.[1] These are limited in view of the many people who would need to be consulted about alterations to the portico and because the sum needed was nearly collected. Requests an early reply so that proposals can be advertised before the assizes. Has introduced a water closet at the end of the portico next to the Crown Court for the use of counsel and jurymen, and proposes another for the Grand Jury.

1. Salisbury Council House, now known as the Guildhall.

699 15 Feb. 1828. Rt Hon Earl of Enniskillen, Florence Court, Ireland.
Has analysed the statement from the executors of the late Mr Wynch about the Grimstead estates. Has not settled Tubbs' large claim for deductions. Hopes to discuss the problem in person if his Lordship is attending parliament.

700 18 Feb. 1828. William Garbett, architect, Winchester.
Reports that Mr Alford expects to meet them at Woolhampton and go on to Maidenhead for the inquest. Discusses at length the problem of their recent business at Romsey [*see* **678**], by which he has been haunted, but does not need an answer.

701 19 Feb. 1828. T Timbrell Esq, Trowbridge.
Has arranged for Mr Wingrove to deal with the complaint about the road adjoining London Bridge [*see* **702**].

702 19 Feb. 1828. Mr Wingrove jun, surveyor, Trowbridge.
Thanks him for attending to Staverton Mill Bridge. Reports complaint [*see* **701**] about road adjoining London Bridge [*Trowbridge*]. If the road is not in his care it should be adopted in the same way as the bridge.

703 22 Feb. 1828. Rev Joah Furey, Fordingbridge.
Reminds him about paying interest on the Ibsley account of £363 17s. 0d. from Christmas 1826.

704 22 Feb. 1828. Rt Hon Lord Bridport, Redlinch.
Sends copy of account for building alterations which had previously been sent through Mr Hopper, the architect, to whom Peniston considered himself assistant [*see* **280**]. Hopper, however, insisted that Peniston was the principal and should submit the account.

705 22 Feb. 1828. Rev Mr Williams, Wishford.
Encloses a charge for an intention not carried into effect.

706 22 Feb. 1828. Phillip Chitty Esq, Shaftesbury.
Encloses account for preparing a survey and report on the direction of Mr Bowles.

707 22 Feb. 1828. Charles Bowles Esq, Shaftesbury.
Encloses a demand on the executors of the late Rev Mr Bingham.[1]

1. Probably Rev Peregrine Bingham, Rector of Edmondsham and Berwick St John, died 28 May 1826: F.

708   22 Feb. 1828.   Thomas Hopper Esq, Sovereign Street, Connaught Terrace, London.
Presses for the return of specification[1] as the building committee have money in their pockets and, anxious to dispose of it in the best posible way, want to advertise the proposals.

1. Salisbury Council House. See **698**.

709   22 Feb. 1828.   J Benett Esq.
Hopes to meet in London to discuss the plan of the [*Fonthill*] abbey campaign.[1]

1. This letter was enclosed in **708**, asking Hopper to forward it to Benett.

710   27 Feb. 1828.[1]   Richard Webb Esq, Melchet Park.
Has purchased six lots of wine but has substituted one lot of madeira for one of sherry. Enquires if it should be kept at Wilton until sent for, or delivered. The permit will be in Mr Webb's name. Has also purchased some fancy lots.

1. MS *Wednesday evening*, not dated.

711   27 Feb. 1828.[1]   Rev Canon Macdonald.
Has purchased five lots of wine which will be delivered to the cellars at Wilton. The permit will be made out in Rev Montgomery's name, and the hampers in which it is packed have to be paid for.

1. MS *Wednesday evening*, not dated.

712   1 March 1828.   Rt Hon Lord Viscount Palmerston, Stanhope Street, London.
[*Broadlands*]: Forming an area on the garden side of the servants' hall and underpinning the wall of the kitchen would cost £25 to £30 plus the cost of the bricks. And the wall under the kitchen to be built with roman cement not common mortar.

713   1 March 1828.   Charles Baker Esq, Southampton.
Asks for the address of a person for disposal of a quantity of old copper.

714   1 March 1828.   Messrs Chinchen, Swanage, Dorset.
Orders seven pump troughs.

715   1 March 1828.   Thomas Fox Esq, Beaminster, Dorset.
Offers to survey property at Bow [*see* **596, 603**] while staying in London at the Sussex Hotel, Bouverie Street.

716 1 March 1828. William Garbett Esq, architect, Winchester.
Confirms meeting at Woolhampton.

717 2 March 1828. James Still Esq, [*East*] Knoyle.
Corrects a mistake (made by his son) about dilapidations caused by fire at Mrs
Davenish's farm at Bulford.[1]

1. The mistake occurred in copying **532**.

718 3 March 1828. Mr Richard Upjohn, upholsterer and builder, Shaftesbury.
Discusses the disposal of some furniture and payment for it. Sends account, and
enquires whether the parties have settled.[1]

1. See **679, 724**.

719 4 March 1828. Richard Webb Esq.
Sends drawing and estimate for Sir William Freemantle [**720**], and may see Sir William
in London. Has been busy with work for the building committee for the
improvement of the town hall.[1] Thanks Mrs Webb for the introduction and
recommendation. Hopes the wine arrived safely and quotes Harrington declaring the
madeira to be worth seven guineas a dozen.

1. Salisbury Council House. See **708**.

720 4 March 1828. Sir William Freemantle Bart.
Outlines extensive alterations and repairs[1] which will cost £3883. The coach house
and stables will cost a further sum between £1000 and £2000.[2]

1. To Clarendon House. See **754**.
2. The estimate for coach house and stables is included in a redrafted paragraph, replacing
another (struck through) in which no figures are given.

721 6 March 1828. J K Beddome Esq, Romsey.
Encloses Humby's bill[1] and has been very moderate with the deductions, taking some
things for granted on which there is doubt.

1. For work at Romsey National School. See **727**.

722 6 March 1828. W Toogood, carpenter, Eling, Hants.
Wishes to see the timber to be used for the bridge at Testwood Mills before work
starts. Hon Mr Sturgess Bouverie has asked him to superintend the works.

723 17 March 1828. G A Underwood Esq, architect, Pierrepoint Street, Bath.
Discusses employment of workmen at Farleigh [*Hungerford*] Bridge.

724 17 March 1828. Mr Richard Upjohn, builder and upholsterer, Shaftesbury.
Surprised not to have heard about the furniture [*see* **718**].

725 17 March 1828. Mr Moody.
Needs to know the weight of lead to complete the school account for Lord
Palmerston.

726 23 March 1828. G Eyre Esq, Warrens, Stoney Cross, Southampton.
Has surveyed the barn at Whaddon and details extensive repairs needed. The old
house suffers from damp. Will prepare estimates.

727 23 March 1828. Mr Humby, builder, Alresford.
The school[1] account will be sent soon.

1. Romsey National School. See **736**.

728 23 March 1828. Mr Crook, Lullington, near Beckington.
Arranges to meet at Farleigh [*Hungerford*] Bridge to discuss work on the Wiltshire part
of it.

729 23 March 1828. R Butler Esq, solicitor, Temple Chambers, London.
Explains that a friend may be able to repay money lent to the late Mr Begin by Mrs
Blatch, if security is available.

730 28 March 1828. Mr Jay.
Agrees to the sale of iron and lead at Fonthill Abbey but not at the price suggested.

731 29 March 1828. Webb Dyke Esq, Laverstock.
Threatens that Messrs Tinney and Cobb will be instructed to recover a debt.

732 4 April 1828. Mr Albury, surveyor, Frimley.
Sends a stamped valuation and an inventory of work at Farnborough Place.[1]

1. Addressed from Devaux Place, not the Close.

733 4 April 1828. Mr Finniman, at the Lodge, Farnborough Place, Blackwater.
Encloses stamped valuation. Asks him to pay Mr Russell for the carriage of the parcel
on the North Devon Coach.

734 4 April 1828. Mr Russell, Swan Inn, Blackwater.
Asks him to deliver packet [**733**] to Mr Finniman.[1]

1. Addressed from Devaux Place, not the Close.

735 5 April 1828. Henry Holmes Esq, Romsey.
Details costs totalling about £540 for work done at the National School at Romsey.

736 5 April 1828. Mr Humby, carpenter,[1] Alresford, Hampshire.
Has forwarded bill for £131 1s. 8d. for work done at the National School at Romsey.

1. MS *builder*, struck through and corrected.

737 5 April 1828. Mr William Floyd, bricklayer, Romsey.
Has forwarded bill for £183 11s. 8d. for work done at the National School at
Romsey.

738 5 April 1828. Mr Crook, mason, Lullington, near Beckington.
Discusses work at Farleigh [*Hungerford*] Bridge.

739 6 April 1828. Rt Hon Lord Viscount Palmerston, Broadlands, Romsey.
Rearranges a meeting at Broadlands.

740 10 April 1828. Thomas Hopper Esq, architect, Sovereign Street, Connaught
Terrace, Edgeware Road, London.
Discusses details of changing the layout under the banqueting room, and other
matters concerning the basement of the [*Salisbury*] Council House.

741 12 April 1828. Earl of Enniskillen, Florence Court, Ireland.
Has sent to William Gregory Esq, at the Castle, Dublin, an abstract of the statement
of the late Mr Wynch's account with the lords of the manor of Dean and Grimstead.
Explains in detail the difficulties of reconciling some of the extraordinary entries.
Cannot offer an explanation for some discrepancies.

742 16 April 1828. George Morant, Cliff House, Dorchester.
Discusses arrangements to be made at Blackwater. Has given the bailiff details of items bought at the auction.

743 16 April 1828. Messrs Chinchen, Swanage, Dorset.
Reminds them about his order for pump troughs [**714**].

744 16 April 1828. Hon W S Ponsonby, Canford (*Camford*) House, Wimborne.
Thinks that the marble chimney pieces at Fonthill Abbey would not be suitable. One heavy moulded large one that had never been fixed might do for an entrance hall or large dining room, but not calculated for apartments of common dimensions.

745 18 April 1828. Mr Stanford.
'Dear Sir, As the time approaches at which I intend that John shall pay you a visit shall I trespass on your kindness to look out for a lodging somewhere in the neighbourhood of your office[1] where he and his brother[2] may be accomodated [*sic*]. I should require for them a double bedded room, and a room in which they could take their breakfast, and sit in the evening - their dinner I calculate they will take out. I shall feel greatly indebted by your assistance in this respect, as also if you can aid me in my views for my younger son, which I believe you are aware is to get him into a respectable carpenters' and joiners' shop.[3] - and if possible not very far removed from his brother. Wages is a very secondary consideration. I should be very willing to rely on the honor of his employer to allow him whatever he may consider his exertions would fairly entitle him to. I propose if no objections should present themselves to go to town with the boys on Monday fortnight, and shall be happy to hear from you in the intermediate time if you will oblige me by making the enquiries I have requested. I have received Mr Hopper's letter in answer to mine [**740**], relative to the proposed alterations at the [*Salisbury*] Council House, and wait the pleasure of seeing him. I am, dear sir, yours very truly, J Peniston.'

1. Stanford worked in Hopper's office, in Connaught Terrace, London. See **1535**.
2. Probably George Peniston. See **894**.
3. MS *office*, struck through and corrected.

746 21 April 1828. P M Chitty Esq, Shaftesbury.
Has examined items numbered 1 to 36 and details comments on each about the prices, percentages, measurements and quantities of various building materials.[1]

1. Probably materials salvaged from Fonthill Abbey. See **748**.

747 25 April 1828. Rev J Lear, Chilmark.
Will call at the public house in Chilmark on the way to Fonthill Abbey for any message about his wish to have some of the Fonthill flooring.

748 25 April 1828. Arthur Legge Esq, Pyt House.
Will be at Fonthill Abbey and will leave with Jay the prices of the articles for sale.

749 25 April 1828. P M Chitty Esq, Shaftesbury.
Will be at Fonthill Abbey and will then sleep at Wardour and attend the service next morning. Can ride over to Shaftesbury to discuss subject of letters personally.

750 27 April 1828. Mr Stanford.
Confirms lodgings[1] are acceptable and will bring the boys to town.

1. 10 Princes Street, Cavendish Square. See **774**.

751 [*undated*]. Edward Blount Esq, 1 Thorney Street, Bloomsbury, London.
At the request of Rev Mr O'Connor, acknowledges receipt of a circular containing the copy of a petition to be presented by the Catholics of Salisbury to both Houses of Parliament, by Captain Bouverie in the Commons and by Lord Radnor in the Lords.

752 30 April 1828. Mrs Berrington, Spetisbury House.
Arranges a meeting.

753 1 May 1828. Rt Hon Sir W H Freemantle, Stanhope Street, London.
Acknowledges plans[1] and will be able to discuss them during forthcoming visit to London.

1. Clarendon House. See **754**.

754 5 May 1828. Sir W H Freemantle.
Indisposed and unable to accompany his son to London [*see* **750**]. The latter, who has assisted with the Clarendon plans, would convey them. Will be pleased to direct the work but has for some years declined the building business himself.

755 5 May 1828. Thomas Hopper Esq.
Prevented by his enemy the gout from introducing in person his son John as Hopper's new assistant, but does not want to delay his departure. The building committee are anxious for Mr Hopper's advice in determining their choice.[1] Is in his new house[2] and can offer a bed and hearty welcome, having next claim after Colonel Baker who is absent. Mrs Peniston joins in these sentiments.

1. Regarding Salisbury Council House. See **745**.
2. In De Vaux Place, Salisbury. See **732, 734**.

756 5 May 1828. Mr Stanford.
Prevented by gout from accompanying his sons to London.

757 6 May 1828. P M Chitty Esq, Shaftesbury.
Requests meeting in Salisbury before starting the business.

758 6 May 1828. Mr Richard Upjohn, builder's upholsterer, Shaftesbury.
Has received the chair and may order more.

759 9 May 1828. John Davis Esq, Fisherton de la Mere.
Has surveyed a house at Amesbury for Mrs Swayne. The house, offices and gardens are worth £37 a year and the detached paddocks occupied by Mr Batho with adjoining garden £5.

760 12 May 1828. Harrington.[1]
Requests that enquiries be made through Mr Jac. Goss, the organist at Chelsea, about the intention of a mad neighbour, Mrs Thomas, who may be selling her property. Her agent, named Spratt, is an intimate of Mr Goss. Outlines a complex family ownership of property in Harnham including a house, cottage, garden and a field let to the Rose and Crown, which Peniston would like to purchase.

1. Addressee not stated, but letter begins *Dear Harrington*.

761 4 May 1828. Mr Flower.[1]
Agrees to use his services, in making a screw pump for the use of the county.

1. William Flower, millwright, Winchester. See **819, 824**.

762 14 May 1828. T Sewell,[1] Clerk to the Commissioner of the Highways, Newport, Isle of Wight.
Recommends Thomas Jeffery as surveyor of roads.

1. Name partly illegible, but Thomas Sewell was Steward and Deputy Recorder of the Isle of Wight: P.

763 17 May 1828. Messrs Grieve, Grellier and Co, cement manufacturers, Millbank, London.
Orders six casks of roman cement. Asks to be distinguished from his cousin James Peniston, who resides in the city of Salisbury, not the Close.

764 18 May 1828. A Wingrove Esq, surveyor, Trowbridge.
Wishes Crook to do any strictly necessary repairs to Trowbridge Bridge while the water is low. Will meet later to discuss Staverton and Trowle Bridges.

765 [*undated*]. Hon John Coventry, Burgate House.
Has sent account to Mr Wood and hopes Mr Coventry's return to Burgate has improved his health.

766 [*undated*]. T Lane Wood Esq, Fordingbridge.
Sends account for work for Mr Coventry.

767 6 June 1828. [*addressee not stated*].[1]
Reports alarm on the part of a Salisbury builder, Fred Fisher, at London tradesmen being employed in the city.

1. Presumably to Mr Hopper. See **769**.

768 9 June 1828. Mr Richard Upjohn, upholsterer, Shaftesbury.
Arranges to meet at Shaftesbury, to complete the measurement of the chapel.

769 10 June 1828. Thomas Atkinson Esq.
Reports that Mr F Fisher has applied to Mr Hopper to be allowed to bid for the work at the Council House. Mr Hopper wishes not to give any offence to the city, and proposes that Fisher submit a sealed bid to Atkinson. Peniston has written to Hopper on the subject [**767**].

770 4 June 1828. Mr John Ward, Farnham, Surrey.
Cannot help with information about brokers and did not buy on his own account at Farnborough Place.

771 16 June 1828. Rt Hon Sir William Freemantle, Stanhope Street, London.
Encloses specification and estimates.[1] Has not included the scagliola[2] columns which are about £30 each, new. But will have his son in London enquire about any that have been removed and also deliver a sketch of the proposed conservatory. Will then get an estimate from Birmingham.

1. Clarendon House. See **754**.
2. Plasterwork imitating stone, of Italian origin, and fashionable in the early nineteenth century: OED.

772 16 June 1828. Messrs Harwood and Co, 11 Upper George Street, Portman Square,[1] London.
Orders quantities of paper.

1. *sic*, cf. **774**, where address is Bryanston Square.

773 17 June 1828. Payne Esq, architect, Gillingham, Dorset.
Arranges to meet. Regrets there has been dissatisfaction about cost of the meeting house[1] compared with estimate.

1. At Shaftesbury. See **768, 780**.

774 18 June 1828. Messrs Harwood and Co, 11 Upper George Street, Bryanston Square,[1] London.
Arranges to pay £14 14s. 8d. Explains that this was to paper one of a series of houses Peniston has built and is building on speculation in Salisbury. Any discount should be sent to Mr J M Peniston at No 10 Prince's Street, Cavendish Square.

1. See **772** and note.

775 18 June 1828. Rev Richard R Mole, Shaftesbury.
Discusses arrangements to consider cost of work on the chapel, and promises to send measurements.

776 18 June 1828. Mr Upjohn, upholsterer, Shaftesbury.
Asks for all bills for the chapel to be sent to Hindon by hand of Mr Payne.

777 16 June 1828. Mr James, Tewkesbury.[1]
'Sir, I have received your letter of the 13th inst. requesting to know if the estate of Harnham can be sold in lots on a long lease. As my nephew, now Captain Born, is expected in England I think the matter had better remain until he arrives, when your letter shall be laid before him. I am obliged by your having made the communication and remain, sir, your most obedient servant, James Meek.'

1. Addressed from Ilfracombe.

778 19 June 1828. J M Peniston.
Has said all that he intends to say on the subject of his remaining in London and hopes that John will not repent his decision. Has been to the [*Salisbury*] Council House with Mr F Fisher and the plans prepared by John. Had not told Mr Fisher of the disinclination of the London tradesmen to enter into competition. Discusses details in the plans at length. Two extra columns needed on the principal front.

779   22 June 1828. Mr A Wingrove, surveyor, Trowbridge.
Enquires about work at Farleigh and two other bridges (unspecified), which Crook
has been directed to repair. Reply to be sent to the Bear Inn, Devizes.

780   26 June 1828. Rev Richard R Mole, Shaftesbury (*Shaston*).
Has rechecked the accounts[1] and found a few omissions, but the prices are those to
which no regular respectable surveyor would object. Mr Payne acted fairly.

1. For the Shaftesbury Wesleyan chapel. See **775, 799**.

781   27 June 1828. Earl of Enniskillen.
Encloses letter from Messrs Tinney and Cobb about an account sent to them by the
proprietor of the Grimstead estate, with reference to the agency of the late Mr
Wynch. Has attended to these very complicated accounts and hopes the matter is
settled. The affairs of the late Mr Wynch wanted for method, and entries tended to be
omitted rather than improper. Asks for determination of the matter by his Lordship
and the other proprietors.

782   28 June 1828. Edward Blore Esq, 62 Welbeck Street, London.
[*Fonthill Abbey*]: Offers, on behalf of Mr Benett, ashlar stone at 6d per foot superficial.[1]
'To be taken down from either face of the gallery now standing, but exclusive of the
tower part over the sanctuary. Or from the unfurnished part of the building which is
over the kitchen, exclusive of the two towers at the external angles.' Does not know
quantity of steps under the fallen tower.

1. i.e. per square foot: OED.

783   28 June 1828. Messrs Jones and Clark, metallic hot house manufacturers,
Birmingham.
Encloses plan of a south facing building.[1] Asks for a design and price for a
conservatory between the wings and in the same style as at Norman Court.

1. Clarendon House. See **771**.

784   28 June 1828. Antony Wingrove Esq, surveyor, Trowbridge.
Acknowledges letter and would like to know how work proceeds in order to arrange
a visit. Other engagements are pressing. Apologizes for not paying postage on a recent
letter.

785 28 June 1828. F Payne Esq,[1] architect, Gillingham, Dorset.
Postpones a visit in order to be able to meet the Earl of Radnor who is only briefly at Longford Castle. The visit has to be on Wednesday because of the need to meet other parties who are only in Salisbury on Tuesday, market day.

1. *sic*, but elsewhere R Payne, i.e. Robert Payne: P.

786 29 June 1828. Mr Jeffery, Wardour Castle.
Has forwarded letter to Mr Hopper, the gentleman wanting a servant. Balance of money referred to by Mr Fraser is Lord Arundell's troop account. Will enquire, through Mr Pettit, whom the Marquess of Bath has appointed as regimental agent. Will ask if Mr Fraser, as Commanding Officer of the Troop in Lord Arundell's absence, will accept any order to transfer the account. Requests Lord Arundell be informed.

787 1 July 1828. Mrs Berrington, Spetisbury House, Blandford.[1]
Apologizes for delay in sending the enclosed sketch of alterations to her chapel. If the present chapel is to be retained there will be a screen to separate the congregation in the new part, but this will not impede the straight forward view of the ladies towards the altar. Will send plan for a new chapel, so that it will be possible to calculate alternative costs.

1. Addressee 'Reverend Mother' struck through, then 'Madam' struck through and corrected to 'Mrs Berrington'. Letter sent to the care of Mr House. Letter begins, 'Reverend Madam'.

788 1 July 1828. Bethel Cox Esq, Quarley House.
Encloses copy of a plan sent to Mr Hodding.

789 2 July 1828. Mrs Graham, Basingstoke.
The two houses adjoining the one in which she is interested are secured by the widow of the late Mr Canon Coxe, whose relations may intend to take her from Salisbury. If so the house can be transferred. Notes the colour of the dining room.

790 2 July 1828. Edward Blore Esq, 62 Welbeck Street, London.
[*Fonthill Abbey*]: Accepts offer for stone of £1 per load, on behalf of Mr Benett. Will accommodate Mr Seymour in taking it down if possible. The lowest price for lead is 18s. per cwt.

791 5 July 1828. Mr Bevis, stonemason, Tisbury.
Arranges to meet at Harnham Bridge.

792 5 July 1828. P M Chitty Esq, Shaftesbury.
Requests help in recovering £33 15s. 0d. from Mr Richard Upjohn, due to be paid
from the monies received from the [*Shaftesbury*] chapel building. Understands that Mr
Upjohn has disposed of his business at Shaftesbury and is about to visit another
hemisphere.

793 5 July 1828. Mr Richard Upjohn, upholsterer, Shaftesbury.
Asks for payment, to Mr Chitty, of £33 15s. 0d. after deducting five guineas for the
chair. Understands that Mr Upjohn is determined on visiting the yankees and sends
best wishes for future success.[1]

1. Richard Upjohn (1802-78) emigrated to Massachusetts in 1829, became a celebrated
architect, and first president (1857-76) of the American Institute of Architects, which he was
instrumental in founding: DAB, vol.10, pp.125-6.

794 5 July 1828. Messrs Jones and Co, metallic hot house manufactory, Mount
Street, Birmingham.
Asks for sketch of proposal,[1] with the addition of a balcony of 32 feet on each side
with a flight of steps to each one. Queries whether estimate of £430 includes a
furnace.

1. Presumably for Clarendon House. See **771, 783**.

795 5 July 1828. William Garbett Esq, architect, Winchester.
Has received the bond for Wilkes versus Stockbridge Trust from Messrs Tinney and
Cobb. Arranges a date to enter the business.

796 5 July 1828. Mr Jay, J Benet's Esq, Pyt House.
Will want some 800 to 1000 feet of floor board. The English will do. Asks for
someone to take up the boards in readiness.

797 7 July 1828. Messrs Hodding.
Tells them that the Building Committee will receive an estimate for alterations to the
[*Salisbury*] Council House from Mr Franks, the London builder, in person.

798 8 July 1828. Mr John Franks, 36 Nutford (*Sutford*) Place, Bryanston (*Byaston*)
Square, London.
Has sent the statement to the secretary of the Building Committee [*see* **797**]. They
will assemble at 48 hours notice to receive the proposal.

799 9 July 1828. P M Chitty Esq, Shaftesbury.
Understands that the trustees are dissatisfied with the result of his valuation with Mr Payne. But thinks it very wrong of them to resist payment having agreed to abide by the decision. Has already told Mr Mole that no respectable surveyor would make a materially different award for the work in the Wesleyan chapel and is willing to meet any regular and respectable man of business to justify it. Suggests that Mr Upjohn may unintentionally have led his employers into greater expenditure than they had a right to expect, and ought to settle the business with the sacrifice of £92.

800 10 July 1828. Rt Hon Earl of Enniskillen, Cheltenham.
Acknowledges a letter and will send the particulars desired.[1]

1. Addressed from 'Close', struck through and corrected to 'De Vaux Place'.

801 10 July 1828. Messrs Crook and son, masons, Lullington near Beckington, Somerset.
Acknowledges a most extraordinary statement demanding £40 for work expressed to be done at Town Bridge, Trowbridge. Asks for minutely detailed particulars of that and work at Staverton Bridge, where there has also been a great waste of labour. Any future work for the county must pay a regard to economy as if the work were done for a private individual.

802 10 July 1828. Mr F Fisher.
Asks if Mr Woolfreys will let the premises at Payne's Hill[1] on a repairing lease for seven years. Agreeing a price now for Mr Figes to buy at the end of the period.[2]

1. Presumably Salisbury. The firm of William and John Woolfryes occupied premises in nearby Culver Street, Salisbury, in 1822: P.
2. Addressed from De Vaux Place. Hereafter many letters are addressed from De Vaux Place, and this fact is not separately noted.

803 10 July 1828. George Eyre Esq, Warrens, Stony Cross.
Confirms that the church belfry[1] is so dilapidated that the bells should not be rung and repair would be false economy. Discusses alterations, including building a gallery at a cost of about £200.

1. Bramshaw. See **812, 828**.

804 11 July 1828. Hon Sturgess Bouverie MP, Testwood House, Hampshire.
Has asked Mr Toogood to deliver a letter reporting on the Testwood Bridge.

805 10 July 1828. Mr Jeffery, Wardour Castle.
Has heard from his son[1] who is with Mr Hopper that the latter will employ the youth [*see* **786**], who is wholly to keep himself, for 12s. weekly and a suit of clothes or a livery. Wages to be advanced according to his deserts.

1. J M Peniston. See **755**.

806 11 July 1828. Mr James Futcher, Fovant.
Arranges to meet at the Fovant Bridges, on the way to sessions at Warminster.

807 11 July 1828. A Wingrove Esq, surveyor, Trowbridge.
Has just received minutes of the commissioners' meeting on 21 May and will pass these to Mr Swayne. Has written to Crook about the account for Town Bridge at Trowbridge, a good round sum wrapt up in a few words. Rehearses details of his letter to Crook [**801**]. Has not seen papers relating to the County Bridge Bill.[1]

1. No such bill was enacted. An act 'to amend the acts for regulating turnpike roads' (9Geo4, c.77) passed on 25 July 1828, but was not directly concerned with county bridges.

808 11 July 1828. Mr Toogood, builder, Totton, Hampshire.
Regrets not having met at Testwood, but has reported to the Hon Sturgess Bouverie that the bridge was satisfactorily finished [*see* **804**]. Payment would be conditional on an agreement to maintain it for three years.

809 12 July 1828.[1] Messrs Hoddings.
Asks for the meeting with Mr Franks [*see* **797-8**].

1. MS *Saturday morn'g*, undated.

810 12 July 1828. Mrs Berrington, Spetisbury House.
Arranges to visit.

811 13 July 1828. R Payne Esq, architect, Gillingham, Dorset.
Delays a meeting because a letter from the proprietor of Clarendon means an earlier return.

812 14 July 1828. G Eyre Esq, Warrens, Stoney Cross.
Arranges to meet at Bramshaw Church. Asks if the mode of repair to the buildings at Whaddon Farm meets with approval.

813   14 July 1828. J Benett Esq MP, 19 Albermarle Street, London.
Has seen nothing further to the papers about the County Bridges Bill.[1] Understands that Lord Lowther is opposed to it. Enquires whether it will pass in the present session. Presumes that Mr Blore is appointed to direct Mr Seymour's intended building,[2] as he has agreed to buy stone and has been sent the price of sheet lead.

1. See **807** note 1.
2. Perhaps Knoyle House or Clouds, East Knoyle. See **790, 968**, and VCH 11, pp.86-8.

814   16 July 1828. W Garbett Esq, architect, Winchester.
Laments the insistence on nominating barristers as umpire,[1] as nothing in the bond suggests that there is likely to be any legal difficulty that cannot be dealt with by the very respectable solicitors employed. The cost may not be important to Mr Garbett's employers, to whom the matter is sport, but his are in a position of the Frogs to whom it is death.[2] If some names suggested were to be barristers attending sessions at Salisbury or Winchester others must not practice or reside in Hampshire.

1. Probably in the case of Wilkes v. Stockbridge Turnpike Trust. See **795**.
2. An allusion to Aesop's fable, of a boy stoning frogs for amusement, and to the expression derived from it, 'it may be fun to you, but it is death to the frogs': Brewer.

815   19 July 1828. Hon Sturgess Bouverie MP, Testwood House, Hants.
Confirms that Toogood had undertaken to repair the bridge for three years, the alternative having been to leave a sum unpaid as security, such an agreement being normal.

816   22 July 1828. William Garbett Esq, architect, Winchester.
Cannot agree to the suggestion about an umpire. Cannot think it right to risk the influence of connection in a business[1] which could ruin his employer. Discusses options of making short lists of barristers or surveyors in reciprocal counties, or possibly both parties could name a list of three surveyors not resident in Hampshire, Wiltshire or Dorset. Umpire should attend the investigation, and the award should be drawn up by respective solicitors without reference to counsel.

1. See **814** note 1.

817   23 July 1828. Elizah[1] Bush Esq.
Sends cheque to be passed as to the parties named in it. The receipt to be given to Mr Wingrove.

1. *sic*, but Elijah Bush: P.

818 23 July 1828. Messrs Crook.
Cheque for £50 for work at Farleigh [*Hungerford*] Bridge has been sent via Elizah Bush Esq. Needs amended estimates for Town Bridge at Trowbridge in order to decide how to act. Encloses a receipt to be stamped.

819 24 July 1828. Mr William Flower, millwright, Winchester.
Asks for information by return of post about the availability of a screw pump [*see* **761, 824**].

820 25 July 1828. W Garbett Esq, architect, Winchester.
Agrees to postpone meeting until the mode of appointing an umpire can be agreed. Is still not convinced of need for a barrister, but accepts that Mr Garbett will list three barristers and three surveyors and he will list six surveyors.

821 25 July 1828. William Gover, architect, Winchester.
Arranges a meeting at Wilton.

822 27 July 1828. Mr Dyer, smith, Stapleford.
Asks if his screw pump is in repair and available for use at Harnham Bridge.

823 27 July 1828. George Eyre Esq, Warrens, Stoney Cross.
Would regret omitting the buttresses which add materially to the strength of the building[1] and add a legitimate ornament at no great expense. Agrees a plain top to the tower is to be preferred. Desirable to postpone the cement to next year. Recommends Coles of Southampton for the slating.

1. Bramshaw Church. See **812, 828**.

824 27 July 1828. Mr William Flower, millwright, Winchester.
Wishes to order a pump for county bridge work, but wants clarification about a price of 20 guineas, with delivery to Salisbury, quoted on 11 May and a more recent price of 63 guineas. Is aware that the general price for the very best description of screw pump is about a guinea a foot.

825 27 July 1828. Rev Edward Scott, 85 Norton Street, Marylebone (*Mary le borne*), London.
Bearer[1] has been a member of the Wardour congregation and is a servant of Mr Hopper, architect at Bayswater, who is anxious that he should perform his religious

duties under the control of a pastor of the Catholic Church. Asks if lodgings can be found with a humble Catholic family near Bayswater. Is there any likelihood of Peniston's son[2] quitting France this autumn for Stonyhurst?

1. Probably the youth referred to in **805**.
2. Probably James Peniston (1809-56). See **1521**. He was ordained a Jesuit priest in 1838: F-L.

826 30 July 1828. William Garbett Esq, architect, Winchester.
Reiterates repugnance at the idea of nominating a barrister. The cost may not affect the public purse but is of the utmost consequence to his employer.[1] Will only consent to name a barrister with the strongest protest about it being wholly unnecessary. Suggests that they should each nominate three surveyors, and the respective solicitors should nominate beforehand a counsel to deal with any matter of law that they could not determine, excluding Hampshire practitioners and those in Wiltshire if desired.

1. ?Wilkes. See **795**.

827 1 Aug. 1828. Rt Hon Sir William Freemantle, Englefield Green, Surrey.
Apologizes for delay with enclosed additional estimates for Clarendon House. Will not decline engaging to get the work done for the sums stated but would prefer, on such work, to engage tradesmen to be paid according to the nature of their work.

828 2 Aug. 1828. George Eyre Esq, Warrens.
Sends plans of Bramshaw Church without buttresses. Warns strongly against a proposal for the roof.

829 4 Aug. 1828. Mrs Berrington, Spetisbury House, Blandford.
Apologises for delay in replying but is often from home. Recommends that the good Sister Procuratrix should not emulate the clown at the fair, who by displaying the contents of a purse, excites the cupidity of bystanders, and often leads, though somewhat surreptitiously, to a transfer of property. Recommends doing no more than securing building material, mainly bricks, for work in the ensuing spring. Has not wholly given up hope, if funds allow, to transfer the school room to the chapel, leaving more room in the dwelling house. Asks if this looks like aiming at the purse of the Procuratrix.

830 5 Aug. 1828. William Garbett Esq, architect, Winchester.
Yields in despair, vanquished but not convinced. Will name three barristers and three surveyors. Would prefer to retire from the business except that further procrastination would further damage a much oppressed man.[1]

1. ?Wilkes. See **795, 826**.

831 5 Aug. 1828. Rev Mr Brook, 85 Norton Street, Marylebone, London.
Laments, for his mother's sake, that his son[1] cannot visit home before returning to the college. Asks if they can meet in London. Is joined by Mrs Peniston in respectful remembrances to the Rev Mr Scott.

1. See **825** and note 2.

832 5 Aug. 1828. Rt Hon Sir William Freemantle, Englefield Green, Surrey.
[*Clarendon House*]: Regards it as unfortunate that a transposition of the offices is adding to the expense while the estimate has to be reduced by nearly £150. Will try to rely on the justice of Sir Frederick Hervey Bathurst if the expenditure is fairly shown to be more than the estimate. The roman cement to be used to stucco the south and west walls of the mansion, but only to colour the walls of the offices with the same materials. If the work is started immediately could be inhabitable by Michaelmas the following year.

833 7 Aug. 1828. Mr Young, carpenter, Bramshaw, Stoney Cross.
Arranges meeting to set out work at Bramshaw Church.

834 9 Aug. 1828. Daniel Brooks Esq, surveyor, Southampton.
Confirms appointment as umpire to value property at Wilton and arranges meeting.

835 10 Aug. 1828. Mr Jay, J Benett Esq MP, Pyt House.
Asks the whereabouts of the statue of the late Alderman Beckford which stood in the entrance hall at Fonthill Abbey. Asks if any copper has been sent to Bristol. Bar iron has been raised 10s. per ton. Asks if Mr Seymour has fetched away any stone [*see* **790**].

836 9 Aug. 1828. W Garbett Esq, architect, Winchester.
Intends to send list. Suggests meeting and that they should be joined by solicitors.

837 12 Aug. 1828. W Garbett Esq.
Offers six names for selection: Mr Hopper, architect London; Mr T Bramah, engineer London; Mr Underwood, architect Bath; and Mr Bingham, Mr Benson and Mr Awdry, barristers.

838 [*undated*]. Mrs Eyre, Warrens, Stoney Cross.
Hopes observations,[1] with former letter, will enable Mr Eyre to exercise his own wishes on return.

1. On Bramshaw Church. See **828**.

839 13 Aug. 1828. Anthony Wingrove Esq, surveyor, Trowbridge.
Discusses Scapin's proposals for repairing a bridge, made more difficult by the most unseasonal of all seasons and having to wait for the water to fall.

840 13 Aug. 1828. Mrs Eyre, Warrens, Stoney Cross.
[*Bramshaw Church*]: Has heard from Mr Eyre in London that he had not understood the buttresses to be so important and they should be built if essential. However the buttresses are only desirable and will add only a little to the cost. Prefers that Mr Eyre should decide on his return.

841 13 Aug. 1828. Rt Hon Sir William Freemantle Bart, Englefield Green, Surrey.
Confirms that a packet with a drawing of the offices at Clarendon had been sent by the Light Salisbury Coach.

842 16 Aug. 1828. [*addressee not stated*[1]].
Discusses the buttresses. Those for the church [*Bramshaw*] should be as before, to conform with the existing ones, and to be able to re-use old material. Those at the external angles of the new tower should correspond with the building erected by Mr Eyre.

1. Letter begins, *Madam*, thus Mrs Eyre. See **840**.

843 17 Aug. 1828. Daniel Brooks Esq, surveyor, Southampton.
Reflects on their recent meeting about valuing a building[1] and cannot agree with Mr Gover's suggestion to put 24 years purchase on buildings which are freehold and 22 years for buildings which should be calculated at 17¾ and 16 years.

1. At Wilton. See **821, 834**.

844 19 Aug. 1828. [*addressee not stated*[1]].
Refers to letter of 4 March, and encloses plan but cannot reduce the estimate if the alterations in the house are completed as proposed. There is now the addition of a brew house, wash house, laundry and bake house with their enclosures and a dairy, changes to farm buildings, alteration and additions to the gardens. However the cost could be kept to as little as £1000 if the alterations to the library and bedroom above were to be accepted.

1. See **720**. The letter was presumably sent to Sir William Freemantle, and the estimate relates to Clarendon House.

845 25 Aug. 1828. Mr Thomas Jay, J Benett Esq, Fonthill Abbey.
Will be visiting the abbey to examine the articles.

846 26 Aug. 1828. Mr John Fowler, Melksham.
Has received accounts for road repairs at Melksham Bridge.

847 26 Aug. 1828. Anthony Wingrove Esq, surveyor, Trowbridge.
Regrets that the dangerous illness of a dear friend[1] prevents a visit. Requests Mr Wingrove to give the directions needed at Farleigh [*Hungerford*] to give security to the public.

1. Harrington. See **850**.

848 31 Aug. 1828. D Brooks Esq, surveyor, Southampton.
Had called hoping to discuss valuations which, with infinite regret, he cannot agree. Will be pleased to meet Mr Gover again to discuss the matter if his opinion is open to revision. Has a duty to protect the interest of the Earl of Malmesbury and the other trustees.[1]

1. Letter is addressed from Portsmouth, later crossed through in pencil. The following note is appended: 'Mem. The above copy of a letter to Mr Brooks is the substance of one written by me from Portsmouth yesterday, though in point of expression may not be an exact copy. JP Sept. 1, 1828.'

849 1 Sept. 1828. Mr J Hurlstone,[1] 5 Grays Inn Place, London.
Has not written about the meeting to Mr Bingham, who should not be taken from the relaxation necessary after the professional exertions he encountered. But as the meeting is postponed he could be asked to come.

1. Name indistinctly written.

850 3 Sept. 1828. Anthony Wingrove Esq, surveyor, Trowbridge.
Encloses cheque for £20 on account for expenditure for Trowbridge. Has lost his poor friend Harrington.[1]

1. Thomas Harrington, proprietor of the Black Horse Inn, Salisbury. Peniston was a trustee of a trust set up to administer his estate, and advanced money to his widow, although it subsequently became apparent that Harrington had died insolvent. See WRO 451/393.

851 5 Sept. 1828. Anthony Wingrove Esq, surveyor, Trowbridge.
Cannot visit Trowbridge and leaves it to Mr Wingrove to judge what needs to be done at the bridge. While not wishing to spend more than is required of the county's money, it would be false economy to leave anything of consequence after the expensive preparations.

852 5 Sept. 1828. Philip Chitty Esq, Shaftesbury.
Laments that exertions in serving poor Upjohn[1] have been of little avail. Is not disposed to aggravate the misfortune and will agree any compromise the creditors may consent to. Is himself owed £28 10s 8d and will accept any proportion that can be agreed.

1. See **793** note 1.

853 6 Sept. 1828. Mr Strong, mason, Box, near Bath.[1]
Orders stone for structure shown on enclosed plan.[2] Sufficient needed for five columns in the entrance hall, and for three windows in the Grand Jury Room.

1. MS *By Devizes Mail, Sept'r 6, 1828.*
2. Of Salisbury Council House.

854 6 Sept. 1828. Samuel Whitchurch Esq.
Has surveyed repairs needed at Bishopdown and agrees with Mr Saph, except about the cottage occupied by the shepherd where the roof has been sunk for twenty years and is good for twenty more. The barn floors are as bad as Mr Saph described. Discusses clause of the lease from William Beckford about the use of timber from the estate. This can be used for repairs but not new buildings. Calculates amounts needed for two-inch oak floors in the barns, and elm or deal needed for barn and other doors and racks. Does not include timber for repair of hatches in the meadows which were under water during the visit.

855 7 Sept. 1828. Mr Harris, Ringwood.[1]
Joins with Mr Parker in the temporary security required for a Mr Jelly and hopes that, in trying him again, Mr Harris will find it 'shooting an arrow the self same way' (Shakespeare).[2] If not, suggests that he deserves to be beaten till he becomes like his own name.

1. Addressed as 'Dear Dan'. Daniel Harris was a currier in Ringwood Market Place, and Joseph Jelly was a clothier in High Street, Ringwood: P.
2. Bassanio in *The Merchant of Venice*, Act 1, Sc.1, 141-5.

856 18 Sept. 1828. Rt Hon Sir William Freemantle, Englefield Green, Surrey.
Arranges to meet in Dorset.

857 18 Sept. 1828. Samuel Whitchurch Esq, Milford Street [*Salisbury*].
Has calculated that to repair the hatches and carriages and to make good the embankment at Bishopdown meadows will need 76 cubic feet of timber. The greater part needed for the bedding and winging of the hatches. Elm would do and little oak is needed.

858 20 Sept. 1828. Mr Bickers, Broadlands, Romsey.
Returns estimates for Wade Farm. Suggests minor changes to Pope's calculations concerning doors and floors. Cannot understand the glazier's estimates and suggests the windows be measured.

859 22 Sept. 1828. W Ledyard Esq, Road Hill, Beckington, Somerset.
Acknowledges letter handed on by Mr Swayne and will be examining Road Bridge before reporting to sessions.

860 22 Sept. 1828. Mr Haywood, governor, Penitentiary, Devizes.
Fears engagements will delay a visit.

861 23 Sept. 1828. Anthony Wingrove Esq, surveyor, Trowbridge.
Dreads what the storm may have done to the works. Urges completion of Farleigh, London and Maiden Bradley Bridges. And for Crook to send the accounts so that they can be checked before submission to the Committee of Accounts and then the Sessions. Otherwise Crook will have to wait twelve months for his money. Encloses cheque for £20. Requests his account for Road.

862 30 Sept. 1828. Mr Bickers, Broadlands, Romsey.
Acknowledges Messrs Pragnall's estimate for glazing at Wade Farm, which is not unreasonable.

863 30 Sept. 1828. R Payne Esq, architect, Gillingham.
Requests a meeting at Shaftesbury to discuss the Hindon memorandum.

864 1 Oct. 1828. G Eyre Esq, Warrens, Stoney Cross.
Agrees to a meeting at Bramshaw.

865 1 Oct. 1828. William Garbett Esq, architect, Winchester.
Passes on details of a meeting to be held with Mr Bingham at Southampton.

866 1 Oct. 1828. Mr James Stent, Antelope Inn, Dorchester.
'Many thanks for your kind remembrance[1] of the son of your old companion in arms. I am now dressed for a Field Day, but it is with regret I am compelled to add, with feelings far different from those with which we[2] used to meet in days of yore. Two and thirty years of service has taken somewhat of the gilt off these said feelings, but the circumstances that occurred at our last permanent duty have so completely disgusted me with everything pertaining to Troop matters that nothing but a sense of duty arising from the vanity of believing that I can still be of service to the Regiment induces me to remain in it.

'I am very much in want of a horse. I am become too weighty for my old charger and mean, if I can procure another, to give him up to my son. Part with him I cannot, it would be another separation from an old friend – will you have the goodness to look out for me. I want something that could be active with sixteen stone on his back, and I could wish him not to exceed six years old and as usual all these good things for as little money as may be – but in the latter respect I should be guided in great measure by your advice.

'If my dear Jem you can assist me in this pursuit it will add to the many kindnesses you have conferred on your old and sincere friend, J Peniston.'

1. MS *present to*, struck through and corrected.
2. MS *we* underlined.

867 1 Oct. 1828. Rt Hon Sir William Freemantle.
Is preparing plans. Neither will reduce the estimates and one will increase it. Therefore states he will execute the alterations, building and repairs including the conservatory according to the plans and specifications agreed for Clarendon House and offices for £8000.

868 3 Oct. 1828. [*addressee not stated*[1]].
Arranges to meet and discuss a problem encountered in the work at Norman Court. Requests that floor boards be lifted so that girders may be inspected. Discusses work at Clarendon, and plans drawn up by J M Peniston.

1. Perhaps Timothy Bramah. See **874**.

869 6 Oct. 1828. [*addressee not stated*[1]].
Acknowledges letter and enclosures. Unfortunate that old Crook's obstinancy has led to further mischief. Stresses that the Trowbridge accounts must not allow any more than the entitlement. Feels more strongly about the shameful accounts for £7 16s. 0d. for labour at Maiden Bradley when the most he can allow is £2 2s. 10d. plus three or four shillings for the cost of lodgings. Is likely to cut any further connection with these worthies.

1. Probably Anthony Wingrove. See **861**.

870 6 Oct. 1828. Rt Hon Sir William Freemantle, Stanhope Street, London.
Has sent another drawing of the garden front and discusses the appearance of the building. Repeats proposal to do the work at Clarendon for £8000.[1] Asks if a meeting in London is required.

1. See **867**, which was written under cover to Lord Clinton, and Peniston was uncertain whether Sir William had seen it.

871 7 Oct. 1828. Mr Guy, George Inn, Portsmouth.
Discusses the payment of Mrs Harrington's bills.

872 [*undated*]. A Wingrove Esq, surveyor, Trowbridge.
The work remaining at the invert[1] may be left another season. Mr Wingrove must exercise his judgement about whether to finish the parapet if the dams are destroyed. Perhaps some of the clay could be saved for future use. Regrets trouble caused by untoward events.[2]

1. 'An inverted arch, as at the bottom of a canal or sewer': OED (where earliest reference is 1838).
2. There is no indication of which bridge is being discussed.

873 18 Oct. 1828. George Morant Esq, Frimley, Surrey.
Will meet Mr Lucas at Farnborough after two days at Southampton. However, if delayed at Southampton the meeting will have to be postponed because of another one with Lord Normanton at Somerley.

874 18 Oct. 1828. C B Wall Esq M.P., Norman Court.
Confirms that there is no immediate danger from the sinking of the bedroom floor at Norman Court. But it is a remarkable settlement of framed floor with trussed girders relative to the width of the room. It should be restored to the proper level. Has consulted Mr Bramah who agrees the plan made to secure it permanently at least expense. This will be between £200 and £300, mainly arising from the iron braces and ties to be affixed to the beams to keep them from sinking again. There should be no cause for alarm.

875 19 Oct. 1828. Anthony Wingrove Esq.
Encloses cheque. Outlines accounts for Staverton, Maiden Bradley, London, Trowbridge and Farleigh Bridges.

876 19 Oct. 1828. Mr Flower, Melksham, Wilts.
Encloses cheque for expenses on the road connected to Melksham Bridge. Asks for a stamped receipt.

877 24 Oct. 1828. Rt Hon Sir William Freemantle, Ramsgate.
Has been to Clarendon House with Mr Webb and arranged for inventories of the furniture and library. Work has started in the house and garden. Will discuss with Mr Webb the nature of security to be given for the money advanced and will then be happy to receive payment as proposed.

878 24 Oct. 1828. H Samuel Whitchurch Esq, Milford Street [*Salisbury*].
Sends the minutes of the repairs required by Mr Saph to be executed at Bishop Down Farm, and his supplementary statement. Has no further comment on these. Returns the lease and laments to learn that the legal construction is opposed to his view, which equity would demand.

879 26 Oct. 1828. Mrs Berrington, Spetisbury.
Replies to query about bricks. Mr Knight should be the judge of their quality. Has not decided for either of the plans. Will call if in the area or could come on purpose if asked.

880 26 Oct. 1828. Charles Baker Esq, timber merchant, Southampton.
Work at Clarendon will require many loads of memel timber and a considerable number of deals. Offers a ready money bargain if terms can be agreed. Asks cost of sawing in scantlings and various thicknesses for doors and windows. Would like well seasoned Christiana deals, red and white, but has been told that they are not to be had out of the London market.

881 [*undated*]. Anthony Wingrove Esq, surveyor, Trowbridge.
Encloses a cheque. Sends Crook's bill and has no compunction in saying they must wait for what is due from the county. Asks for old Crook to be told to make the slight repair in Road Bridge. Sends best respects to Wingrove's father.

882 30 Oct. 1828. Charles Baker Esq, timber merchant, Southampton.
Encloses a cheque for £200 and suggests future payments. Will send details of scantlings. Asks when a load of deals prepared for doors and windows can be collected.

883 1 Nov. 1828. Rt Hon Earl of Enniskillen.
[*Grimstead*]: Has been unable to verify the claim of Feltham, farm agent to the late Mr Wynch, and Hobbs who provided material for repairs. Thinks Feltham has no claim and has been cautious with Hobbs, who has twice been a bankrupt, since any admission may induce his assignees to make a demand. Lists demands from executors of the late Mr Wynch totalling £2006. Has explained that that delay in paying results from his enquiries. And suggests that executors might abate their demand for immediate settlement.

884 1 Nov. 1828. Charles Baker Esq, timber merchant, Southampton.
Returns two bills, having accepted them and made them payable in London at Remington's, the agents for his bankers. If the waggon arrives before deals are ready it should be sent with part of the consignment unsawn.

885 1 Nov. 1828. W Bellamy, builder, 'Whitchurch',[1] Dorset.
Has discussed alterations at Thornhill House with Mr Boucher and work should begin, starting with that above stairs. Mr Boucher is anxious for a suitable man to be engaged for the tiling. Well seasoned oak laths should be preferred to deal.

1. Bellamy's address is later given as Har(t)foot Lane [e.g. **1201**], a hamlet in Melcombe Bingham and Hilton 8km WNW of Winterbourne Whitechurch.

886 1 Nov. 1828. George Morant Esq, Frimley, Surrey.
Discusses alterations at Farnborough House. Suggests that the staircase from the basement to the principal floor should be moved because its vicinity to the gentlemens' water closet is objectionable. Has left written instructions with Mr Mathews about fitting up the stables and the rooms over and adjoining. The situation selected for a servants' hall is the best that could be found. Agrees site for new kennels as it is a moderate distance from the stables, desirable either for going or coming in from the field and with easy access to water. A list of repairs to the farm house and buildings is to follow.

887 3 Nov. 1828. Richard Webb Esq, Melchet.
Says that Perry [*see* **890**] consents to receive their paintings and glasses and will therefore send them forthwith. Encloses a receipt for £1000 and will send a draft of the proposed bond if Cobb can prepare it in time for George.

888 4 Nov. 1828. Richard Eldridge Esq, timber merchant, Southampton.
Asks for account for timber and deals had by Wells.

889 5 Nov. 1828. E R Butler Esq, Temple Chambers, London.
Writes about the account of the late Rev Mr Begin. Will be paid through Remington and Co. Expects the return of Dr Baines from Rome when something will be definitely settled. Regrets not hearing previously, and a friend who had money out of use and would have invested it for 5% had placed it elsewhere.

890 7 Nov. 1828. Rt Hon Sir William Freemantle, Englefield Green, Surrey.[1]
[*Clarendon House*]: Has received £1000 from Mr Webb. Reports on progress. Fine weather has enabled the footings of new garden walls to be done. Old bricks and tiles have been removed, stacked and covered. In the house has removed partitioning and timbers above drawing and dining rooms but timber is worse than expected. Is annoyed by the great quantity of furniture in the house, much of it classed in the inventory as unfit for use. Describes in which rooms articles are being stored. Has arranged for a Clarendon tenant, Mr Perry, to take the pictures and glasses. Has made extensive purchases of timber and brick.

1. Addressee written vertically across the letter.

891 7 Nov. 1828. Rt Hon Earl of Normanton, Somerley House, Hampshire.
Sends sketches for alterations to Somerley House by the Poole Coach. Will visit
Somerley to see Mr Webb's recommended course for the conveyance of the beer from
brewhouse to cellar.

892 9 Nov. 1828. Mrs Barrow, Spetisbury.
Agrees to examine the bills. Sends respects to the Reverend Mother.[1]

1. Mrs Berrington. See **787**.

893 10 Nov. 1828. Messrs Jones and Co, Mount (*Moun*) Street, Birmingham.
Had written earlier about a conservatory at Clarendon House. Has unexpectedly
become contractor for the alterations. Wishes it to be erected early the following
summer. Asks for plan and section of the flues. Asks them to advise his son[1] (if he
calls), on the best conveyance from Birmingham to Penrhyn (*Penryn*) Castle near
Bangor.

1. George Peniston. See **909**.

894 11 Nov. 1828. Mr Baxter.[1]
Provides letter of introduction for his son,[2] who has been recommended by Mr
Hopper, and who has worked briefly in London. He will explain the accident that
had retained [*sic*] his journey.

1. William Baxter was clerk of works at Penrhyn Castle, Bangor: P.
2. George Peniston. See **909**.

895 14 Nov. 1828. Mr G Short.
Has assessed rateable value of a dwelling house at £1 2s. 6d., and a shop and stores at
£1 11s. 6d.

896 14 Nov. 1828. Thomas Bolton Esq, Brickworth House.
Encloses Read's bill for new sashes at the house at Landford. Having deducted the
value of the old windows the balance due is £35 11s. 9d.

897 15 Nov. 1828. George Eyre, Warrens, Stoney Cross.
Sends accounts for carpenter and bricklayer at Bramshaw Church.

898 15 Nov. 1828. R Webb Esq.
Finds that pipes 1½ inches in bore are generally used to convey beer, and the price varies from 2s. to 3s. per foot. Discusses route for the 270 feet of pipe.[1] Has also reported to Sir William about securing the pictures and glasses with Mr Perry.[2] And had suggested disposing of furniture. Encloses a letter from Sir William. Has seen the Rev Mr Eddy and thanks Mr Webb for the kind recommendation. 'My brain is pretty much in a dodder, which I hope will plead my apology for the many inaccuracies of this scrawl...'

1. Somerley House. See **891**.
2. Clarendon House. See **890**.

899 15 Nov. 1828. John Jones Esq, Lincoln's Inn, London.
Apologizes for delay in sending the Hindon and Berwick accounts. Will examine and measure works at Shaftesbury Town Hall when they are completed.

900 17 Nov. 1828. Mr Eldridge, timber merchant, Southampton.
Pays bill for £46 19s 9d by cheque.

901 17 Nov. 1828. [*addressee not stated*].[1]
Encloses valuation by himself and Mr Fisher for signature. Should be sent on to the Rev Canon Bowles, Bremhill near Calne, Wilts. Asks to be sent the charge for acting as their umpire.

1. Presumably Mr Garbett of Winchester. See **902**.

902 19 Nov. 1828. Rev Canon Bowles, Bremhill near Calne.
Has completed valuation of dilapidations at the canonry house in [*Salisbury*] Close [*see* **901**]. Statement of sum will be sent by Mr Garbett of Winchester who has been the umpire between himself and Mr Fisher. The amount at the canonry is £239 12s. 0d. and at Mrs Hinxman's residence £75 15s. 0d. But the latter will not be paid until the end of the remaining six years of the lease.

903 19 Nov. 1828. Rt Hon Earl of Normanton, Somerley House, Hants.
Will send sketch and details for the entrance front and part of the offices by the Poole Coach.

904 20 Nov. 1828. Rev William Heath, West Dean Rectory.
Agrees that in the circumstances Beauchamp is not entitled to make a demand for the sketch and estimates for the windows. In the normal way of business a party not employed to do the work could make a charge of 2½% on the amount for a plan and estimates.

905 22 Nov. 1828. Charles Baker Esq, timber merchant, Southampton.
Orders quantities of beams, rafters, purlins and other timber.

906 25 Nov. 1828. Messrs Jones and Co, Mount Street, Birmingham.
Encloses plans. Has heard of the method of heating by warm water but not seen it.
Asks for details of operation and costs for his employer to consider.

907 25 Nov. 1828. Rt Hon Earl of Normanton, Somerley House, Hants.
Estimates cost of the ballustrading and offices, according to the plan sent previously,
at £552 15s. 0d.

908 26 Nov. 1828. Rt Hon Sir William Freemantle, Englefield Green, Surrey.
[*Clarendon House*]: Provides detailed report on progress. Ground for new wing has
been excavated. Furniture will be stored in staddle barn, but the storage of the books
remains a problem. Discusses size of kitchen fireplaces and chimneys. There have been
nearly a hundred employees on the premises for three or four weeks during the fine
weather; most have now been discharged and it is raining decidedly.

909 29 Nov. 1828. Mr H P Burt, Devizes.
Says that his son George has not received his chest. Asks to be told by return how and
when it was sent, and to whom it was assigned at Birmingham. Is expecting the bill.

910 30 Nov. 1828. Mr Henry Potter Burt, Devizes.
Queries bill. Asks for replies about George Peniston's chest. Asks for
acknowledgement of note from Mr Haywood to be passed on.

911 30 Nov. 1828. Joseph Pitt Esq M.P., Estcourt House, near Malmesbury.
Has been told by Mr Swayne to survey a bridge or bridges near Cricklade and asks
for information.

912 2 Dec. 1828. George Morant Esq, Frimley, Surrey.
Sends per Magnet[1] a plan of the principal floor of Farnborough House with the
alterations. The dotted red line at the end of the hall shows the enclosure above which
he proposes the ladies' water closet, taken out of the dressing room and
communicating with the common sewer beneath. Suggests removing the staircase by
the gentlemen's water closet. Includes a sketch of a rustic veranda added to the dairy.
Is pleased to hear that Mr Mathews has made fair progress and will visit to examine
the Street Farm cottages.

1. A stagecoach which ran between Weymouth and London via Salisbury: P.

913 6 Dec. 1828. Mr Macklin.
The charge for valuing the house in [*Salisbury*] Close was three guineas. Encloses bill for Mr Tanner.

914 9 Dec. 1828. Rt Hon Sir William Freemantle, Englefield Green, Surrey.
[*Clarendon House*]: Provides detailed answers to a series of numbered questions about the work. Asks for arrangements to be made for payment of the first instalment for the work.

915 9 Dec. 1828. John Knapp Esq, 1 Bridge Road, Bath.
Does not know Mr Wheeler of Redbridge personally, only as a lime burner. He is apparently industrious and respectable, mainly in the brick and tile business, and in the timber trade as agent of a person in Petersfield. Returns Mr Wheeler's letter, discusses his financial soundness and offers to make further enquiries.

916 12 Dec. 1828. C Baker, Southampton.
Regrets to have learned from the clerk of works at Clarendon that two of the beams sent could not be used. Orders replacements and two girders. The deals received are of excellent quality.

917 15 Dec. 1828. Mrs Grubbe.[1]
Has met Mr Hunott, who is willing to do anything reasonable to render her abode at Whaddon comfortable, and will not forgo the agreement to a lease. Offers a temporary residence for her and her servants in one of his houses, and invites her to look over one that is already inhabited.

1. Written on the verso of an envelope addressed, 'Mr Peniston, Surveyor, Salisbury', from Malmesbury 9 Dec. 1828, and endorsed, 'Copy of a letter [*to*] Mrs Grubbe relative to Mr Hunott's house at Whaddon'. Found loose in letter book between **916** and **918**.

918 13 Dec. 1828. [*addressee not stated*].[1]
Writes that he will be given an allowance of £20 a year in addition to his earnings, and encloses a £5 note for the first quarter in advance.

1. Letter begins, 'My Dear George', and so was presumably to his son, George Peniston.

919 15 Dec. 1828. Mr Bellamy, builder, Whitchurch, Dorset.
Will be at Thornhill House.

920 15 Dec. 1828. P M Chitty Esq, Shaftesbury.
Will deliver the Berwick and Hindon accounts which will require verbal explanation.

921 15 Dec. 1828. R Payne Esq, surveyor, Gillingham.
Regrets delay with the Hindon and Berwick accounts. Arranges meeting to discuss these before they are presented to Mr Chitty.

922 15 Dec. 1828. C Millet Esq, Hindon.
Arranges to deliver Lord Grosvenor's Hindon accounts and regrets keeping them for so long for examination and arrangement. The late Mr Norton's has been finished for some time but could not be forwarded alone.

923 18 Dec. 1828. Mr Bellamy, builder, Whitchurch, Dorset.
Delays meeting at Thornhill House because of an unexpected occurrence.

924 18 Dec. 1828. R Payne Esq, architect, Gillingham, Dorset.
Delays meeting because Mr Chitty will not be at home. Discusses discrepancies in the accounts relating mainly to the stone dwelling at Berwick.

925 19 Dec. 1828. [addressee not stated].
Refers to letter to Mr Baker [**916**] requesting replacement tie beams and girders. This order has been misunderstood and the wrong items sent.

926 [undated]. [addressee not stated].
Has several marble chimneypieces for re-erection at Clarendon House. Laid out for examination at Mr Brown's store in Exeter Street [?Salisbury].

927 22 Dec. 1828. Mr Haywood, Penitentiary, Devizes.
Arranges to visit before pasing some bills.

928 26 Dec. 1828. Earl of Enniskillen, Florence Court, Ireland.
Encloses copy of a letter and will await a reply before communicating with Messrs Tinney and Cobb.

929 26 Dec. 1828. John Jones Esq, Lincoln's Inn, London.
Has delivered Lord Grosvenor's Hindon and Berwick accounts to Mr Chitty. Discusses some discrepancies.

930 26 Dec. 1828. Joseph Pitt Esq M.P., Estcourt House, Malmesbury.
Will be at Cricklade to survey the bridges.

931 [*undated*]. Charles Baker Esq, Southampton.
Says the £100 bill is now payable at Messrs William Deacon & Co. instead of
Remington & Co. as Messrs Brodie & Co. have transferred their payments.[1]

1. Written by J M Peniston, on father's behalf.

932 31 Dec. 1828. Mr Adjutant Pettit.
Encloses a memorandum of the sum due from the regiment.

1829

933 2 Jan. 1829. Rt Hon Sir William Freemantle, Englefield Green, Surrey.
[*Clarendon House*]: Acknowledges £500 payment. Reports better than expected progress because of good weather. Discusses possible difficulties about the water closet and balustrade because of wall weakened by previous alterations.

934 7 Jan. 1829. Mr Ledyard, Road Hill, near Beckington.
Has received both applications about the road adjoining the Wiltshire part of Road Bridge, and will present them to the forthcoming sessions. Cannot give directions without their orders.

935 7 Jan. 1829. Mr A Goodwin, Guildford Street, Southwark.
Will be in town and will pay for the plaster purchased by Potter.

936 7 Jan. 1829. James Tanner, Scavenger of the Tithing, Atworth, near Bradford, Wilts.
Will state the application concerning Ganbrook Bridge to the forthcoming sessions.

937 7 Jan. 1829. A Wingrove Esq, surveyor, Trowbridge.
Does not doubt that the application of the owner of the mill will be properly considered by the court at the sessions. Has written to Mr Ledyard [**934**]. Asks for stamped receipt for last year's Road account and those for Trowbridge Bridge.

938 8 Jan. 1829. Charles Millet Esq, Hindon.
Regrets sending a substitute but gout prevents him keeping a promise. Asks that his son[1] be shown the building to be altered.

1. John M Peniston, who appears to have returned from London, and was assisting his father. See **931, 943**.

939 8 Jan. 1829.[1] [*addressee not stated*].
Regrets having been so long in debt, and £10 poorer. Has no doubts about the bill but requests an annual account in future.

1. MS *Thursday evening*.

940 8 Jan. 1829. [*addressee not stated*].
Receives from Mr Joseph Saunders, by contra account, £8 for one year's rent of storeroom in St Martin's Church Street [*Salisbury*], due at Michaelmas for Lord Arundell.

941 9 Jan. 1829. T Fleming Esq.
Asks for a letter [**942**] to Mr Hopper to be passed on at Stoneham Park.

942 9 Jan. 1829. Thomas Hopper Esq.
Reports on building progress at Salisbury Council House.

943 12 Jan. 1829. J Swayne Esq.
Had booked a place in the Mail for Devizes but was advised by his doctor not to travel. Is sending John with the report. Encloses statement [**944**] describing condition of the Seven Bridges. Describes issues relating to the town bridge at Cricklade and the stream flowing under it; also Ganbrook in Atworth; and Road Bridge.

1. MS *9th*, corrected to 12th.

944 12 Jan. 1829. Chairman of the Wilts Sessions, Devizes.
Reports on the Seven Bridges near Cricklade.[1] The so-called bridges are a mile and a half from Cricklade on the road to Swindon and consist of a series of causeways of about 250 ft. with four arches, two of them over the principal course of the stream and in decent repair, but the rest very dilapidated. Encloses also a report[1] on the Town Bridge, Cricklade, some parts of which are in a dangerous condition.

1. Both reports are dated 29 Dec. 1829 [*recte* 1828].

945 14 Jan. 1829. Charles Millet Esq, Hindon.
Sends plan and elevation of proposed alterations to the clergyman's house at Hindon.

946 23 Jan. 1829. Mr Henry Martin, Close.
Discusses a bill for glazing which is not excessive.

947 [*undated*]. [*addressee not stated*[1]].
Discusses taking possession of a property.

1. Letter begins *Dear Madam*.

948 23 Jan. 1829. Mr Ambrose Fisher, South Gate, Tetbury, Glostershire.
Has received bill for repairs at Tetbury Bridge, under a frank from Mr Pitt. Had no knowledge of this and will need to examine the work.

949 23 Jan. 1829.[1] Rt Hon Sir William Freemantle, Englefield Green.
Explains that an attack of gout and a visit to London have prevented a meeting. Reports details of work at Clarendon.

1. MS *1828*, in error.

950 26 Jan. 1829.[1] J Hodding Esq.
Will be able to attend a meeting of the Building Committee.[2]

1. MS *Monday morning*, undated.
2. Probably in relation to Salisbury Council House.

951 27 Jan. 1829.[1] Hatcher.[2]
'Dear Hatcher, I am quite ashamed at having been so long in deciding whether to return William to you or to take him to school a year at my office. A balance of pros and cons determine me on the latter course, but if you can without inconvenience to yourself allow him to join your mathematical class at such hours as they usually assemble for that purpose, I shall be most happy to balance as far as a pecuniary compensate can do so desirable a favor. Allow me to take this opportunity of thanking you for the advantages my boys have received for your kind attentions and instruction, and believe me to be, dear Hatcher, very sincerely yours, J Peniston.'

1. MS *Tuesday morning*, undated.
2. Henry Hatcher, historian, taught school in Endless Street, Salisbury, at this period: P.

952 2 Feb. 1829. Rev F Baker, Wylye.
Has re-examined Titt's bill and cannot, with justice, make the deduction that had been proposed.

953 [*undated*]. J K Beddome (*J W Bedham*)[1] Esq, Romsey.
Discusses measurement of Moody's work.

1. Elsewhere (e.g. **967**) the name is Beddome. Beddome and Winter were Romsey surgeons: P.

954 7 Feb. 1829. Rt Hon Sir William Freemantle, Stanhope Street, London.
'I am much gratified at the kind manner in which you have been pleased to approve of the progress of the works at Clarendon House, and be assured no exertion shall be spared to fulfil all the engagements I have made for its completion. The several

observations you have made in your last letter shall be attended to but I fear the alteration of the fire place in the north west bedroom cannot well be effective without cutting more into the old wall than I would wish to do.

'You will be pleased to learn, Sir, that we have taken off the whole of the old roof and have nearly replaced it with the timbers of the new one. We hope to put on the plumber on Thursday next to lay a portion of the gutters and, the present weather continuing, we calculate the slaters may begin on the Monday following and hope the bricklayers will succeed in raising the walls of the additional building to enable them to continue and cover in the whole.

'We found the timbers of the old roof even worse than I had expected, many of them rotted off in the walls. One of the beams over the old staircase gave way with a carpenter on it who went with the timber to the bottom and though pretty much shaken and taken to the Infirmary as a matter of precaution is not very seriously hurt and hope in a few days he will be able to resume his work.

'We have found it necessary to take down the whole of the chimney to the level of the chamber ceiling, they [sic] being too much shattered to remain with safety.

'I have received at Mr Webb's office the farther sum of £500, making in the whole £2000. I make this particular acknowledgement because I have not given a stamped receipt for the last £500. I believe the law does not require it when an acknowledgement is made by letter and a general receipt is afterwards given on a stamp. If this mode, Sir, is satisfactory to you it will save me as [sic] 7s 6d stamp on each payment. If not I will of course meet your wishes.

'With the sincerest respect I remain, Sir, Your faithful and obedient servant.'

955   10 Feb. 1829. Mrs Berrington, Spetisbury House.[1]
Warns that as the building season approaches the costs ought to be looked at more closely. If she will send back the drawing of the new chapel with Mr O'Connor working drawings will be prepared. Sends good wishes to the ladies of the community.

1. MS note: *Favoured by* [delivered by] *Mr O'Connor.*

956   [*undated*] R Webb Esq, Melchett.
Returns stamped receipt for £2000 on the Clarendon account. Had written to Sir William Freemantle [**954**] about his dislike of stamped receipts, and copies letter to Webb.

957   12 Feb. 1829. T Bramah, Pimlico.
Will discuss drawings with Sir William Freemantle. Discusses wedges needed to secure girders at Norman Court. Will be in town again in the spring and hopes to have determined what will be needed at Clarendon House.

958   12 Feb. 1829. Charles Baker Esq, timber merchant, Southampton.
Encloses cheque for balance of account.

959 14 Feb. 1829. John Swayne Esq, Wilton.
Could not sign Mr Brook's valuation award for the Seagrim property at Wilton.[1]
Explains at length how the arrangements for surveying and umpiring the proceedings
had been unsatisfactory.

1. See **843**. cf William Segram, gent., Minster Street, Wilton: P.

960 14 Feb. 1829. Rev Charles Eddy, Guilsborough, near Northampton.
Has completed valuation of dilapidations at Bemerton.

961 16 Feb. 1829.[1] William Boucher Esq, Close.
Intends visiting London to get the judges' views on plan for fitting out the Crown
Court [*Salisbury Council House*]. Can also give orders for Mr Boucher's chimney
pieces.

1. MS *Monday morning.*

962 16 Feb. 1829. Messrs Winckfield and Co.
Discusses order for building materials.

963 17 Feb. 1829. Mr Bellamy, builder, Whitchurch, Dorset.
Sorry to learn from Mr Boucher that work at Thornhill House is going so slowly. If
Mr Bellamy cannot supervise the work himself he must send someone who is willing
and confident to direct. Asks for sketches of the two fireplaces with exact dimensions
of the openings and the chimneypieces of the rooms made from the gallery.

964 19 Feb. 1829. Messrs Winkfield and Co.
Has told his bankers to pay their bill of £1 9s 4d through Messrs Deacons and Co.

965 [*undated*]. Mr Adjutant Pettit.
Acknowledges a letter from the Marquess of Bath and enclosures from Lord Arundell.
Expects to hear from Lord Arundell with authority to transfer the balance of the
Troop fund from Mr Fraser to the present regimental agent.

966 20 Feb. 1829. T Hopper Esq.
Encloses estimate received for the railing in front of the [*Salisbury*] Council House.
Engages in lengthy discussion about work in the building.

967 21 Feb. 1829. J K Beddome Esq, Romsey.
Reports that Mr Moody is anxious for the accounts to be settled. Discusses the bills
and recommends some deductions. Will keep some until he visits Romsey.

968 25 Feb. 1829. Messrs Brockway and Taylor.
Encloses measurement and valuation, dated 20 Feb. 1829, of £3 5s. 0d. of their work for Mr Seymour at East Knoyle (*Knowle*).

969 24 Feb. 1829. Rev Mr Dullard, Cannington House, near Bridgwater.
Apologizes for delay. Sends proposed plan for Spetisbury and hopes its expedition may tend to forward his wishes at Cannington.

970 25 Feb. 1829. Anthony Wingrove Esq, surveyor, Trowbridge.
Has received a peevish letter from Mr Ledyard about Road Bridge. Discusses intended work on the bridge and asks for any temporary work needed to be done.

971 26 Feb. 1829. Mrs Berrington, Spetisbury House, Blandford.
Arranges to delay a visit when he will bring a carpenter.

972 27 Feb. 1829. James C Sharp Esq, Southampton.
Arranges to be at home to receive a visit.

973 1 March 1829. Rt Hon Sir William Freemantle, Stanhope Street [*London*].
Reports that the greater part of the work at Clarendon has been done despite the rain. Details progress.

974 3 March 1829. James Cobb Esq.
Has dissected the carpenter's accounts for work done at Mr Mundy's. Specifies detailed adjustments.

975 3 March 1829.[1] Mrs Ellary.
Has waited for accounts before replying. Discusses a rent.

1. MS *Tuesday morn.*

976 5 March 1829. Messrs Chinchen, Swanage.
Vouches for Mr Francis Brown, who has applied for stone, and guarantees payment.

977 8 March 1829. Richard Webb Esq, Melchet.
Takes advantage of Mr Nightingale's visit to Melchet to forward remarks about Ibsley church, consisting of a belfry, chancel and central nave, the whole in a wretched state of repair. Some parts had been rebuilt. Trusses had decayed and iron ties and braces corroded. A detailed report would follow. Pavings and fittings were much decayed and only the tiles could be used again.

978 9 March 1829. Messrs Jones and Co, Metallic Hot House Manufactory, Mount Street, Birmingham.
Takes advantage of Mr Vandenhoff's intention of visiting Birmingham to enquire if there is any circumstance that may have delayed the hot house. The building is advanced and preparations need to be made for footings and flues.

979 9 March 1829. Joseph Tanner Esq, Castle Street [*Salisbury*].
Calculates values of theatre and a tenement at Salisbury, totalling £389 6s [*see* **395**].

980 9 March 1829. W E Griffin, statuary mason, 63 Quadrant, Regent's Street, London.
Chimney pieces purchased by Mr Hopper to be sent by Woolcott's Salisbury Waggon, directed to William Boucher Esq, Thornhill House, Dorsetshire. Slabs are not needed. Gives dimensions of openings. Asks for bill.

981 9 March 1829. George Morant Esq, Farnborough Place, Blackwater.
Has some minor objections to Mr Matthews' bills. Has marked inaccuracies. Asks if visit to Farnborough is needed.

982 9 March 1829. Mr Bellamy.
Sends pattern for the ceiling coffers at Thornhill House. Will get the work done himself if the plasterer is unable to work from the pattern.

983 10 March 1829. Mr Strong, mason, Box near Bath.
Surprised not to have a reply to the earlier request.[1]

1. Written by J M Peniston, on father's behalf. But no letter to Strong survives more recent than 6 Sept. 1828 [**853**]. See also **995**.

984 10 March 1829. Rt Hon Sir William Freemantle, Stanhope Street, London.
[*Clarendon House*]: Had expected Mr Webb to notify the payments. The offices connected with the mansion at the first floor level and the stables would be started. Had met Mr Webb at Melchet and hopes the report will be satisfactory.

985 11 March 1829. W E Griffin, statuary mason, 63 Quadrant, Regent's Street, London.
The fire places not to be less than 4 ft., as the rooms are large. Thus £2 to be added to the statuary chimney piece.

986 [*undated*].[1] Sir William Freemantle.
[*Clarendon House*]: Discusses cost of altering the roof, substituting slates for tile, which would improve the appearance of the building. The space is cleared for the intended staircase.

1. Acknowledges a letter dated 10th.

987 13 March 1829. Mrs Berrington, Spetisbury House, Blandford.
Discusses orders for various lots of timbers.

988 23 March 1829. Rt Hon Sir William Freemantle, Stanhope Street, London.
[*Clarendon House*]: Regrets that it is too late to alter the basement floor of the offices as building is complete to the first floor. Discusses plans for the principal rooms, bedrooms and roof. Asks for agreement and hopes that when next honoured with a visit they will not be found to have been idle in endeavouring to meet his wishes.

989 23 March 1829. Mr Franks.
Asks if he intends to undertake the staircase at Clarendon.

990 26 March 1829. Rev R Parker.
Writes in the middle of military arrangements to say that they are equally busy in getting up a counter-petition to the Anti Catholic.[1] Hopes to send a few sheets for signatures. Cannot send particulars but will request Mrs P [*sic*] to do so. There are great and good names with them. Is anxious about Mr Arundell's resignation.

1. A petition to the king, opposing Catholic emancipation, was circulating among Wiltshire gentry during March 1829, and was printed in *Salisbury and Winchester Journal*, 16 March 1829, p.4. A heated correspondence on the issue was maintained in the newspaper during March and April.

991 27 March 1829. [*addressee not stated*[1]].
Is able to send a copy of the petition as Mrs P forgot to send the letter by the morning mail. Describes how the petition should be completed. Urges the speedy collection of as many respectable names as possible but no XX: Mr Henry Everett the banker is the most zealous, active and useful friend and *entre nous* is the gentleman to replace Mr B- A-[2] should he resign.

1. Probably Rev Parker. See **990**.
2. Perhaps Mr B Arundell. See **990**.

992 27 March 1829. Mr Thomas Lucas, builder, Chertsey.
Thinks the price for plastering[1] to be fair. The price per rod of brickwork is excessive and asks about the charge for mortar and labour as he cannot recommend Mr Morant to agree.

1. At Farnborough House. See **993**.

993 27 March 1829. G Morant Esq, Farnborough House, Frimley, Surrey.
Forwards copies of a letter from Mr Lucas and the reply [**992**]. Was away when his son sent off the plans and enquires if they were explanatory [*sic*]. Has not yet made accounts of Mr Matthews' works.

994 27 March 1829. Messrs Winkfield and Co.
Regrets the roman cement sent is unfit for use. Has tried two casks and will keep them but is sending back the other four in accordance with the agreement. Requires a guarantee before ordering large quantities of cement and plaster or will go elsewhere.

995 31 March 1829. Mr Strong, mason, Box.
Disappointed not to hear about the balustrading for Lord Normanton.[1] Wishes to know when a load will be ready and at which part of the house scaffolding should be erected.[2]

1. For Somerley House. See **907, 983**.
2. Written by J M Peniston, on father's behalf.

996 31 March 1829. Rev Mr Dewdney.
Encloses a valuation.[1]

1. Written by J M Peniston, on father's behalf. The property was presumably at Fovant. See **1008**.

997 1 April 1829. Samuel Foot Esq, Endless Street [*Salisbury*].
Agrees a price for wood, subject to usual discount.

998 1 April 1829. G Morant Esq, Farnborough Place, Surrey.
Dissatisfied with reply from Mr Lucas about cost of brickwork. Discusses cost and undertakes to make best bargain possible. Suggests that Mr Matthews be allowed to make a proposal to do the work.

999 2 April 1829. Winkfield and Co, Grove Street, Southwark.
Reiterates that unsatisfactory cement must be taken back. Judges this on the basis of 20 years as a surveyor. Will accept a further shipment of 12 casks subject to the conditions already proposed.

1000 4 April 1829. Mr Strong, mason, Box near Bath.
[*Somerley House*]: Encloses drawings of baluster caps and base, and of the mouldings of the bases of balustrading to the house. Seeks agreement that the scaffolding will be erected first over the colonnade on the south front.[1]

1. Written by J M Peniston on father's behalf.

1001 7 April 1829. Rt Hon Sir William Freemantle, Stanhope Street, London.
Acknowledges further advance of £500. Will meet wishes about chimney piece and asks address of party on whom he is to call in town. Discusses bedroom doors and progress being made by bricklayers, carpenters and plasterers at Clarendon.

1002 7 April 1829. George Morant Esq, Farnborough Place.
Acknowledges letter containing Mathews's proposals for brickwork but does not know whether he was aware of Lucas's prices. Will send accounts in a day or two. Mathews's proposals are exactly 20s. per rod less than Lucas's, and are fair. Peniston insists that he has no motive in preferring one tradesman to another, farther than to protect Morant's interests.

1003 7 April 1829. Mr E Griffin, 63 Quadrant, London.
Encloses draft for the amount of a bill and asks for a stamped receipt [*see* **980, 985**].

1004 9 April 1829. Wadham Wyndham Esq, College.[1]
Has analysed ten bills and lists the proportions for Mr Wyndham and Mr Munday.

1. The College, Bourne Hill, Salisbury: P.

1005 11 April 1829. W D Whitmarsh Esq, Endless Street.
Has surveyed the house in [*Salisbury*] Close occupied by Miss May and values it at £670.

1006 11 April 1829. Messrs Winkfield and Co, Grove Street, Southwark.
Assumes that the proposed terms of dealing [*see* **994, 999**] were not acceptable as there had been no reply. Requests reply by return or will have to go elsewhere, as he is in urgent need of plaster and 15 to 20 more casks of roman cement. Depends on their honour to take back the useless cement.

1007 11 April 1829. [*addressee not stated*].

Regrets cannot name Monday or Tuesday to meet the tradesmen at Bramshaw Church. Is waiting hourly to receive a gentleman from Ireland to settle some accounts of the late Mr Wynch with the Lords of the Manor of Dean and Grimstead. Will write again to arrange the meeting.

1008 11 April 1829. Rev Mr Dewdney, Fovant Rectory.

Has seen Mr Brownjohn who valued the fixtures at Fovant. Lists some reductions.

1009 11 April 1829. Charles Millet Esq, Hindon.

Forwards amended plan and estimate.[1] The additional bedroom, the second staircase and new sash windows in the front will increase the cost to £530. Suggests a way of raising the drawing room ceiling without taking the roof off.

1. Probably relates to the clergyman's house at Hindon. See **945, 1056**.

1010 13 April 1829. G Morant Esq, Farnborough Place, Surrey.

Has completed most of Mathews' bills. Details some queries about ironmongery, smithwork and bricks. Encloses amended plan moving the main staircase into the intended drawing room by permitting the existing bathroom to form part of the conservatory, and communicating with it by a pair of folding glass doors. Has proposed some alterations in and adjoining the lobby leading to the water closet to make it more private. Proposes arrangements for servants' staircase. Has received from Mr Mathews the prices for brickwork, and Strong promises to do the work in the best possible manner, but will not answer until he has heard from Morant.

1011 13 April 1829. Mr Bellamy, builder, Whitchurch, Dorset.

Says that Mr Boucher is anxious that work on the staircase at Thornhill should proceed. Asks for plan of the lodge gates and adjoining roads.

1012 15 April 1829. Mr Sworn, Oatmeal Row [*Salisbury*].

Had intended to answer personally the previous day but seeing the shop full of customers thought the visit would be ill-timed. The sentiments in the letter did him great credit and removed a disagreeable impression. Had been informed by someone at the time that he had employed King to post the bills and was only prevented by the city authorities. Is pleased that this was void of truth.[1]

1. Perhaps relates to anti-catholic feeling in Salisbury. See **990** note 1.

1013 15 April 1829. Mr Franks, builder, 36 Nutford Place, Bryanston Square, London.
The estimate[1] so much exceeds the calculation that he will trouble him no further.

1. Perhaps for the staircase at Clarendon. See **989**.

1014 16 April 1829. Mr Strong.
[*Somerley House*]: Has only just received the letter of 11th and no scaffolding can be ready until the 27th. Is going immediately to Mr Webb, Lord Normanton's steward, who is arranging the poles. Regrets the delay as Lord Normanton is impatient. Suspects the letter which had arrived by post had been carried in someone's pocket. Is replying by post because Mr Strong's man chooses to stay although there was nothing to do until the 27th.

1015 17 April 1829. Colonel The Marquis of Bath, Grosvenor (*Grovesnor*) Square, London.
Accepts frankly and respectfully the cap[1] His Lordship has been pleased to offer. Welcomes it with a consciousness of having at least endeavoured to deserve it. Will inform Lord Arundell on his return. Hopes that, when the Regiment meets, the Troop will meet with approval. Offers help to Mr Adjutant Pettit if needed.

1. Perhaps formal ratification of Peniston's yeomanry commission following the passing of the Catholic Relief Act.

1016 20 April 1829. George Morant Esq, Farnborough Place, Surrey.
Feels regret at the change made before the house is finished, but the event is too common to excite surprise. Knows Mr Tatham to be a gentleman of ability and does not have the vanity to compete with London architects.

1017 [*undated*]. [*addressee not stated*].
Notes that Salisbury Fair is not until 20th October and that Weyhill starts on the 10th for five days. Lord Bath proposes Troops march to quarters on the 13th and return on the 20th, both Tuesdays. Suggests gentlemen with business at the market could delay their arrival or leave early.

1018 21 April 1829. Samuel Foot Esq, Endless Street.
Encloses a cheque.

1019 22 April 1829. Philip Chitty Esq, Shaftesbury.
Cannot move until after the sessions but makes appointment afterwards to meet Mr Down and bring accounts of Lord Grosvenor.

1020 23 April 1829. [*addressee not stated*].
Orders two casks of mastic, to be sent by Mr Woolcott's waggon.

1021 23 April 1829. [*addressee not stated*[1]].
Cannot understand delay about conservatory at Clarendon. Unless there is a satisfactory reply will have to apply elsewhere.

1. Messrs Jones and Co of Birmingham. See **978**.

1022 23 April 1829. Messrs Winkfield and Co.
Acknowledges that the first cask opened proved very good and expects the rest to be the same [*see* **1006**].

1023 23 April 1829. C Millet Esq, Hindon.
Will visit Hindon. Wants to employ a particular carpenter and any bricklayer who is preferred.

1024 24 April 1829. Mr Strong.
Reports that Lord Normanton is at Somerley but that Mr Webb, his steward, does not wish him to be annoyed sooner than absolutely necessary. But all the stone for the work should be sent with the greatest expedition.

1025 24 April 1829.[1] [*addressee not stated*].
'Dear John, There appears a precious paucity of brains with members of my family. Ellen & Will[2] in the plenitude of their epistolary knowledge direct their letter to "Mrs Peniston, Hartford Bridge". I wonder they had not directed it to "My Mother, Hart Bridge". And Mrs P and my son John expecting an answer to their letter consider it an act of superogation to make any enquirement at the Post Office. The consequence is that Thomas with Mrs Harrington's horse has been waiting all day at Andover and most likely, hearing from no-one, will return tonight or tomorrow morning; and I relying on your return this evening and arranging accordingly have to pay the penalty of the combined stupidity of all the party with all the patience I can muster. I remain very affectionately yours, J Peniston.'

1. MS *Friday eve*.
2. Presumably Eleanora Arundell Peniston (born 1812) and William Michael Peniston (born 1814), son and daughter of John Peniston: WAM, vol.80, p.186. The identity of the addressee and the frustrating circumstances which occasioned the letter are unclear.

1026 [*undated*]. Mr Swayne.
The number of old tiles wanted is available for Mr Thring at Clarendon.[1]

1. Written by J M Peniston, on father's behalf.

1027 25 April 1829. Mr James Bowerman, Bugle, Southampton.
Has been asked by Mr Marett to send plans of the interior of the church[1] with the new seating.

1. No indication is given of which church, perhaps St Michael's, Southampton. See **1575**.

1028 25 April 1829. Winkfield and Co, Cement Works, Grove Street, Southwark.
Has received their bill for £34 19s. 5d. and has directed his bankers, Messrs Deacon and Co, to pay it.

1029 26 April 1829. Rt Hon Sir William Freemantle.
Reports on progress at Clarendon.

1030 3 May 1829.   Sir W Freemantle
Reports that windows in the south front at Clarendon are finished as desired. Discusses various aspects of the work, including drainage and timber to be used for the roof.

1031 [*undated*]. Messrs Winkfield and Co.
Specifies details for delivery of casks of plaster.

1032 [*undated*]. Rt Hon Earl of Enniskillen.
Acknowledges request for Mr Baker to send the balance of account to Messrs Drummond and Co.

1033 3 May 1829. Mr Strong, mason, Box near Bath.
'I have had a letter from L'd Normanton complaining of the small quantity of stone yet sent for the proposed ballustrade. I have written in answer that I have every reason to believe that you are preparing at the quarry with all possible expedition. I most earnestly entreat you to lose no time in meeting his wishes. I know he contemplates extensive alterations and it may be of consequence not to offend him. He is at present residing at Somerly – and I understand from Mr Webb his Steward it is doubtful whether he may not continue there during the summer – it would therefore be madness to begin setting till the whole of the part connected with the mansion is prepared. If you will give me due notice of this I will take care that scaffolding bricklayers and coppersmiths shall be in readiness to get on with the work but do not I entreat you let us begin to pull the house about till we are prepared to go regularly on with the completion. I am dear Sir, very faithfully yours.'

1034 3 May 1829. Rt Hon Earl of Normanton, Somerley House, Hants.
Confirms that the mason has been urged to get forward with the stonework for the balustrade [*see* **1033**]. Will arrange to erect scaffolding when the poles arrive from Lord Malmesbury's bailiff.[1] 'I am aware My Lord that the label for the windows is not strictly architectural as connected with a brick front, and that to make them so the architrave should be continued round the windows so as to make the dressings complete. But I am also aware that much greater liberties are taken with the regular orders in modern buildings. If the desired effect be produced regularity is not considered of much consequence.' However perhaps a decision should be delayed until completion of the balustrade.

1. Presumably Mr Hart, Hurn Court, Christchurch. See **1047**.

1035 4 May 1829. Rev Charles Wrottesly, East Knoyle.
With an early start it should only take one day to inspect the proposed alterations.[1] The charge would be three guineas, or five if it took two days.

1. Probably to East Knoyle church. See **1223**.

1036 4 May 1829. R Payne Esq. architect, Gillingham.
Puzzled about mason's account at the Town Hall[1] because local customs of measurement are contradictory. Asks for help so as not to injure Mr Downs with the report. Agrees price for Tisbury stone but does not know what to allow for setting. Encloses accounts and discusses variations to several entries. Apologizes for troubling him while he is indisposed.

1. Shaftesbury. See **899**.

1037 6 May 1829. Rev C Wrottesley, East Knoyle, Wilts.
Proposes to arrive not later than nine o'clock on Friday morning.

1038 [*undated*]. Messrs Winkfield and Co, cement manufacturer, Grove Street, Southwark.
Had not received six casks of coarse plaster ordered to be sent by Russell's waggon from Friday Street [*see* **1031**]. Nor heard anything of cement and plaster by the Albion. The disappointments are very serious to the plasterers who are standing idle for want of material. Requests immediate attention.

1039 7 May 1829. George Morant Esq, E J Shirley Esq, Eastington Park, Shipston-on-Stour.
Has received packet of Matthews' bills and regrets many appear exceptionable. Will meet Matthews at Farnborough to measure the work. Asks for permission to see the day work book which he had recommended be kept.

1040 10 May 1829. Rt Hon Lord Viscount Palmerston, Stanhope Street, London. [*Broadlands*]: Sketches section of the ground and foundation exposed by lifting the hall paving. Satisfied that stains are not damp but more likely grease acted on by the adjoining flues. Will be in London later in the week at the Sussex Hotel in Bouverie Street. Has directed Marsh to send a report to him there on an experimental reworking of the stones, and will discuss it with Lord Palmerston if he wishes.

1041 10 May 1829. Sir William Freemantle.
Arranges to call when in London.

1042 10 May 1829. Rev William Arundell Bouverie, under cover to Hon B Bouverie M.P., 21 Edwards Street, Portman Square, London.
Offers to meet at Tytherley or in London.

1043 10 May 1829. Mr John Matthews, builder, Frimley, Surrey.
Will be travelling on the following day's Salisbury coach and asks to be met at Blackwater.

1044 15 May 1829. Rt Hon Earl of Normanton.
Has enquired about the poles which should be at Somerley. As soon as they are, Mr Strong's men will begin. Encloses elevation of the alterations of the label and architraves for the windows.[1]

1. Written by J M Peniston, on father's behalf.

1045 1 [*sic*] May 1829. [*addressee not stated*[1]].
Order for timber, so that Haggar may finish a roof.

1. Probably Messrs Baker and Fox. See **1066**.

1046 19 May 1829. Mr Jones, Birmingham.
Replies that Sir William Freemantle agrees to the conservatory being heated by warm water. Thinks it will come cheaper from Birmingham than casting at Salisbury. Asks the weight and freight per ton cost to Southampton. A local gentleman has procured one from London at considerably less expense. But the difference would be the freight charge from Birmingham versus London. However one prepared under Mr Jones' direction would be preferred. Asks when erection could start at Clarendon.

1047 19 May 1829. Mr Hart,[1] Hurn Court, Christchurch (*XtChurch*).
Understands that Mr Webb has spoken about the fir poles for Lord Normanton.
Needs 6 from 30 feet to 35 feet, and 20 from 25 feet to 30 feet, and 14 any length.

1. Presumably Lord Malmesbury's bailiff. See **1034**. The poles were for scaffolding at Somerley.

1048 19 May 1829. Arthur Baker Esq, 6 Great George Street North, Dublin.
Pleased to hear of his safe arrival at the capital of hospitality, and that Mrs and Miss
Baker are well. Copies a statement of sums, amounting in all to to about £500, lodged
with Messrs Drummonds between 1825 and 1829. Discusses details of some of the
payments.

1049 20 May 1829. George Morant Esq, E J Shirly's Esq, Eastington Park, Shipston-
on-Stour.
Has measured Mathews' work and corrected the bills as far as possible. Discusses some
points in detail.

1050 [*undated*]. Charles Bowles Esq, Shaftesbury (*Shaston*).
Has inspected the Punch [*sic*] of the prison with Mr Knight, millwright, and to put
the punch tackle at Fisherton gaol in repair with a cast iron housing for the wheel
will cost about £6 9s 0d. Suggests alteration worked by capstan. Reports on other
work at the gaol.

1051 22 May 1829. Mr Bouverie, Edward Street, Portman Square, London.
Reports on dilapidations at Tytherley, totalling £99 12s. 2d. Encloses plan and
elevation for a stable and coach house.

1052 22 May 1829. [*addressee not stated*].
Prevented from commencing the race stand[1] but will start the foundations in the
ensuing week.

1. Salisbury Racecourse. See **1054** note 1.

1053 23 May 1829. Rt Hon Earl of Normanton.
Apologizes for the delay caused by the want of scaffolding poles. But no time will be
lost when it is fixed and Peniston will visit Somerley to direct the masons. Sends a
new elevation showing alterations.[1]

1. Written by J M Peniston, on father's behalf.

1054 24 May 1829.[1] Mr Windham Esq.
Discusses location of the new race stand, relative to the property of G T Jervoise and the Earl of Pembroke.[2]

1. MS *23* corrected.
2. Presumably at Salisbury Racecourse. Jervoise owned land at Stratford Toney, and Pembroke at Netherhampton and Wilton, adjoining the course. See WRS vol.30.

1055 26 May 1829. Rev Aurundell Bouverie, Tytherley.
Has received Crooks' estimates and discusses alterations.

1056 29 May 1829. Charles Millet Esq, Hindon.
Encloses an elevation for the proposed alterations to the house at Hindon, and discusses details of the plan.

1057 1 June 1829. Mr Strong.
Scaffolding at Somerley will be finished by the following day. Understands that Strong is to visit Somerley and asks to know when, so that their visits may coincide.

1058 2 June 1829. Mr Mark Hanks.
Encloses cheque for A Fisher of Tetbury as the balance of account of £9 18s. 9d. Requests a stamped receipt for £11 18s. 9d. as £2 has already been paid. The receipt is to be sent to Peniston if Hanks can procure a frank, otherwise he can bring it to the ensuing sessions. Asks for immediate settlement with Fisher as the poor man is distressed and writes frequently.

1059 2 June 1829. A Wingrove Esq, Trowbridge.
Encloses cheque for sundry accounts. Will be visiting soon so will be able to offer thanks for all the kindness and good wishes. Sends best respects to Mrs Wingrove.

1060 4 June 1829. Mr Strong, mason, Box near Bath.
Scaffolding on the east front at Somerley is complete and Strong's man is cutting down the blocking course in preparation for fixing the new base. Needs a drawing of how many pedestals are intended on the front. Lady Normanton is anxious to know when Strong will visit. Lord Normanton is away but writes every day to urge the work on. Men may be sent as the bricklayers and others will keep out of the way. Asks for an urgent reply.

1061 5 June 1829. Messrs Harwood (*Haywood*) and Co, paper stainers, Upper George Street, Portman Square, London.
Has been waiting for the paper-hanger to measure the walls of his houses.[1] Orders six times the previous quantity of the drawing room paper and three times that of the other papers with their corresponding borders.

1. Probably De Vaux Place, Salisbury. See WAM, vol.80, p.186.

1062 5 June 1829. Messrs Grieve, Grellier and Morgan.
Orders via Southampton 20 casks of roman cement, 14 of coarse plaster and six of fine plaster.

1063 5 June 1829. Lord Viscount Palmerston, Stanhope Street, London.
Reports on work at Broadlands and discusses some aspects.

1064 5 June 1829. Captain Tayler, Devizes.
Will vote for Mr Silvester and try to induce others to do so, unless Mr Sutton renews his intention of proposing for the office.[1]

1. Possibly connected with the Bear Club, Devizes, of which all were members: information from Mr John Hurley.

1065 7 June 1829.[1] Rt Hon Sir William Freemantle.
[*Clarendon House*]: Annexes plan and section of the roof of the offices which will be put on in the ensuing week. Reports on work in various parts of the house. Sums up by observing that every part of the work is as forward as is desirable, if he can believe the party who is preparing the conservatory who assures him that it should be ready for erection about the end of the month. Is obliged by the punctuality of the payment.

1. MS *6 June* corrected.

1066 10 June 1829. Messrs Baker and Fox.
Sends cheque for £216 17s. 11d. [*see* **1045**] but queries the charge for sawing. Has left the bill with Haggar to determine the number of feet charged.

1067 10 June 1829.[1] A Wingrove Esq.
Instructs that work on Road Bridge should continue the footpath on the Somerset line. Necessary repairs should be done but Crook must not be the judge of this. Agrees about Crook's charge which is why his is not among the accounts to be discharged. Is about to visit Box and Bath.

1. MS *May* corrected.

1068 12 June 1829. Rev A Bouverie.
'My father is at present from home but has desired me to go to Tytherley and report to you on the progress of the work. I have done so today and find the painters have finished the outside and are now cleaning and painting in the attics. The bricklayers have opened the footings for the coach house and stable etc, and I have altered the size of the coach houses as you wished from 10 feet to 14 feet. Beauchamp's work is in preparation for fixing and he has promised to prepare the estimate for the water closet by Tuesday next.[1] My father will then be at home and will forward it to you immediately.

'I remain, Sir, very respectfully your obedient servant, J M Peniston.'[2]

1. MS *by Tuesday next* interlined.
2. This letter written on a loose sheet, and inserted in letter book with sealing wax.

1069 16 June 1829. Charles Bowles Esq, Shaftesbury (*Shaston*).
Encloses Whitmarsh's account, with remarks on specific points.

1070 16 June 1829. Lord Viscount Palmerston, Stanhope Street, London.
Acknowledges instructions that are so explicit that it should not be necessary to send the butler down to Broadlands. Will visit Broadlands and give Floyd his final directions.

1071 21 June 1829. [*addressee not stated*[1]].
Will tour the county in the ensuing week and arranges to meet at Road Bridge on Tuesday at about eleven in the morning on his route through Trowbridge to Devizes. If they do not meet at the bridge will call on the recipient at his residence.

1. Perhaps A Wingrove. See **1067**.

1072 21 June 1829. Rt Hon Earl of Normanton.
Sincerely regrets that His Lordship has had to complain about the slowness of the work at Somerley and explains the arrangements with the mason.

1073 21 June 1829. Lord Viscount Palmerston.
Reports that he has visited Broadlands and instructed the workmen. Discusses various details of the work.

1074 22 June 1829. A Bouverie, Merton College, Oxford.
Has received estimates for building and apparatus of water closet of £75 4s. 0d., not including painting and glazing. The whole lot may be estimated at £80. Was at Tytherley and reports on work.

1075 [*undated*]. Mr Strong, mason, Box, near Bath.
Finds that two men promised at Somerley were not there. Everything is ready to erect the balustrading. Wishes to hear by return how many men he proposes to send.

1076 26 June 1829. Mathews, Frimley, Surrey.
Extracts general statement of account and passes on Mr Morant's request for discount for prompt payment.

1077 26 June 1829. Mr Marsh, mason, Romsey.
[*Broadlands*]: Passes on Lord Palmerston's instructions that all the stones in the Hall that are stained [*see* **1040**] should be reworked. Acknowledges letter from Floyd, and will visit.

1078 26 June 1829. Joshua Robinson Esq, Paddington Cottage, London.
Replies that Mr May has left for France. Is anxious about Mr Hopper's health as Colonel Baker found him indisposed. But assumes that no news is good news, and conveys his best wishes.

1079 26 June 1829. Timothy Bramah Esq, Pimlico.
Orders four sets of apparatus for that number of water closets. Confirms that he is a contractor and a ready money dealer.

1080 21 June 1829. Lambert Esq, Bridzor, Wardour Castle.
Commends a young friend, Mr John Alford, as a candidate to supply poor Dudley's situation as clerk to the Turnpike Commission. Adds a postscript that, if successful, Mr Alford will support poor Dudley's family for six years.

1081 26 June 1829. J Bennet Esq MP, Pyt House.
Commends Mr John Alford, for his talents and character, to the vacancy caused by death of Charles Dudley as clerk to the Turnpike Commission, as Mr Alford has recently been admitted to the honorable corps of solicitors.

1082 26 June 1829. Mrs Berrington, Spetisbury House, near Blandford.
Asks her to make enquiries of Wells about an order for laths.[1]

1. Written by J M Peniston, on father's behalf.

1083 27 June 1829. Mr Richard Downs, builder, Shaftesbury (*Shaston*).
Responds at length to query about masonry. Will meet him at Fovant and suggests employing Mr Payne.

1084 27 June 1829. Haywood Esq, Penitentiary, Devizes.
Encloses sketches of methods proposed to prevent the boundary walls spreading further outwards, and to increase ventilation over the treadwheels. These should be sufficient to explain measures to the visiting justices.

1085 28 June 1829. Strong, mason, Box, near Bath.
Passes on Lord Normanton's anxiety about the balustrades to the offices. Asks Strong when he will call at Salisbury.[1]

1. Written by J M Peniston, on father's behalf.

1086 29 June 1829. Messrs Harwood (*Haywood*) and Co, paper etc. etc. [*sic*], 11 Upper George Street, Bryanston Square.
Acknowledges a paquet of paper and discusses some future needs [*see* **1061**].

1087 29 June 1829. Lord Normanton.
Answers letter about balustrade on the offices. Arranges to visit Somerley to give directions.

1088 29 June 1829. [*addressee not stated*[1]].
Discusses work at Tytherley and possible changes to the windows. Has directed work to start on the water closet. Is sending oak joists, and asks about requirements for other materials.

1. Probably Rev Arundell Bouverie. See **1068, 1074**.

1089 1 July 1829. Arthur Baker Esq, 5 Great George Street, Dublin.
Reports on discussion with Mr Cobb about the late Mr Wynch's business with the Grimstead estate.

1090 1 July 1829. Thomas Hopper Esq.
Enquires about his health [*see* **1078**]. Discusses progress of work at the [*Salisbury*] Council House and relates local opinions of it.

1091 3 July 1829. Timothy Bramah Esq, Pimlico.
Has arranged payment of £32 14s. 0d. Mr Bramah's few observations made when at Salisbury have induced his boy to apply himself to his algebra.

1092 3 July 1829. George Morant Esq.
Passes on a letter from Mathews about accounts for work at Farnborough. Comments on the confusion about these.

1093 [*undated*]. Mr Wells, carpenter, Spetisbury House, near Blandford.
Disappointed in connection with the work. Discusses problem about the supply of laths.

1094 5 July 1829. Mr Jones, Birmingham.
Apologizes for the inaccuracies in dimensions given to help judge the most desirable course for the boiler reservoir and pipes. Sends plan of the basement and suggests a layout.[1]

1. Probably relates to warm-water heating for the conservatory at Clarendon House. See **1046**.

1095 5 July 1829. Bennet Esq M.P.
Explains that a letter [**1081**] had been sent to Pyt House recommending a young friend for the post of clerk to the Turnpike Commissioners.

1096 5 July 1829. E Baker Esq, 145 Regent Street [*London*].
Reports on the state of the canvass for Alford's election as clerk to the Commissioners. Stresses Alford's generous intention for poor Dudley's family. Reports support from Mr Swayne and the great majority of the county commissioners, but the corporation of Salisbury supports Messrs Hodding, who are also candidates. Seeks Baker's assistance in gaining support of county magistrates, or at least to neutralize them as opponents.

1097 5 July 1829. [*addressee not stated*[1]].
On counting the office windows a second time there were eleven instead of ten. Estimate is now £138 6s. 0d. to finish the architraves and cases to the windows in the south. Will commence work if his Lordship agrees.

1. Letter begins *My Lord*. Perhaps Lord Normanton. See **1109**.

1098 6 July 1829. John Swayne Esq, Wilton.
Explains that comments made on the draft award are incorrect. There are differences of opinion about drawing up the instrument between Mr Swayne and Mr Blackmore. It would be desirable for Mr Stevens and himself to so word the documents that it would not be offensive to either party.[1]

1. Peniston appears to have been arbitrating in a dispute between Messrs Blackmore and Messrs Sargeant and Thring. See **1101, 1326**. Both firms were carpet manufacturers in Wilton: P.

1099 6 July 1829. A Baker, 5 Great George Street, Dublin.
Reports further unsatisfactory discussion with Mr Cobb. Has had a letter from Mr Freemantle's agent arranging the quit rent in the next month.

1100   7 July 1829.   Rt Hon Sir W Freemantle, Stanhope Street, London.
Acknowledges that Mr Webb has paid him the instalment of £500. Expects to meet at Clarendon so will not be very minute in reporting progress. They were fortunate in covering the roof of the kitchen offices before the last stem [*sic*] of wet weather. The garden walls may be delayed because they cannot get the bricks across the fields in the wet weather.

1101   8 July 1829.   Messrs Sargeant and Thring, Wilton.
Gives notice of meeting with Mr T O Stevens. Encloses the demands of the late partners but wants [*i.e. lacks*] the key to understand the nature of them.[1]

1. See **1098** note 1.

1102   9 July 1829.   [*addressee not stated*].
Expects Alford's success. Discusses aspects of the election. Has heard from Hopper, who is feeling much better.

1103   13 July 1829.   J W Ledyard Esq, Road Hill.
Has directed Mr Wingrove to repair the road, pavement and coping at Road Bridge, provided Mr Blandford would do the work for under ten pounds.

1104   13 July 1829.   George Morant Esq, Farnborough House, Surrey.
Acknowledges a cheque for £75 4s. 0d. and discusses Mathews' work. Mathews has prepared some sashes for Farnborough, but as Mr Tatham will apply them,[1] Peniston leaves it to Tatham to decide.

1. Tatham had replaced Peniston as architect responsible for work at Farnborough Place. See **1016**.

1105   13 July 1829.   Mr Gardiner, builder, Ringwood, Hants.
Orders stone lime from Poole and two loads of sharp sand for the plasterers at Somerley.

1106   [*undated*].   Messrs Grieve, Grellier and Morgan, Belvedere Road, Waterloo Bridge, London.
Orders 20 casks of plaster to be sent to Southampton. And seven casks of mastic warranted to Poole.[1]

1. Written by J M Peniston, on father's behalf.

1107 14 July 1829. Messrs Grieve, etc.
Requests that half of the foregoing order be sent by Woolcott's waggon from the Elephant, as work has stopped for want of materials.[1]

1. Written by J M Peniston, on father's behalf.

1108 20 July 1829. [*addressee not stated*].
Has been preparing for movement in the north but the plan of campaign has been altered by orders from headquarters. Discusses church matters, and requests that he adds correct dimensions to a rough sketch.

1109 21 July 1829. Mr Strong, mason, Box near Bath.
Reports that Lord Normanton still writes in the language of complaint relative to the non-arrival of the blocking course for the offices. Asks for account of expense so far in order to keep with the estimate for which Lord Normanton holds him responsible.

1110 21 July 1829. Grieve, Grellier and Morgan.
Surprised to receive no answer to the order for plaster and mastic.[1]

1. Written by J M Peniston, on father's behalf.

1111 24 July 1829. [*addressee not stated*].
Complains of certain hatches in the parish of Dinton being in such disrepair that Mr Wyndham's tenants cannot water their meadows.[1]

1. A letter, writ and plans on this matter are in WRO 451/536.

1112 24 July 1829. Rev Arundell Bouverie, Merton College, Oxford.
Reports work at Tytherley is slow, as bricks from the adjoining kiln cannot be provided as fast as needed because waggons from all parts of the county are in waiting when a kiln is ready to be drawn. Discusses progress of various parts of the building in detail.

1113 26 July 1829. Mr Gardiner, builder, Ringwood, Hants.
Enquires if any mastic has arrived at Poole, which was shipped by the Rose on 16 July [*see* **1105**].

1114 27 July 1829. G Morant Esq, Bangor, North Wales.
Discusses measurements and costs for Mr Mathews work at Farnborough.

1115 27 July 1829. Messrs Jones and Co, Mount Street, Birmingham.
Has received letter and drawings, and confirms that preparations are being made.[1]

1. Presumably to erect the conservatory for Clarendon House. See **1046, 1094, 1130**.

1116 29 July 1829. Lord Normanton, Somerley, Ringwood.
Discusses the masons at Somerley, particularly one named John Austin who had been exerting [*sic*] dissatisfaction, and who might be discharged as an example to the others.

1117 29 July 1829. Messrs Grieve, Grellier and Morgan.
Orders 10 casks of roman cement via Southampton.

1118 29 July 1829. [*addressee not stated*].
Copies correspondence with Mr Morant about work at Farnborough, as he no longer has the accounts. Discusses various deductions and alterations. Hopes that the information will enable the accounts to be closed satisfactorily.

1119 30 July 1829. Mr Tarrant, mason. Swindon.
Asks about progress at the Seven Bridges. Wishes to have a report each week.

1120 3 Aug. 1829. Mr R Downs, builder, Shaftesbury (*Shaston*).
Acknowledges letter, bill and parcel. Encloses cheque.

1121 4 Aug. 1829. G Morant Esq, P.O. Bangor.
Replies to query about Mathews' work on stable building.

1122 5 Aug. 1829. Mr Strong, etc.
Surprised to have had no answer to two letters. Requests reply by return of post. Has been to Somerley and 180 more balusters must be sent. Asks when Strong will visit.[1]

1. Written by J M Peniston, on father's behalf.

1123 [*undated*]. Thomas Hopper Esq.
Writes with reminder that the assizes are past and a visit is expected. Has heard no very heavy complaints and some approvals, pretty well as the world goes. Expects a line so that the mayor and committee can be notified. Mr Hopper will be his guest if the Colonel[1] is absent.

1. Colonel Baker. See **755**.

1124 7 Aug. 1829. R Webb Esq.
Discusses water supply and pumps.[1]

1. Probably for Clarendon House. See **1129**.

1125 7 Aug. 1829. Sir W Freemantle, etc.
Sends a plan, but the situation of the new farm buildings is not yet fixed.[1]

1. Written by J M Peniston, on father's behalf.

1126 9 Aug. 1829. Mr Richard Tarrant, mason, Swindon.
Acknowledges account of progress.[1] Regrets cannot confer a right to the scrapings of
the road. It is usually considered that 100 yds. on either side of the bridge is kept in
repair by the county, and where this has been done at county expense the scrapings
would be their property. But this has not hitherto been done. Complains about the
position of the commissioners who were released from the repair of the bridge.

1. Seven Bridges, near Cricklade. See **1119**.

1127 11 Aug. 1829. John Coventry, Burgate House.
Will visit Burgate to examine a settlement.

1128 11 Aug. 1829. Rev Mr Dullard, Court House, Cannington, Bridgwater.
Asks for reply to questions about dimensions arising from the change of situation
determined by Lord Clifford and the good ladies.

1129 12 Aug. 1829. R Webb Esq.
[*Clarendon House*]: Notes surprise at copies of letter attached to a plan that should not
have been included. Discusses the cost of laying on water which had not been in the
specification, but Sir William Freemantle had subsequently observed that the house
could not be complete without it.

1130 17 Aug. 1829. Mr[1] Jones, Birmingham.
[*Clarendon House*]: Assures them that his employer is very fidgety about the
conservatory. Fears the summer will pass away before it is erected. Enquires about a
warm air stove, castings for the balustrade of the back stair, and mortice locks for
doors and windows.

1. MS *Messrs*, deleted and corrected.

1131 20 Aug. 1829. Mr R Tarrant, Swindon.
[*Seven Bridges*]: Regrets that there has been annoyance by the water, and from the appearance of the weather thinks the annoyance likely to continue. The description of the watercourse being stopped is not confined to that part of the county and many statements to the court of sessions had no effect. Understands that the carriages with material for the repair of county bridges should, under the Turnpike Act, pass toll free.

1132 20 Aug. 1829. Messrs Harwood, 11 Upper George Street, Bryanston Square, London.
Discusses quantities and cost of paper. Has more paper than needed for his houses[1] but will keep it for future use [*but see* **1142**].

1. Probably De Vaux Place, Salisbury. See **1061**.

1133 20 Aug. 1829. Mr John Wright, (schooner Pomana, from Southampton), Chamberlains Wharf, London.
Replies that casks marked G are intended for Grieve, Grellier and Co. at Waterloo Bridge; those marked W for Messrs Winkfield and Co, Grove Street, Southwark.

1134 23 Aug. 1829. Mr Bevis, mason, Tisbury.
'What I feared has come to pass. The excessive indolence of your men at Fisherton Bridge has so far attracted public notice that I have received a formal application on the subject. My answer was any delay or neglect on the part of your men would not be to the loss of the county but yours, as the work would be measured and valued when done. This will certainly be the case. I therefore give you this notice that you may prevent any further loss from the same cause.'

1135 23 Aug. 1829. Messrs Jones, Birmingham.
Will arrange waggons when the cargo [*see* **1130**] reaches Southampton. Suggests that it is not worth Mr Thomas paying a visit as the requirement is small.

1136 31 Aug. 1829. Mr G Short.
Confirms that he has been appointed to value certain properties on the part of Mr W Figes.

1137 31 Aug. 1829. P M Chitty Esq.
Regrets delaying settlement of the Town Hall account. Will have to visit Shaftesbury. Enquires about commitment to Mr Downs.

1138 [*undated*]. Messrs Baker and Fox.
Encloses cheque for £128 8s 4d.

1139 4 Sept. 1829. Col the Marquis of Bath.
'My Lord. I am honoured by your Lordship's letter of yesterday and shall have great pleasure in meeting your Lordship's wishes of undertaking the duty of Adjutant of the Wilts Yeomanry[1] during the period they assemble for permanent duty. I shall always My Lord be most happy to render the regiment any services in my power.'

1. MS *of the Wilts Yeomanry* interlined.

1140 4 Sept. 1829. Sir W Freemantle.
Regrets not acknowledging two recents payments of £500. Reports progress at Clarendon on stables, washhouse, laundry, brewhouse, bakehouse and dairy.

1141 6 Sept. 1829. Sir W Freemantle.
[*Clarendon House*]: Regrets that Sir William considers some estimates too high. There were several things mixed up. Discusses costs of various parts of the work.

1142 6 Sept. 1829. Messrs Harwood and Co, 11 Upper George Street, Bryanston Square, London.
Has sent 21 pieces of paper and sundry bordering to Woolcott's warehouse to be forwarded by waggon. To be exchanged for drawing room paper, the same as before [*see* **1132**].

1143 10 Sept. 1829. Rt Hon Lord Arundell.
Has just learnt of his Lordship's arrival in England. Sends three notes from the Marquis of Bath for calling out the regiment and proposing to march to Devizes. Has, in conjunction with Colonel Baker, recommended Mr Henry Everett of Salisbury to succeed the Hon Mr Arundell who has resigned as Cornet of the Salisbury Troop. Otherwise the troop would have had no officer. Hopes the action will be approved. Proposes a field day to prepare for the period at Devizes.

1144 10 Sept. 1829. M Hodding Esq.
Writes hastily that he will attend to Stapleford Bridge, and is preparing to put up posts and rails adjoining Codford Bridge.

1145 [*undated*[1]]. Grieve, Grellier and Co.
Acknowledges a request to pay them on behalf of Mr Paulter.

1. Apparently written in haste on the same occasion as **1144**.

1146 12 Sept. 1829. Messrs Grieve and Co.
Commissions two chimneypieces from Mr Paulter, for small parsonage houses in the county.[1]

1. Both appear to have been for Hindon. See **1171, 1203**.

1147 [*undated*]. Sir W Freemantle.
Gratified that his good faith is appreciated about the business at Clarendon [*see* **1141**]. Discusses the accounts, progress on work and the need for an additional well and pump.

1148 14 Sept. 1829. Mr Dullard.
Has made some progress on plans for the site apparently determined on.[1]

1. Cannington chapel. See **1342, 1368**.

1149 14 Sept. 1829. Lord Normanton.
Regrets to learn that his Lordship considered the estimates for balustrades at Somerley to be a contract. Expenses will considerably exceed it. Discusses the work and queries the existence of plans and drawings.

1150 16 Sept. 1829. [*addressee not stated*[1]].
Sends drawings of posts and railings at Codford Bridge and asks for estimates to do the work.[2]

1. Presumably Messrs Carson and Miller. See **1152**.
2. Written by J M Peniston, on father's behalf.

1151 17 Sept. 1829. Grieve and Grellier.
Orders five casks of coarse plaster and three of fine.

1152 20 Sept. 1829. Messrs Carson and Miller, ironfounders, Warminster.
Has received proposals for erecting railings at Codford Bridge. Will arrange to meet at the bridge to assess the necessary preparations.

1153 21 Sept. 1829. [*addressee not stated*].
Sends copy of letter for Mr Downs with list of extras. Discusses details, including quantities of lead, fittings, doors, stairs and locks. Lord Normanton is much annoyed at the recipient disappointing him again. Will arrange a meeting at Somerley.[1]

1. Written by J M Peniston, on father's behalf.

1154 [*undated*]. Messrs Colley and Sutton.
Forwards a resolution of the committee of cottage owners proposed by Mr Peniston and seconded by Mr Seymour and unanimously agreed, 'that Messrs Tinney and Cobb and Mr George Sutton be requested to act as solicitors to the committee for such legal business as may be required in opposing the intended application to parliament'.[1]

1. The circumstances are explained in **1250**.

1155   21 Sept. 1829. Rev C Eddy, Guilsborough, Northampton.
Understands him to be the purchaser of a piece of land at Bemerton. Had previously arranged a plan of operation with Mr Swayne and Mr Handcock.

1156   22 Sept. 1829. Sir W Freemantle.
Pleased that Sir F Bathurst and Mr Harvy approve of the operations at Clarendon House. Discusses a window for the gentlemen's room. The conservatory has arrived [*see* **1135**].

1157   2 Oct. 1829. Mr Jay.
Delays a meeting at [*Fonthill*] Abbey.

1158   2 Oct. 1829. Thomas Culling, stonemason, Kinton[1] near Somerton, Somerset. Agrees to pay 1s. 8d. per foot for stone to be delivered to Mr Payne three miles beyond Salisbury.[2] Will discuss the hearth stones.

1. Probably Keinton Mandeville.
2. Clarendon House. See **1259**.

1159   5 Oct. 1829. [*addressee not stated*].
Encloses cheque for repair of bridge roads for Michaelmas 1827 to Michaelmas 1828. Requests a stamped receipt.

1160   5 Oct. 1829. [*addressee not stated*[1]].
Lists weapons held in store and by the six Troops. Reports that nine of the swords received from the Marlborough Troop were not of the up-to-date regulation pattern and some were unfit for use.[2]

1. Letter begins *My Lord*. Probably Lord Bath. See **1139, 1163**.
2. An unfinished letter, to *My Lord*, dated 3 Oct. 1829, is pinned to the letter book. It gives the same lists and more detail.

1161 [*undated*]. Messrs Grieve, Grellier.
Complains that nothing has been heard of the last parcel of goods, and orders eight more casks of coarse plaster.

1162 [*undated*]. [*addressee not stated*].
Encloses measurement of the works at Shaftesbury Town Hall. Describes aspects of the work and various bills.

1163 8 Oct. 1829. [*addressee not stated*[1]].
Has referred to the Adjutant's copy of the pay list and has found that nine days stationary [*sic*] has been charged instead of eight, which would have been correct. Mr Lawrence had said it was usual to charge an extra day's postage. Can vouch for Lieutenant Ward and Cornet Codrington of the Marlborough Troop having been on duty for the whole of the stay at Devizes. Encloses a certificate from the Clerk of the Lieutenancy of Cornet Estcourt's commission, this having been overlooked by the War Office as His Lordship had thought. Lists those officers who had two horses at Devizes but had learnt from Mr Petitt that the whole of the officers there returned two horses. Outlines his expected journey to Malmesbury, Bath, Frome, Maiden Bradley, Warminster and back to Salisbury, and notes where a message could be left for him.

1. Presumably Lord Bath, since an inn is described in the letter as, 'your Lordship's arms at Warminster'.

1164 8 Oct. 1829. [*addressee not stated*[1]].
Will be at Marlborough sessions on 20 [*Oct.*], the day named to meet at Clarendon. Suggests 22 [*Oct.*]. The monthly payment of £500 is due and he has made engagements in expectancy. Discusses the agreed method of payments.

1. Probably Mr Webb, who was responsible for Clarendon House payments. See **1100**.

1165 [*undated*]. Mr Collis.
Weather had prevented him from calling at Frogham. Returns key of cottages and cannot consent to receive it with the regular notice to quit which the law requires between landlord and tenant. Returns the bills, not understanding what they are for.

1166 12 Oct. 1829. Dyke Whitmarsh Esq.
Has surveyed the house in High Street[1] occupied by Mr Dennis and found it dilapidated, with portions really dangerous. A stack of chimneys adjoining the Rose and Crown Inn is fractured in many places, and should be removed with as little delay as possible. Discusses other defects and their remedies.

1. Salisbury. John Dennis was a confectioner in High Street (P, 1822) and there was a Rose and Crown Inn in High Street: P.

1167 [*undated*]. [*addressee not stated*].
Complies with the wishes of the Commissioners of the Fisherton Turnpike to survey the bridge at Stapleford. Details some parts which are decayed and need replacement. Some posts and rails are defective.

1168 [*undated*]. Mr Bevis, stonemason, Tisbury.
Asks for accounts of the county. Will measure work on Fisherton Bridge and prepare the bill.[1]

1. Written by J M Peniston, on father's behalf.

1169 [*undated*]. Thomas Culling, near Somerton, Somerset.
The stone may be laid immediately. The building[1] is on the Southampton road and the carter will be shown where.[2]

1. Clarendon House. See **1259**.
2. Written by J M Peniston, on father's behalf.

1170 16 Oct. 1829. Rt Hon Earl of Normanton, Somerley, Ringwood.
Will convey necessary information to the plasterer, whose brother will not be paid for the time spent idling at Ringwood.

1171 16 Oct. 1829. C Millet Esq, Hindon.
The chimneypieces [*see* **1146**] are on the eve of embarkation from London. But will write again [**1172**] urging expedition.

1172 16 Oct. 1829. Messrs Grieve, Grellier and Morgan, Belvedere Road.
The first consignment of plaster has arrived but not the chimneypieces. When they arrive the cases will immediately be returned.

1173 16 Oct. 1829. J W Ledyard Esq, Road Hill.
Considers that the person employed[1] has not done justice to the undertaking. Accounts to be sent to Mr Wingrove [*see* **1189**]. The costs already exceed the estimate.

1. Perhaps Mr Blandford. See **1103**.

1174 16 Oct. 1829. W Boucher Esq, Recorder, Close.
Agrees suggestion and proposed arrangement for 5 November.

1175 [*undated*]. Mr G Green, plasterer, Hindon.
Consents to his fixing the stones even though this is a bricklayer's work.

1176 [*undated*]. Mr Parsons, Bear Inn. [?*Devizes*]
Wishes Parsons to retain the bag he has sent until his own is returned.

1177 [*undated*]. Mr Saunders, waiter, Dukes Arms, Marlborough.
Had brought the wrong bag and asks for enquiries to be made. The correct bag to be
forwarded by Mr Brownjohn.

1178 [*undated*]. [*addressee not stated*].
Regrets that Henry Harris is gone.[1]

1. Appears to be signed *W M Peniston*. The letter is written around a large ink blot, and may
merely be a doodle.

1179 [*undated*]. P M Chitty Esq.
Sends an account,[1] and assumes, as Mr Downs has not commented, that he abides by
the calculation.

1. Probably relating to Shaftesbury Town Hall. See **1137**.

1180 [*undated*[1]]. Messrs Grieve, Grellier and Morgan.
Chimneypieces should be sent by waggon. The four for Clarendon will be paid for
on arrival, and the other two soon after.

1. Must post-date 30 Oct., as letter of that date referred to.

1181 [*undated*[1]]. Lord Bath.
Considers that the War Office remarks mean that each officer can draw forage for two
horses if he has two on duty. Should keep the carabines [*sic*] used to fire over the grave
when members of the troops attend to pay the last tribute of respect to a deceased
comrade. These were not originally supplied from the government store. Damaged
arms will be returned to the Ordnance Stores.

1. Must be Nov., as letter of 28th ult. referred to.

1182 [*undated*]. Messrs Reeves and Son, 80 Holborn Bridge, London.
Orders six quires of common cartridge and one dozen HH and one dozen HHH
pencils. Was away when their agent called.

1183 [*undated*]. Mr Downs.
Discusses account with Lord Gr...[1] but cannot submit report for inspection as this would be unusual and improper. Refers to details of the inspection.

1. Name crowded and indistinct. Probably Lord Grosvenor is intended.

1184 [*undated*]. Samuel Whitchurch Esq.
Calculates timber used at Bishopdown Farm for boards, planks and scantling.

1185 [*undated*]. Butler Esq, Temple, London.
Discusses payment of interest for the chapel property. Rev Dr Baines is now the principal trustee.

1186 [*undated*]. Mr Garbett Esq.
Discusses valuation of articles over which they have agreed to differ. Attempts to compromise, so that they can submit a joint report.

1187 [*undated*]. R Webb Esq, Melchet.
Reports on correspondence with Mr Garbett [**1186**], and discusses the likelihood of inducing him to raise his valuation.

1188 9 Nov. 1829. Mr Tarrant, mason, Swindon, Wilts.
Encloses cheque for £300 on account for work at the Seven Bridges near Cricklade. Requests a stamped receipt.

1189 9 Nov. 1829. Anthony Wingrove Esq, Trowbridge.
'My Dear Sir, Your letter which I have this moment received announcing the death of our poor friend Underwood both surprizes and grieves me. It is a very short time since I received a letter from him on his road to Ilchester requesting an inquiry for a greatcoat he had left in his passage through Salisbury, which I was fortunate enough to recover and forward him to Ilchester; a circumstance trifling in itself but now of comparative importance as the last connecting link with one who ceases to exist. Requiescat in pace.
    'I have to apologise for not having before sent you the cheque which I now enclose. I have it is true been much engaged and great part of my time from home, but not sufficient to warrent this neglect for which I request your forbearance. In the following statement you will perceive that £10 is placed to the account of Road Bridge, on which I have written to Mr Ledyard [**1173**] to inform him that I should request your examination of the work done, and would pay the accounts if you deemed them fair. But I really see no reason to pay one shilling more than the value of the work done. The accounts transmitted to me I believe amounted to £10 5s. 10d. I have asked only for £10 and this from Mr Ledyard's assurance was to have completed the job, and now informs me an additional coat of stone is immediately

required. This cannot be right and compromises me with the county for an improvident engagement. I have allowed Crook for Road Bridge £7 7s. 0d. for which I must trouble you to get me a proper receipt. I believe the following statement will be found to be correct.

'Mr Wingrove's account for the repair of sundry roads as noted: £99 5s. 5d. For repairs of Kington Bridge: £4 7s. 2d. For alterations and repairs of Road Bridge: £10 0s. 0d. Crook's bill for mason's work at Road Bridge: £7 7s. 0d. [Total:] £120 19s. 7d.

'Will you also be kind enough to forward me a stamped receipt for £32 16s. 9d. paid on account of Trowbridge Bridge since our last annual settlement.

'Sincerely hoping that this may find you in better health than when last we met. Best wishes to your father. I remain most truly yours.'

1190　10 Nov. 1829.　W Garbett Esq, Winchester.
Expects reply to earlier letter [**1186**] by return or will give his own statement [*see* **1207**] and let the result be decided by consequences.

1191　10 Nov. 1829.　Sir W Freemantle.
Acknowledges £500. The staircase at Clarendon might need apertures in the stairs as well as the risers.

1192　12 Nov. 1829.　Messrs Grieve and Grillie [*sic*].
Orders, by Southampton, six cases of roman cement.

1193　13 Nov. 1829.　Mrs Berrington.
Will be visiting Spetisbury when the plasterers are there, which he hopes will be the following week.

1194　13 Nov. 1829.　W Garbett Esq.
Regrets great difference in their valuation which precludes coming together. Has sent own valuation [*see* **1207**] to his employer.

1195　[*undated*].　Mr Downs, Shaftesbury (*Shaston*).
Accepts that Mr Payne should correct the measurements and will adjust the amount to be paid if necessary.

1196　[*undated*].　Messrs Carson and Miller, Warminster.
[*Codford Bridge*]: Has written to Mr Marsh of Tisbury relative to the stones to receive the posts [**1197**]. Asks them to give Marsh instructions about the brick piers also.

1197 14 Nov. 1829. Mr Marsh, mason, Tisbury.
Informs him that Messrs Carson and Miller are ready for the standard stones for Codford Bridge. They need not be tooled. Mr Miller will specify the number and size of holes to be cut to receive the foot of the standard bar.

1198 [*undated*]. [*addressee not stated*[1]].
Believes that he has collected the surplus arms except those that his Lordship allowed to be kept by the Marlborough and Swindon troops. Lists good and bad swords and pistols.

1. Letter begins *My Lord*, probably Lord Bath. See **1181**.

1199 [*undated*]. Messrs Grieve, Grellier.
Has asked his bankers to pay £86. The chimney pieces [*see* **1203**] had arrived safely despite damage to the packing because they were at the bottom of the waggon. Lists consignments of cement.

1200 18 Nov. 1829. Mr C Jones, chandelier manufactory, Birmingham.
Is not concerned with fitting up the rooms at Clarendon, but will pass details to his employer providing anything is sent free of carriage or post. There are four rooms of about 27 x 24 feet, 14 feet high; an entrance hall 20 x 14 feet; a staircase 20 x 20 and 30 feet high; a conservatory 27 x 20.

1201 18 Nov. 1829. W Bellamy, Hartfoot Lane,[1] Dorset.
Should address the request to Mr Boucher. Will measure the work at Thornhill House.

1. Former name for a hamlet now regarded as part of Melcombe Horsey and Ansty (in Hilton). See Hutchins, vol.4, p.373.

1202 19 Nov. 1829. F Attwood Esq, Close.
The three reserved rents of the East Grimstead estate which appertain to Mr Freemantle total £5 18s. 0d. per year, and 14 years are due.

1203 19 Nov. 1829. C Millet Esq.
Has discovered that the chimneypieces did not arrive with the others, but are now on the road to Hindon.[1]

1. See **1171, 1199**.

1204 19 Nov. 1829. Messrs Grieve, Grellier.
Orders 20 casks of coarse and two of fine plaster via Poole to Spetisbury, Blandford.[1]

1. The letter book does not contain a copy of this letter, but a summary of its contents, noting that there was not time to copy it.

1205 [*undated*]. Mrs Berrington, Spetisbury House.
Acknowledges wishes about trees to be felled in the garden. Suggests those to be felled first, in order to judge effect. The plasterers may proceed with lathing the ribs in the ceiling.

1206 [*undated*]. Messrs H and C Price, Bristol.[1]
Will visit in January and inspect the invention.

1. John, Henry and Charles Price, iron founders, 11 Clare Street, Bristol: P. The invention was some form of heating apparatus. See **1274**.

1207 [*undated*[1]]. [*addressee not stated*].
Encloses measurement and valuation of Ploughman's[2] work at Compton Bridge, totalling £19 14s. 0d.

1. The valuation is dated 11 Nov. 1829, so is to be associated with **1190, 1194**.
2. MS *contractors*, deleted, and *Ploughman's* interlined.

1208 26 Nov. 1829. Trustees of the Harnham, Dorchester and Blandford Turnpike.
As the architect appointed to inspect the new toll house at Coombe built by Charles Meaden of Coombe Bissett, certifies it has been completed according to the agreement.

1209 25 Nov. 1829.[1] [*addressee not stated*].
Wishes Mr Boucher to be told that Meaden has replaced the portico covering with lead of a proper weight. Encloses bill for planning and supervising the erection of new toll house at Coombe.

1. MS *Wednesday evening*, undated.

1210 27 Nov. 1829. Sir W Freemantle, Brunswick Terrace, Brighton.
Quotes estimates for a pipe of 170 feet and fittings to convey beer from the brewhouse to the cellar. Has taken a gilder to Clarendon to estimate for gilding two brackets for marbles slabs and bronzing three eagles. Discusses other work.

1211 [*undated*]. Rev C Wrottesly, [*East*] Knoyle.
Arranges to visit, and will be happy to meet Mr Seymour's wishes.

1212 27 Nov. 1829. Rt Hon Lord Arundell, Upton House, Poole.
Has told Brown to collect the Troop bills. Mr Pitt has been recommended as lieutenant of Malmesbury troop, which may assist in reviving it.

1213 28 Nov. 1829. Mr Porter, plasterer, Spetisbury House, near Blandford.
Approves mode of finishing the ribs adjoining the sanctuary.[1]

1. Written by J M Peniston, on father's behalf.

1214 [*undated*]. Mrs Berrington.
Prefers to write instructions rather than visit because of recent indisposition. Does not wish to renew it by exposure to the Dorsetshire hills. Wells' difficulties are often more imaginary than real. Porter thoroughly understands his business.

1215 4 Dec. 1829. Rev C Wrottesly, Knoyle.
Arranges to visit.

1216 4 Dec. 1829. Sir W Freemantle, Brunswick Terrace, Brighton.
Acknowledges £500. Cannot agree about alterations connected with the northern entrance. Convinced that when Sir Frederick takes up residence at Clarendon he will fund a further alteration. Discusses other work. The drawing room is complete except for doors and shutters.

1217 [*undated*]. Arthur Baker Esq, 5 Great George Street North, Dublin.
[*Grimstead*]: Has received quit rents of £82 12s. 0d. from Mrs Freemantle and various sums from other people. Discusses investigation about problems dating from Mr Wynch's time, and consequent on the death of Wynch the younger.

1218 [*undated*]. Mrs Dyke.
Requests settlement of an account.

1219 [*undated*]. C Harcourt Esq, Ringwood.
Requests settlement of an account, as referee between Compton Esq and Dyett.[1]

1. Dilapidations at Red Lion, Totton. See **594**.

1220 11 Dec. 1829. Mr Bellamy, Hartfoot Lane.
Postpones visit to Thornhill, as the work is not yet finished.

1221 12 Dec. 1829. [*addressee not stated*].
Has checked and encloses abstract of accounts for work on Knoyle Church and its gallery, executed by Elliott [*see* **1392**].

1222 14 Dec. 1829. Messrs Grieve, Grillier and Morgan.
Obliged for notice of sale of chimneypieces but has nothing in prospect for them.

1223 [*undated*]. The Incorporated Society for Promoting the Enlargement Building and Repairing of Churches and Chapels, No 2 Parliament Street, Westminster.
Certifies that work in East Knoyle Church has been completed in a substantial and workmanlike manner. Has obtained 122 additional sittings, of which 82 are free and unappropriated in consequence of a grant of £50 from the Society. Signatories are Charles Wrottesley (minister), William Wigmore and Thomas Compton (churchwardens), Henry Seymour MP (inhabitant) and J Peniston (surveyor). Includes a plan of the work.

1224 17 Dec. 1829. Mr E Bracher, mason, Hindon.
Has received original bill from Mr Seymour and returned it [**1225**] with remarks. The price for labour is reasonable but the time excessive, and this must be settled with Mr Seymour.

1225 [*undated*]. H Seymour Esq MP, Knoyle.
Has examined the work done by Bracher [*see* **1224**]. Has been assisted by Mr Seymour's bailiff. Explains discrepancies noted in red ink on the bill.

1226 17 Dec. 1829. Rev A Bouverie.
Encloses a corrected bill.

1227 18 Dec. 1829.[1] James Sutton Esq.
Tries to re-arrange a meeting because the mayor could not name a day in the ensuing week. Messrs Leach and Squarey advise that there should be notice in the next [*Salisbury*] *Journal*.

1. MS *Friday morning*, undated.

1228 18 Dec. 1829.[1] Mr Squarey.
Thinks his remarks are cogent but better not put in writing.

1. MS *Friday ½ past one*, undated.

1229 18 Dec. 1829. Rt Hon Earl of Normanton.
Regrets cannot measure work at Somerley until after Christmas [*see* **1231**].

1230 22 Dec. 1829. Samuel Whitchurch Esq, Milford Street, [*Salisbury*].
Sets out in detail the extensive repairs and alterations proposed by Mr Whitchurch to
be executed at the Mitre Inn, Southampton.

1231 24 Dec. 1829. Rt Hon Earl of Normanton.
Will measure work at Somerley. Feels little compunction at making Strong wait for
his money after the long delays he has caused. Is also induced not to hasten because
the weather would be sure to prove any defect in the stone used.

1232 24 Dec. 1829. Edward Pearce Esq, Ringwood.
Acknowledges £4 1s. 0d., being a moiety of the charge as an umpire, between H C
Compton Esq and J Dyett.[1]

1. See **1219** note 1.

1233 26 Dec. 1829. J Swayne Esq.
Has seen Governor Dowding and examined bills for work done by Coombs on the
prison [*Devizes*]. Discusses the relative costs of masons and labourers. Writes in haste
as is about to set off by coach for Bath.

1234 [*undated*[1]]. Earl of Enniskillen, Florence Court, Ireland.
Regrets that his son has neglected to remit £200 to his lordship's accounts but has
now done so.

1. Presumably several days after 26 Dec., as letter implies that Peniston has been from home for
some time.

1830

1235 7 Jan. 1830. Rt Hon Sir William Freemantle, Englefield Green (*E Green*), Surrey.
Acknowledges £500. Discusses payment for the whole project. The billiard room will be ready in a fortnight for the table to be put up. Little progress made since Sir Frederick Bathurst left Clarendon. The catacombes [*sic*] are finished in the wine cellar. The well diggers have not yet reached a natural spring for the brew house. Asks for directions about the bell hanger.

1236 8 Jan. 1830. Messrs Grieve, Grillie and Morgan.
Has paid £43 9s. 6d. via Deacon and Co. Discusses payment for chimneypieces.

1237 8 Jan. 1830. Messrs Carson and Miller.
Protests that some post and rails at Codford Bridge had been burnt to melt the lead. Criticizes the lime used for the brick piers.

1238 [*undated*]. Mr Porter.
Gives a reference for satisfactory plastering at Clarendon.

1239 8 Jan. 1830. Lord Normanton.
Intends to spend the week after next examining tradesmen's work at Somerley.

1240 8 Jan. 1830. Lord Arundell.
Notes extravagance of the troop bills for the years 1827, 1828 and 1829, which he has finally collected. This applies particularly to Sergeant Mackrell for cleaning the arms and Saunders for repair of saddlery. Has made reductions and told the Quartermaster of his dissatisfaction. Suggests system of control for the future. Encloses abstract of accounts totalling £200 5s. 3d.

1241 11 Jan. 1830. Messrs Eyre and Coverdale, solicitors, 3 Grays Inn Square, London.
Sends an account for the late Hon John Coventry.[1]

1. Written by J M Peniston, on father's behalf.

1242 [*undated*]. Mr Strong, mason, Box near Bath.
Arranges to to meet at Somerley House.[1]

1. Written by J M Peniston, on father's behalf.

1243 [*undated*]. Marquess of Bath.
Points out that if the Quartermaster's return was correct they have been credited by the Ordnance Board with 2 swords more than they have and 3 pistols fewer. The 10 carbines for the Devizes Troop are with a gunsmith, having been returned by the Everley Troop in a wretched state. The 10 carbines for Marlborough were in excellent condition. Had not known the Hindon Troop had 6 carbines. Acknowledges a basket of game.

1244 [*undated*]. Mr Cotman, carpenter, Ringwood, Hants.
Wishes to meet him at Somerley.[1]

1. Written by J M Peniston, on father's behalf. MS note: *Mr Porter, plasterer etc, Mr Gardiner, bricklayer, Ringwood, the same as above.*

1245 20 Jan. 1830. Lord Normanton, Somerley.
Postpones visiting Somerley because of the weather, and intends to let the severe part of the winter pass. Suggests sums that the various tradesmen may be paid on account.

1246 21 Jan. 1830. Messrs Grieve, Grillie and Morgan.
Discusses problem of paying Brown. Has received their bill of parcels for plaster [*sic*] which he was unaware of ordering, but would find a use for.

1247 [*undated*]. Right Reverend Dr Baines.
Reports arrangements with the Reverend Mother[1] about work to be started at Cannington. Cannot visit until the ensuing month.

1. Mrs Knight. See **1249**.

1248 25 Jan. 1830. Mr Hopper.
Invites Hopper to a meeting at Devizes to discuss the enlargement of the prison, 'the march of intellect' having produced 'more candidates for admission at the Devizes college than the present establishment can conveniently accommodate'. Discusses various ways in which the prison may be enlarged. Work on the [*Salisbury*] Council House will not be finished before the March assizes.

1249 [*undated*]. Mrs Knight, Lady Prioress, Cannington Priory.
Honoured by letter wishing him to superintend erection of the new chapel. Discusses a future visit. Has made enquiries about timber from a Bridgwater ironmonger. Believes that work may commence in early March.

1250 28 Jan. 1830. J Bennett Esq M.P., Pyt House.
Regrets entering on a tiresome subject. A committee has been set up [*see* **1154**] to oppose the churchwardens and overseers, who are promoting a parliamentary bill to transfer poor rate assessment from cottage occupiers to owners. Sets out the arguments and resolution of the committee.

1251 [*undated*]. Mr Bellamy.
Weather has been a barrier to meeting at Thornhill House but expects to do so later in February.

1252 [*undated*]. Rt Hon Sir William Freemantle.
Considers the bellhanger's estimate by no means unreasonable for hanging 17 bells complete in the principal part of the house for £35, and six bells in the office for £10. Suggests that the clock should be in a turret with north and south faces. Has given directions to prevent damage to the billiard table. Pleased that Sir Frederick [*Bathurst*] is satisfied. Points out that letters should be addressed to him at the Close so as not to be confused with a relation of the same name[1] who is a builder.

1. James Peniston. See **763**.

1253 3 Feb. 1830. [*addressee not stated*[1]].
Acknowledges letter and will comment on one opinion expressed. Agrees that the compulsory rate for the maintenance of poor relief should be equally levelled against all property and stock in trade. Disagrees about comparing the situation with tithes. Compares the Salisbury proposal unfavourably with the Bristol local act. Wants a clause inserted that rates houses let by the year to the occupier and not the owner. The committee will not have funds to employ professional assistance and seeks his help during the progress of the bill.

'I am glad to learn Lord Arundell has been with you. The pleasure of such a meeting I am sure must have been mutual, and I sincerely join you in the gratifying feelings his friends must experience on such a man resuming his hereditary rights.[2] I should be laughed at were I to express my feelings in becoming really a free man. It was easy for those who felt no privation to consider ours[3] imaginary. Bitterly I felt them and not the less so from endeavouring to conceal their effects. Deo Gratia est nos amis. However defective the language the sentiment is gratefully remembered.'

1. Presumably John Benett. See **1250**.
2. The Roman Catholic Relief Act (10Geo4, c.7), passed in April 1829, enabled Catholics to enter Parliament.
3. Badly written, but probably what was intended.

1254 6 Feb. 1830. Lord Bath.
Reconciles a discrepancy in the return to the War Office of 349 men in June 1829 and 361 in December. Understands that the establishment was limited to 583, the strength in 1808. Cannot understand the deficiency in carbines.

1255 7 Feb. 1830. Most Noble Col the Marquis of Bath.
Acknowledges his Lordship's wishes. Suggests that if the return of arms was forwarded to the Ordnance it would prove that his Lordship had not been inattentive to their wishes.

1256 [undated]. Lord Normanton.
Arranges to visit Somerley and meet the tradesmen.

1257 [undated]. Messrs Cottman, Gardiner (Ringwood) and Strong (Box near Bath). Requests meeting at Somerley.[1]

1. Written by J M Peniston, on father's behalf. Presumably similar letters sent to each. Ringwood applies to Cottman also.

1258 9 Feb. 1830. Lord Bath.
Acknowledges £49 10s. 10d. Ordnance return should be sanctioned by his Lordship. Has procured copies of the letter but cannot frank certificates to the captains, and will wait until many are at Salisbury as grand jurors.

1259 [undated]. Mr Thomas Culling, Keinton Mandeville (Kinton), Somerset.
Encloses cheque for work at Clarendon House.

1260 [undated]. Mr John Hunter. Post Office, Warminster.
Has no expectation of meeting wishes, as the Quartermaster, Mr Brown, takes the drill duties of the Troop, receives a salary, is very competent and much respected. And no change is expected. Has no knowledge of Cooper's business but business is at a very low ebb.

1261 [undated]. E Baker Esq M.P.
Refers to attempts of certain parties here to rate owners instead of occupiers [see **1250, 1253**]. Discusses forthcoming second reading of the bill and asks Mr Baker to present the petition if Mr Bennet is not at the House.

1262 [undated]. Mr Bennet, Pyt House.
Discusses first and second readings of the bill. Has asked Mr Baker to present the petition [**1261**].

1263 [*undated*]. Thomas Fox Esq, Beaminster, Dorset.
Rearranges visit to Thornhill, delayed by weather.

1264 17 Feb. 1830. Messrs Carson and Miller, ironfounders, Warminster.
Asks them to join a meeting at Codford Bridge with Mr Biggs and Col A'Court.

1265 [*undated*]. Arthur Baker Esq, 5 Great George Street North, Dublin.
[*Grimstead*]: Encloses letter from the executors of Mr Wynch who are waxing wrath.
Asks for directions on the subject. Tubbs has died. And his son now residing in the
farm is joined in the lease and appears anxious to renew it. Suggests farm is surveyed
so fixing the annual value.

1266 [*undated*]. John Bennett M.P., 19 Albermarle Street, London.
Seeks an opinion on a clause in the bill by which the owner of a property worth more
than £10 a year would be liable to the rate. Will be at Cannington House and
Thornhill House the following week. Col Baker has presented the petition.

1267 [*undated*]. Messrs Grieve, Grillie and Morgan.
Intends to procure the amount of their bill from Brown who is from home.[1]

1. Letter is crossed through in red ink, with note: 'This letter was not sent, as Mr Brown called
before it went to post to say that he had paid the money to Messrs Grieve and Grelly. JMP.'

1268 26 Feb. 1830. R Payne, architect, Gillingham.
Regrets has no information but a friend going to Andover will make enquiries.[1]

1. Written by J M Peniston, apologizing that his father had to leave at short notice.

1269 [*undated*]. Messrs Grieve and Co.
Has been told by Brown that the money has been forwarded [*but see* **1272**]. Reiterates
part of earlier letter [**1267**].[1]

1. Written by J M Peniston, on father's behalf.

1270 [*undated*]. Mr Webb.
Has returned from Devizes and not heard from Mr Garbett. Has heard from Mr
Hodding how stock in the garden will be valued.[1]

1. At Lainston. This letter is related to **1271**.

1271 [*undated*]. Mr Garbett.
Presses for reply about Lainston (*Lainstone*) dilapidations.

1272 1 March 1830. Grieve, Grillier and Co.
Explains that he does not have the means to secure payment of the balance of Brown's account. Regrets that Brown deceived him [*see* **1267, 1269**].

1273 2 March 1830. Sir William Freemantle, etc, etc, [*sic*] London.
The person who was to erect the billiard table at Clarendon has not conformed to Sir Frederick's [*Bathurst*] direction that it be fixed on solid piers above the cellar groins. The old bookcases are defective and will cost more to reassemble. Work will be completed on the house in a fortnight except for the entrance hall. Wishes work not specifically agreed to be valued before his assistant leaves for another post. In a postscript notes that Mr Hughes says he has completed the table, thinks it unnecessary to strengthen the floor and wishes to be advanced £6.

1274 [*undated*]. Messrs J H and C Price, Bristol.
Annexes plan and section of hall and staircase referred to when examining model. Asks how much it will cost to heat the space.[1]

1. See **1206**, note 1.

1275 9 March 1830. R Edwards Esq, Castle Street, Holborn, London.
Prepared to subscribe to the draft lease of Mrs Thomas's property for seven years, but only subject to some changes about payment for property tax and repair. State of the property which demands caution when binding himself on execution to a repairing lease, the consequences of which he frequently sees in his professional avocation. Does not wish to take advantage of Mrs Thomas. An early decision is needed as much must be done before the house is habitable.

1276 [*undated*]. Mr Porter.
Cannot agree the ladies' wishes to substitute corbels for columns.[1] Has returned from London with the gout and cannot visit. The altar with its dressing and the painting should fill a large part of the end wall. Asks for sketch of the Reverend Mother's[2] and Rev Mr Lee's wishes.

1. Spetisbury chapel. See **1213-14**.
2. Mrs Berrington. See **1214**.

1277 [*undated*]. Lord Bath, Grosvenor Square, London.
Disputes the instructions of the Ordnance Board to return weapons purchased by Lord Bath for use of the regiment. Suggests that the intention of the government is to limit the strength of the regiment to 353. Has discussed with Colonel Baker how to control and thus lessen expenditure and will call when in London to submit a plan.

1278 [*undated*]. Mr Bellamy, Harfoot Lane, near Blandford.
Had sent copy by the Magnet[1] on Saturday but expects it to be waiting at Blandford. Agrees to postpone meeting.[2]

1. See **912** note 1.
2. Written by J M Peniston, on father's behalf.

1279 9 March 1830. C Millet Esq, Hindon.
Arranges to meet tradesmen at Hindon to measure their work.[1]

1. Written by J M Peniston, who is to attend meeting because his father has gout.

1280 10 March 1830. Rt Hon Sir William Freemantle.
Acknowledges £10 advance to Hughes[1] and will answer the queries in a few days.[2]

1. Apparently for erecting the billiard table at Clarendon House. See **1273**.
2. Written by J M Peniston, on father's behalf.

1281 13 March 1830. Mr Cutler.
Has visited Wishford Bridge and finds that no attention has been paid to the direction given. The wall is to be taken down and rebuilt. Sketch plan included.[1]

1. Written by J M Peniston, who also visited on father's behalf.

1282 [*undated*]. Rt Hon Sir William Freemantle, Stanhope Street, London.
Repeats acknowledgement that might have miscarried for cheque for £5. Awaits arrival of ballusters, but is unwilling to proceed because of the cost. Has the gout but hopes to send the list of extras next week.

1283 [*undated*]. Mr Goodfellow.
'On the receipt of your letter proposing to pay two thirds of the sum for which you stand engaged for your father I wrote stating his want of means as described by you. I have permission from the parties for whom I act to acquiesce in your proposal and cancel the note upon the understanding that if Mr Goodfellow should ever be in a situation to enable him to pay the difference that he will pledge his word to do so.'

1284 14 March 1830. R Edwards Esq, Castle Street, Holborn, London.
Substitutes tenantable repair for wind and water tight relative to Mrs Thomas's house [*see* **1275**]. Premises must be repaired before payment will start.

1285 [*undated*]. R Edwards Esq, Castle Street [*Holborn, London*].[1]
Has no objection to an annual inspection of repairs by Mrs Thomas's attorney or builder but objects to the clause as it stands.

1. See **1284**.

1286 [*undated*]. Mr Bellamy, Hartfoot Lane.
Cannot allow a list of work done for the London painters unless it is in addition to that already measured. Reminds Bellamy of his promise respecting the elm timber at Spetisbury.

1287 [*undated*]. [*addressee not stated*[1]].
Regrets did not send dimensions by Mr Haycock. Lists details of doors, and hopes that this will enable them to make calculations, so that their discovery can be given a fair trial.

1. Evidently Messrs Price of Bristol. See **1274**.

1288 [*undated*]. Mr R Tarrant, mason, Swindon.
Is confined with gout and postpones inspection of bridge.

1289 19 March 1830.[1] T Bramah Esq, Pimlico.
Gratefully accepts proposals and will send his son[2] on his trial, he nothing loath.

1. MS adds *½ past 7 o'clock AM*.
2. William Peniston, who was offered employment with Messrs Bramah. See **1358-9**.

1290 19 March 1830. Messrs Carson and Miller, Warminster.
Anxious to know about preparation for work at Codford Bridge. Must procure and verify accounts for work independent of their contract. Asks if steps have been taken to widen the road by removing the mud wall where the drain will be put in. The brick piers should be taken up and the bricks cleaned and safely stacked for future use.

1291 19 March 1830. E Doughty Esq, Mivarts Hotel, Brooke Street, London.
Arranges meeting at Upton.

1292 [*undated*]. Mr Cottman.
Expects to be at Ringwood at Russells and will pay his bill on Lord Normanton of £26 0s. 3½d. This deduction from the original bill has been agreed by the referee.

1293 21 March 1830. Rt Hon Sir William Freemantle.
Agrees that the estimate for the ballustre [*sic*] was 5s. per foot, but to that has to be added the cost of carriage, packing cases, wrought iron sinking screws and labour for fixing, so that the total must exceed £10.

1294 [*undated*]. Mr Garbett (*Garbutt*), architect, Winchester.
Does not have the valuations of the horticultural dilapidations. Asks for details so that their statements should not clash.

1295 21 March 1830. Mr Gardiner (*Gardener*).
Has altered the bill for Lord Normanton. Allowed 4s. a day for Mr Gardiner, 3s. for a bricklayer, and 1s. 6d. for a labourer, totalling £74 9s. 5d. Is waiting for the charge for scaffolding. Will be at Ringwood at Mr Russell's at the Crown with a cheque.

1296 22 March 1830. Mr Haywood, Penitentiary, Devizes.
Sends estimates for alteration to the prison for the Committee of Justices in case he is delayed and unable to attend in person. The aggregate expense will be £530.

1297 22 March 1830. [*addressee not stated*¹].
Encloses a cheque for £250 as part payment of Lord Normanton's bill, and recapitulates totals of bills and payments. The last £69 16s. 3d. will be paid when the remaining vase is received.

1. Mr Strong. See **1305**.

1298 22 March 1830. E Doughty Esq, Upton House, Poole.
Arranges to visit Spetisbury, at the request of the Reverend Mother, and Upton House to discuss proposed alterations. His son will be driving their chaise.

1299 23 March 1830. Messrs May and Merrit, 367 Oxford Street, London.
[*Clarendon House*]: Asks the cost of supplying a ballustre [*sic*] for a staircase being erected for Sir William Freemantle.

1300 23 March[1] 1830. Messrs Carson and Miller, Warminster.
Arranges meeting at Codford. The county settle their accounts annually but he will apply for an advance.

1. MS *May*, corrected.

1301 25 March 1830. Thomas Fox Esq, Beaminster.
Has marked the bill in pencil with various adjustments. Agrees to survey dilapidations at Lydlinch and discusses other delayed business concerning Mr Bellamy.

1302 [*undated*]. Mr Bellamy, Hartfoot Lane, near Blandford, Dorset.
Unexpectedly called to London. J M Peniston can attend instead of his father, but cannot deal with prices which can be settled by letter.[1]

1. Written by J M Peniston, on father's behalf.

1303 19 March 1830.[1] Mr Bellamy, Hartfoot Lane, near Blandford, Dorset.
Postpones an engagement.

1. Addressed from Hartford Bridge, Hants.

1304 20 March 1830.[1] G Morant Esq.
Submits survey of work at the Farnborough house. General repair of the main house has been done economically and well executed. But has to condemn some of the work on the offices and elsewhere. Has never before seen a roof so badly constructed. Other possible defects require further investigation. Urges caution before agreeing to further expenditure and suggests that detailed accounts should be provided.

1. Addressed from Hartford Bridge, Hants.

1305 27 March 1830. Mr Strong, mason, Box near Bath.
Presses for a receipt. The money held back will be paid when the other vase is sent to Somerley [*see* **1297**].[1]

1. Written by J M Peniston, on father's behalf.

1306 27 March 1830. W Garbett Esq, Winchester.
Has seen Mr Webb who is anxious to receive award of dilapidations at Lainston.[1] If sent to Salisbury J M Peniston will send them to his father in London.[2]

1. See **1270-1, 1308**.
2. Written by J M Peniston, on father's behalf.

1307 [*undated*]. [*addressee not stated*[1]].
Assures Peniston's attention after business in London.[2]

1. Letter begins *Madam*.
2. Unsigned, but presumably written by J M Peniston, on father's behalf.

1308 29 March 1830. W Garbett Esq, architect, Winchester.
Reiterates request [**1306**] for particulars of award of dilapidations at Lainston as Mr
Webb has again asked for the report.[1]

1. Written by J M Peniston, on father's behalf.

1309 30 March 1830. W Hart, Heron Court, near Ringwood.
Forwards cheque for scaffolding poles sent to Lord Normanton at Somerley [*see*
1047].[1]

1. Written by J M Peniston, on father's behalf.

1310 [*undated*]. W Garbett Esq.
Peniston has returned to London but has signed the papers.[1] Payment is enclosed.[2]

1. Presumably relating to Lainston dilapidations. See **1306, 1308**.
2. Written by J M Peniston, on father's behalf.

1311 2 April 1830. E Baker Esq MP, 213 Regent Street, London.
Thanks him for some financial support. Is opposed to the New Sarum Poor Bill and
outlines the position of some other M.Ps: Mr Dickinson, the member for Somerset;
Mr Littleton, member for Stafford; Sir John Astley; Mr C B Wall; Mr Robert Gordon;
Marquis of Blandford; and Mr Gye, member for Chippenham.

1312 4 April 1830. Rt Hon Earl of Normanton, Somerley.
Tradesmen's receipts will be delivered except for those of Cottman and Gardiner,
who both object to deductions made from their accounts. Is not convinced of any
injustice. Strong will not be wholly paid despite a full receipt until he has completed
the vases.

1313 [*undated*]. Mrs Knight, Cannington.
Is at a loss to know how to meet the bishop's objection. The plan presented was
recommended by Dr Baines himself. The change proposed will prevent the nuns from
seeing the altar.

1314 [*undated*]. J Bennett Esq, 19 Albemarle Street, London.
Has been informed by Mr Foote that the second reading is postponed. The public meeting will consider a proposition about the bill,[1] but, in view of the cupidity and obstinacy of many of the parties, not much can be expected of it. Affirms belief that bill's effects will be as unpolitic as they will be unjust.

1. New Sarum Poor Bill. See **1311**.

1315 [*undated*]. Mr Laurence.
Regrets that settling tradesmen's accounts at Hindon has been delayed by his gout and absence on parliamentary business in London. Arranges to visit Hindon.

1316 [*undated*]. Messrs Carson and Miller.
Discusses work at Codford bridge.

1317 [*undated*]. Mr Hacker, Hindon.
Will be at Hindon to measure the work at the parsonage house.

1318 [*undated*]. David Foot Esq.
Enquires on behalf of Colonel the Marquess of Bath whether the Lord Lieutenant knows that the Wiltshire Yeomanry are to be inspected this year and will assemble on permanent duty.

1319 [*undated*]. Lord Bath, Grosvenor Square, London.
Has passed the query to Mr Foot [**1318**]. Has ordered the appointments[1] from Messrs Hawkes for the Malmesbury Troop recruits [**1320**] and informed Mr Pitt [**1321**].

1. Used here, as elsewhere (e.g. **1321**, **1672**) in the sense of 'equipment, outfits': OED.

1320 [*undated*]. Messrs Hawkes and Co, army saddlers, Piccadilly.
Orders various items of saddlery to be sent to Mr Pitt Jun, Esq, Lieutenant of the Malmesbury Troop, W.Y.C., including sword belts, bridles and saddle bags.

1321 [*undated*]. James Pitt Esq, Estcourt, near Malmesbury.
Reports that Messrs Hawkes will be sending some appointments. Discusses troop equipment.

1322 15 April 1830. Mr Bellamy, surveyor, Hartfoot Lane near Blandford.
Will send accounts as soon as possible.[1]

1. Written by J M Peniston, on father's behalf.

1323 [*undated*[1]]. Edward Doughty Esq, 43 Lower Brook Street, London.
Has marked out the ground to be removed at Upton with Mr Parker. Will take the masons to set out the work when it can start. A store of sand and lime will be needed to begin the foundation. Will use old bricks from the present cellars and can wait a few days for new ones.[2]

1. Presumably 15 April, since it refers to **1324** as if written on the same occasion.
2. Written by J M Peniston, on father's behalf.

1324 15 April 1830. Mr Parker, Upton House, Poole, Dorset.
Requests that directions are given to make some of his sharpest pit sand dry and to secure some fresh lime from Conway's kiln to begin work.[1]

1. Written by J M Peniston, on father's behalf.

1325 18 April 1830. Mr Parker, Upton House near Poole.
Will be meeting the bricklayer at Upton, and wishes the lime and sand to be ready.[1]

1. Written by J M Peniston, on father's behalf.

1326 [*undated*]. T O Stevens Esq.
Regrets that another meeting of the arbitrators and referee is necessary to deal with Messrs Sergeant and Thring's accounts with Messrs Blackmore.[1] Asks for an early meeting because Mr Squarey is about quitting house for some time.

1. See **1098** note 1, **1101**.

1327 19 April 1830. Mr Bellamy, Hartfoot Lane.
Regrets some mistakes in Clarke's bill, and will deal with this after attendance on the magistrates and a possible call to London on Parliamentary business.

1328 [*undated*]. Mr Clarke, mason, Blandford.
Thinks it better for any explanation about the work at Thornhill to be sent to Mr Bellamy [*see* **1327**].

1329 [*undated*]. J Bennett Esq, 19 Albemarle Street, London.
Has consulted the leading cottage owners who have agreed to forgo opposition to the bill[1] on several conditions, set out in detail.

1. New Sarum Poor Bill. See **1311**.

1454 12 July 1830. William Garbett Esq, architect, Winchester.
Arranges a meeting to enter on Miss Wyndham's business.

1455 12 July 1830. [*addressee not stated*].
The account for the dilapidations of Mr Edgecombe's house[1] amounts to £7 7s. 9d.,
which may have to be made out on a stamp.

1. In Gigant Street, Salisbury. See **1379**.

1456 12 July 1830. Most Noble Col Marquis of Bath WYC, Longleat.
Encloses regimental returns for 1829 and 1830, and comments on an apparent
discrepancy. There has been an overall increase of troops from 349 to 370, but whereas
the Chippenham and Marlborough troops in particular have increased, the Salisbury,
Hindon and Warminster troops have diminished numbers. Queries whether the
recruitment limit was not established by reference to the 1808 figure, 583 men.

1457 18 July 1830. Mr Hacker, builder, Hindon, Wilts.[1]
Responds to a dispute over the cost of a door.

1. Addressed from Hartford Bridge.

1458 18 July 1830. W Garbett Esq, architect, Winchester.[1]
Rearranges a meeting after their respective assize weeks, which will enable them to
attend the running for the King's Plate.[2] Has agreed a date to meet Mr Percy of
Sherborne [*see* **1459**].

1. Addressed from Hartford Bridge.
2. A royal plate was awarded annually at the three-day Salisbury race meeting, generally held in
July or August: VCH 4, p.380.

1459 18 July 1830. Edward Percy Esq, architect, Sherborne, Dorset.[1]
Arranges a meeting.

1. Addressed from Hartford Bridge.

1460 25 July 1830. Most Noble Marquis of Bath, Longleat.
Has referred to the adjutant's papers, and finds that on the only occasion when the
regiment was inspected, in June 1824, the Salisbury and Hindon troops were allowed
three days pay, the remaining troops two days only. Lord Bath may from his military
correspondence be able to ascertain the precise allowance on that occasion.

1461   25 July 1830.[1]   William Garbett Esq, architect, Winchester.
Cannot offer him a bed as visitors are accommodating them all at present.

1. MS omits year.

1462   25 July 1830.[1]   Messrs Smith and Bayly, solicitors, Basinghall Street, London.
At Mr Morant's request has examined, measured and valued the works executed by
Mr Thornton at Farnborough House, and believes that Thornton has grossly
overcharged. His demand exceeds £6,000, but the valuation comes to under £4,000.
To corroborate this opinion the accounts of brickwork are detailed, and show a
glaring discrepancy. It is strange too that Mr Thornton should be charging for
alterations to chimneys when a Mr Hiorts of London has already been paid on
account for the work.

1. MS omits year.

1463   26 July 1830.   George Morant Esq, Sunninghill, Bagshot, Surrey.
[*Farnborough House*]: Regrets the mistake which prevented their meeting at the
Gloster Coffee House in London. Encloses a copy of the report which he has sent to
Messrs Smith and Bayly [**1462**]. He forgot to mention to them that, when Hawkins
is paid, he should be required to submit his books and vouchers. Will write again to
Smith and Bayly on this matter [**1464**]. Has written to Mr Harding[1] for his proposals
for a garden wall but has not yet received them. Cannot send a plan for the cottages
immediately because his long absence has produced a fearful arrears of business.

1. No such letter appears to have been copied into the letter-book.

1464   26 July 1830.   Messrs Smith and Bayley, Basinghall Street, London.
Before paying Hawkins his claim as clerk of the works it is desirable that he should
give up the whole of his books, papers, vouchers and other items connected with the
works at Farnborough. If the business is taken to court the trial would be held at
Winchester. Has discussed with a respectable Winchester architect[1] what fee he would
charge to remeasure and value the work. This would be 25 guineas. It would be
desirable for two respectable builders also to express their opinion, for which a charge
of 10 guineas each and travel expenses might be expected.

1. Presumably William Garbett, with whom he was in frequent contact at this period.

1465   26 July 1830.   Edward M Foxhall Esq, architect, 18 South Audley Street,
London.
Had been asked by Rev Mr Watkins to help his tradesmen to interpet Foxhall's
instructions, since like Foxhall Peniston is a catholic chapel builder. Concerned that
Mr Watkins, in his anxiety to complete the chapel, may have expressed himself
unreasonably towards Foxhall, and hopes that this will not prevent him from receiving

further assistance. Discusses carpentry and plastering, and offers (since he is frequently in the neighbourhood) to act as Foxhall's clerk of works, and will have working drawings prepared from his sketches if desired.

1466 26 July 1830. Mr Lawrence, carpenter, Hindon.
Discusses disputed allowances for various items, and suggests a day when Lawrence might call. If not at home, Peniston's son will be able to deal with the matter. Has no personal objection to referring the dispute to Mr Fisher, but not without his employer's consent.

1467 26 July 1830. William Garbett Esq, architect, Winchester.
Cannot attend a meeting on the date proposed.[1]

1. J M Peniston writes in his father's absence.

1468 28 July 1830. Richard Attwood Esq.
Has examined his bills and returns them, but requires further particulars of quantities in order to determine Bastable's bill. Longs to see Attwood about Farnborough, but at present has not a moment to spare.

1469 28 July 1830. George Morant Esq, Sunninghill, Bagshot, Surrey.
[*Farnborough House*]: Intends to set out for Newbury for an appointment, and then travel on to London. Asks that a note fixing a meeting be left for him at the Gloster Coffee House. Postage should be paid on the letter, or else they might decline to receive it in his absence.

1470 28 July 1830. Mr Hagger.
Will endeavour to visit Cannington at about the time when Dr Baines is expected. Discusses details of columns and the roof, preferring the original plan. Offers best respects to the ladies and Rev Mr Dullard.

1471 28 July 1830. Mr Jeffery, Wardour Castle.
The mastic for Mr Parker's house has arrived, and the plasterer will be ready to execute the work during the ensuing week.

1472 29 July 1830. Rt Hon Earl of Normanton, Somerley, Ringwood.
Has made enquiries about coaches, and gives details of coaches from Salisbury to Bath and from Bath to Gloucester.

1473   31 July 1830. Mr Trapp, bricklayer, Warminster.
Gives instructions for making a drain at Codford Bridge.[1]

1. Written by J M Peniston, on father's behalf.

1474   6 Aug. 1830. William Garbett Esq, architect, Winchester.
Is away from home, and will be engaged all next week.[1]

1. Written by J M Peniston, on father's behalf.

1475   8 Aug. 1830. Most Noble the Marquis of Bath, Longleat, Warminster.
Letter and enclosure have been forwarded to Peniston, who is from home.[1]

1. Written by J M Peniston, on father's behalf.

1476   13 Aug. 1830. Mrs Berrington, Spetisbury House, near Blandford.
Apologizing for his father's absence, J M Peniston can see no reason why the workmen cannot comply with her wishes of repairing the altar at Spetisbury. He will visit next week if his father does not return.[1]

1. Written by J M Peniston, on father's behalf.

1477   15 Aug. 1830. Rev Mr Casey, Marnhull Cottage, Dorset.
Will arrange to visit on his return home.[1]

1. Written by J M Peniston, on father's behalf. This letter has been struck through, but a marginal note reads, 'This letter was afterwards sent'.

1478   15 Aug. 1830.[1] Mr Trapp, bricklayer, Warminster, Wilts.
No grating is needed. J M Peniston arranges to meet at Codford.[2]

1. MS omits year. Hereafter the year is usually omitted in the MS.
2. Written by J M Peniston, on father's behalf.

1479   15 Aug. 1830. Rev Archdeacon Macdonald, Bishop's Cannings (*B Cannings*), Devizes.
Since it is his turn to nominate a boy for admission to an education in the school of the Bear Club,[1] agrees to nominate George Coles, residing in Devizes Green. Is concerned that the nomination was required by 12 Aug., but has only just returned home after a long absence. Asks that the cause of the delay should be made clear.

1. An educational and apprenticing charity, originating in a social gathering at the Bear Inn, Devizes: VCH 10, p.302.

1480 15 Aug. 1830. Rt Hon Sir William Freemantle, Stanhope Street, London.
Apologizes for not having had time to complete the account of extras. Encloses a copy of a note which he has received from Mr Hunt,[1] the clockmaker.

1. Name poorly written. Henry Hunt and Son were Salisbury watch and clock makers: P.

1481 15 Aug. 1830. Mr W Daniel, Warminster.
Remits £15 8s. payment for bricks used at Codford Bridge, apologizes for the delay, and asks for a stamped receipt.

1482 15 Aug. 1830. Most Noble the Marquess of Bath, Longleat, Warminster.
Cannot immediately complete the return of arms required by the Board of Ordnance, but will do so at the earliest opportunity. Confirms that the strength of the regiment at the period referred to had been 541, leaving 494 after the 47 members of the Everley troop are deducted. The 1808 return totalled 583, less 50 in the Everley troop, but probably better to confine themselves to the numbers stated in correspondence.

'Lieut Col Baker being from home prevents my having the benefit of his advice on the subject, but I most respectfully submit to your Lordship whether in the present state of political affairs it may not be desirable to reserve the power of completing your numbers to the establishment allowed. It is with great deference I make these remarks, but your Lordship will always have the power of reducing your numbers should circumstances render it desirable.'

1483 15 Aug. 1830. Rev James Watkins, Bugle Street, Southampton.
Wrote to Mr Foxhall [1465], who refused very ungraciously any further assistance. Peniston's son has retrieved the drawing sent to Foxhall, has discussed the business with Peniston, and will call on Rev Watkins to leave directions with the workmen.

1484 15 Aug. 1830. Arthur Baker Esq.
[*Grimstead*]: Discusses bills. Has received nothing from Tubb, but promises. Proposes to wait until Michaelmas.

1485 15 Aug. 1830. Mr Hagger.
Circumstances prevented him from being at Cannington to meet Rev Bishop Dr Baines, but will visit as early as possible. Discusses progress on the chapel. Suggests that Mr Carver (surveyor for the county of Somerset) may recommend a competent slater. Will send a plasterer when required. Has advanced Mrs Haggar £5 as requested. Conveys to the Mr Knights the kindest wishes of their brother, a priest whom Peniston met at New Hall convent in Essex.

1486   15 Aug. 1830. Rt Rev Dr Baines, Prior Park, Bath.
Encloses a letter from Rev Mareste for his perusal and reply, and expresses anxiety about the delay which Peniston's absence will cause. Has written to Rev Mareste observing that any arrangements should be adjusted before Michaelmas.

1487   15 Aug. 1830. Rev B Marest.
Sincerely laments his situation in France, and hopes to make arrangements which will afford the good ladies and himself a tranquil and comfortable asylum in the chapel houses. Apologizes for the delay, but has sent Marest's letter to the bishop, and has no doubt that he will be acquiescent. However, the houses are occupied, and some time must elapse before Marest and the ladies could be accommodated. The arrangements should be made before Michaelmas.

1488   21 Aug. 1830. Rt Hon Sir William Freemantle, Stanhope Street, London.
Acknowledges a letter, and is surprised and hurt by part of its contents. Recounts the arrangements for valuing the items undertaken which were extra to the original contract, and lists them. Is hurt by the implication that Peniston has tried to vitiate the original contract, which he feels is not merited. Asks that an independent arbiter be appointed to determine for what Peniston is entitled to charge, and to fix the value.

1489   22 Aug. 1830. Mr Haywood, House of Correction, Devizes.
Will visit Devizes on his way to Bath, and hopes to see Mr Edmonstone there.

1490   23 Aug. 1830. Messrs Carson and Miller, iron foundry, Warminster, Wilts.
Asks that the stays for the railing at Codford Bridge be finished, and that all loose posts be fixed.[1]

1. Written by J M Peniston, on father's behalf.

1491   25 Aug. 1830. Messrs Smith and Bayley.
Acknowledges safe arrival of two books.[1]

1. Written by Sarah Peniston in the absence of both her husband and son.

1492   25 Aug. 1830. George Morant Esq, Sunninghill, Bagshot, Surrey.
[*Farnborough House*]: Acknowledges letters notifying that Thornton has accepted the proposed terms for refereeing his work. As this may lead to a speedy adjustment suggests that work on the greenhouse be deferred. Offers to go with him to discuss the matter with Messrs Bramah when in London.

1493 29 Aug. 1830. Messrs Smith and Bayley, Basinghall Street, London.
[*Farnborough House*]: Expresses pleasure that Mr Thornton has agreed to the proposition and that Mr Morant has approved it. But is apprehensive of the possibility that the referee might refuse to enter into the real merits of the value of the work done, because it was done under the direction of Mr Morant's former agent, Mr Tatham. Is writing to Mr Hopperton to arrange a meeting.

1494 29 Aug. 1830. Hopperton Esq, 23 Ranelagh Street, Pimlico.
[*Farnborough House*]: Suggests a meeting, since Mr Thornton has appointed Hopperton to agree with Peniston the third party as referee to the dispute.

1495 29 Aug. 1830.[1] William Minty Esq.
Having returned home last night and compelled to set out again today, has not had time to comply with his request, but will do so on his return.

1. MS *Sunday morning*, undated.

1496 29 Aug. 1830. Mr Thomas Hawkins jun,[1] 44 Minshull Street, Golden Square, London.
Messrs Deacon, Williams and Co are directed to pay him the balance of his account if he leaves a stamped receipt.

1. Perhaps the clerk of works at Farnborough House. See **1463-4**.

1497 31 Aug. 1830. Visiting Magistrates, House of Correction, Devizes.
Encloses a plan for an erection to accommodate the female prisoners. Discusses details. Ladders to be used instead of staircases, and the roof to be of zinc, and flat so as not to out-top the boundary wall. Estimates the expense at £314 10s.

1498 31 Aug. 1830. Mr Haywood, House of Correction, Devizes.
Encloses plan for the proposed building for female prisoners. Asks that enclosed letters [**1499-1500**] be sent to Messrs Burt and Carnell.

1499 31 Aug. 1830. Mr H P Burt, ironmonger, Devizes.
Asks his opinion whether a bridge constructed of iron would be eligible at Rangebourne, and seeks an estimate for iron railings to both sides of a wooden bridge at the same place.

1500 31 Aug. 1830. Mr Carnell.
Requests his proposal for Rangebourne Bridge speedily.

1501 31 Aug. 1830. Messrs Smith and Bayley, Basinghall Street, London.
[*Farnborough House*]: Encloses his correspondence with Mr Hopperton [*see* **1494, 1502**], and seeks approval for the course which he has adopted.

1502 31 Aug. 1830. W Hopperton Esq, 23 Ranelagh Street, Pimlico.
[*Farnborough House*]: Has received his letter, which seems somewhat more dictatorial than is consistent with the equality of their appointment. Discusses the procedure to be adopted for agreeing a referee.

1503 31 Aug. 1830. Rev Mr Casey, Marnhull, Dorset.
Apologizes that he could not give notice of his visit to Marnhull, as he was returning from Cannington. Discusses architectural details which he has directed Harding and Johnson to undertake subject to Casey's approval. Regrets that Harding has not followed his directions about the roof.

1504 31 Aug. 1830. William Sargeant Esq, Wilton.
Accepts an invitation to dinner.

1505 3 Sept. 1830. Most Noble the Marquess of Bath, Longleat.
Encloses the return of arms in the regiment's possession, and a copy of the last return. Explains an apparent discrepancy.

1506 3 Sept. 1830. Sir William Freemantle.
Rearranges a meeting at Clarendon.[1]

1. Written by J M Peniston, on father's behalf.

1507 3 Sept. 1830. Richard Cooe Esq.
Submits cheque for £60, being three years' interest due on Lord Arundell's property in St Martin's Church Street. Asks for a receipt.

1508 10 Sept. 1830. W Garbett Esq, architect, Winchester.
'I fear you will be of opinion that I had forgotten our engagement altogether. It is not so, but a series of uncontrollable circumstances have [*sic*] driven me from place to place for the last months that I have not been for any one time 48 hours at home.' Arranges a meeting at Winchester for the morning after his return from a magistrates' meeting at Devizes.

1509 10 Sept. 1830. Mr Matthews, builder, Frimley, Surrey.
Plans to visit Farnborough and discuss the garden fence.

1510 10 Sept. 1830. Messrs Carson and Miller, Warminster.
Discusses the stays at Codford Bridge. It is very important to get the morticed stones
properly run with lead so that the posts are immovable. Urges haste as the Michaelmas
sessions is the only occasion when accounts can be passed. Requires similar posts and
railings for Fonthill Bridge.

1511 10 Sept. 1830. William Percy Esq, Sherborne.
Did not receive letter sent by his brother to Hartford Bridge. Arranges a meeting.

1512   10 Sept. 1830.   Capt Lord Bruce, Savernake Lodge, Tottenham Park [*and
others*[1]].
Is requested by Lt Col Baker to call attention to the WYC[2] regimental inspection
during the ensuing month, and recommends that troops assemble in pairs to practice
the parade movements.[3]

1. The letter was sent also to the following captains: Lord Andover, Malmesbury; Locke,
Rowdeford House; Wyndham, Dinton House; Starkie, Spye Park; Goddard, Swindon; Long, at
Mr Lawrances's, Warminster; Phipps, Wans House.
2. Wiltshire Yeomanry Cavalry.
3. Peniston signs as Acting Adjutant.

1513 11 Sept. 1830. Mr Hagger.
[*Cannington*]: Requests a correct plan of the chapel showing various features.

1514 11 Sept. 1830. Mr Moore, carpenter, Upton House.
Asks him to lose no time finishing at Upton as other work is waiting.

1515 12 Sept. 1830. J T Tyrell Esq, MP, Boreham House, Chelmsford.
'I had forgotten when I addressed you a few hasty lines of congratulation to you [*sic*]
from Marnhull to inform you that I was there but a bird of passage, but I believe I
left my address as above (*Close, Salisbury*) with Sir John Tyrell, which is my home
when I can get here. This has been very rarely of late.
     'I am much pleased to learn your expences do not exceed your expectation. I
am only sorry you think it necessary to increase them on my account. I do assure you
I neither wished nor expected it, but after what has passed I will not risk offending
you by a further refusal. And however I may regret the cause which limits the amount
of your wishes it more than equals mine. My gratification has been of a higher cast.
To serve my much valued friend Hopper was the first motive. I could not reside long
at Boreham House without others springing up, independent of a little ill-natured

gratification arising from opposing Long Wellesley. By the bye I am not at all surprised at him and his friend Dan falling out. I charitably hope they may be enabled to torment each other.

'Have the kindness to present my most respectful regards to Sir John Tyrell, and congratulatory remembrances to such of our committee as will do me the honor to receive them. More particularly to the Rev George Tuffnell with whose zeal and energy in your cause I was much delighted.'[1]

1. John Tyssen Tyrell (1795-1877), elder son of Sir John Tyrell, was elected MP for Essex on 23 Aug. 1830: Boase, vol.3, p.1062.

1516 12 Sept. 1830. Rev B Marest, Volognes, Cherbourg, France.[1]
Had assumed that Dr Baines had replied to his letter [*see* **1486-7**], but having called at Prior Park, discovered that he had not done so, and referred Peniston to Lord Arundell. His only objection was that the premises might not be extensive enough to receive the ladies without considerable expense to enlarge them. Lord Arundell and Rev Mr Parker suggested a house in Shaftesbury belonging to Lord Grosvenor, now inhabited but about to be quitted. Invites Rev Marest to come over and judge for himself, making Peniston's house his headquarters while in England.

1. Next to the address is written 'Mr Devereux, Gosport, Hants'; and vertically across the letter is 'A Monsieur, Monsieur B Marestes, Aux Carmelites Anglaise, Torigni Pres St Lo, Dept. de la Manche, a Torigni.'

1517 12 Sept. 1830. Mr Kent, Chancery Lane, London.
Apologizes that he did not, as intended, answer the letter received in London. Has not communicated with the committee since leaving Chelmsford on the Friday preceding the termination of the Essex election.[1] Is ready to bear testimony to Kent's assiduity and utility, but is unwilling to interfere unasked with the arrangements.

1. See **1515** note 1.

1518 12 Sept. 1830. W Hopperton Esq, 23 Ranelagh Street, London.
[*Farnborough House*]: From Hopperton's list selects Mr Charles Adams, and submits his own list from which Hopperton is to select. Proposes a meeting to decide which of the two names selected is then chosen.

1519 12 Sept. 1830. Messrs Smith and Bayley, Basinghall Street, London.
[*Farnborough House*]: Informs them that, having consulted Mr Hopper and Mr Bramah, he has selected Mr Charles Adams, and drawn up his own list of six names. Also consulted Mr Hopper about approaching Higgins to value the work at Farnborough, but this would be expensive, and the umpire selected would probably measure the work himself. Seeks advice and asks of any other circumstances which would render further delay desirable.

1520 14 Sept. 1830. Mr Wells, carpenter, Spetisbury House.
The dimensions taken the other day were insufficient to complete the new plan, and asks for specific measurements.[1]

1. Signed by J M Peniston. MS note: 'A copy of this letter was sent to Mr Wells on the 16th of Sept. his plans not being correct.'

1521 14 Sept. 1830. Rt Hon Lord Arundell, Wardour Castle, Wilts.
Forwards a circular from Lord Bath for the march of his troop to assemble with the regiment at Devizes on 5 Oct. Discusses glass for a skylight. Peniston is at present laid by with the gout and has sad prospects for military duty. Asks for a frank addressed to James Peniston, Stony Hurst.

1522 14 Sept. 1830. W Hopperton Esq, 23 Ranelagh Street, London.
[*Farnborough House*]: Agrees that a meeting is desirable to determine the referee, but unable to travel because of gout. Invites Hopperton to visit him at Salisbury, otherwise he will attempt to travel to Hartford Bridge.

1523 15 Sept. 1830. Mr Crook, Governor, Marlborough (*Marlbro'*) Bridewell.
Returns his bills approved. Has no hesitation in accepting the correctness of Mr Brown's charges.

1524 15 Sept. 1830. Mr Bastable, carpenter, Shaftesbury.
Acknowledges a parcel. Cannot settle account [*see* **1468**] until the thatcher's bill is supplied.

1525 16 Sept. 1830. W Hopperton Esq, Gloster Coach Office, Piccadilly.
[*Farnborough House*]: Although considerably better, cannot travel on medical advice. Asks if Hopperton will continue his journey to Salisbury.

1526 18 Sept. 1830. Mr Wells, carpenter, Spetisbury House, near Blandford.
The drawing he has sent is of no use. Reiterates the measurements required, with a sketch.[1]

1. Signed by J M Peniston.

1527 18 Sept. 1830. Mr Marsh, mason, Tisbury, Wilts.
Asks him to call for directions about a bridge.[1]

1. Written by J M Peniston on his father's behalf.

1528 17 Sept. 1830. Charles Adams Esq, Elm Cottage, Chelsea.
[*Farnborough House*]: Thornton v Morant. Informs Adams that he has been named as sole referee under a judge's order, in consequence of an action pending in the Court of Common Pleas. Suggests a meeting at Farnborough Place.[1]

1. Signed by Hopperton and Peniston.

1529 18 Sept. 1830. Most Noble Col the Marquis of Bath, Longleat, Warminster.
Encloses the regimental return sent by the Board of Ordnance, but has filled the blanks in pencil only, not understanding exactly how it should be filled up. Discusses discrepancies and uncertain calculations.

1530 18 Sept. 1830. Thomas Brown Esq, Burderop Park, Swindon.
Writes on behalf of Mr Robert Mackrell about a bill of more than £18 for work done in 1825-6, which remains unpaid. Suggests a meeting during the ensuing sessions at Marlborough to discuss the matter.

1531 20 Sept. 1830. Mr Jeffrey, Wardour Castle, Wilts.
Can dispose of a cask of mastic if sent to Salisbury the next day.[1]

1. Signed by J M Peniston.

1532 21 Sept. 1830. Mr Haywood, House of Correction, Devizes.
Encloses with son's plans for the prison some plans and an estimate for Rangebourne Bridge. Asks Haywood to submit these to Mr Edmonston recommending that Mr Carnell's (*Carnal's*) proposal be accepted, and if it is that he should lose no time in undertaking the work.

1533 21 Sept. 1830. Charles Adams Esq, Elm Cottage, Chelsea, London.
Thornton v Morant. Suggests travel and other arrangements for their meeting at Farnborough House. Is travelling to London and may be reached at 29 Norfolk Street, Park Lane. Is at a loss to say what time may be employed in the investigation.

1534 21 Sept. 1830. W Hopperton Esq, 23 Ranelagh Street, Pimlico.[1]
Suggests arrangements for their meeting with Mr Adams at Farnborough.

1. MS *London*, struck through.

1535 21 Sept. 1830. Mr Stanford, T Hopper Esq, 1 Sovereign Street, Connaught Terrace, London.
Asks whether Mr Hopper is in London, and whether a message to him or a meeting can be arranged.

1536 [*undated*]. Mr Haywood.
[*Devizes Penitentiary*]: Encloses two plans of the proposed female ward, and discusses details and estimates.[1]

1. Signed by J M Peniston, and with a note, 'written on the same sheet as Mr P's'.

1537 22 Sept. 1830. Mr Dyer, blacksmith, Stapleford.
Invites Dyer to collect a cheque from his office for the amount of the bill.[1]

1. Signed by J M Peniston.

1538 22 Sept. 1830. Mrs Berrington, Spetisbury House, Blandford.
Peniston has left for London. Before the plan can be completed needs from Wells details of a doorway. Wells has been sent three letters [**1520,1526**] but does not appear to understand what is required.[1]

1. Signed by J M Peniston; sketch included.

1539 22 Sept. 1830. Rev Mr Watkins, Bugle Street, Southampton.
Asks to be excused the delay, caused by Peniston's confinement.[1]

1. Signed by J M Peniston.

1540 23 Sept. 1830. Mr Hagger, carpenter, Court House, Cannington, near Bridgwater.
Has not received a reply to his request for a plan [**1513**], and cannot prepare to finish the interior. Asks for immediate attention.[1]

1. Signed by J M Peniston.

1541 23 Sept. 1830. Edward Doughty Esq, Upton House, near Poole, Dorset.
Awaits the return of a workman who will then be sent to Upton immediately. J M Peniston will meet him there to give directions.[1]

1. Signed by J M Peniston.

1542 24 Sept. 1830. W Hopperton Esq, 23 Ranelagh Street, London.
Received his letter at Farnborough five minutes too late to catch a coach to London. Sorely laments having literally wasted four days. Explains his movements, and regrets that Hopperton did not keep the appointment. Cannot arrange another meeting until 8 Oct., either at Hartford Bridge or Farnborough.

1543 24 Sept. 1830.[1] Charles Adams Esq, Elm Cottage, Chelsea, London.
[*Farnborough House*]: Encloses a copy of his letter to Hopperton [**1542**], explaining his movements and suggesting a future meeting.

1. MS *5 pm.*

1544 24 Sept. 1830. Messrs Smith & Bayley.
Reports that he waited at Farnborough one day and part of another to keep his appointment with Messrs Adams and Hopperton. Having received notice of Mr Adams acceptance, travelled to London to discuss the business with Mr Morant, and with Smith and Bayley. Learnt, however, that they were both out of London. Did not realise that the agreement needed signature before entering into the business. Received Hopperton's letter at Farnborough breaking the appointment too late to return by coach to London. Cannot arrange another meeting until 8 Oct. On Mr Hopper's advice determined not to employ a London surveyor to measure the work, and will now endeavour to make Mr Adams survey it himself. If he will not do this will throw the whole into day work to reduce Mr Morant's losses. Will use the delay to correspond with Mr Hopper[1] on the subject, and as he is a London architect of some celebrity will endeavour to throw his weight into Peniston's zeal to counterbalance the deficiencies his country breeding may produce in the mind of Mr Adams.

1. MS *Hopperton*, but Hopper is clearly intended. See **1545, 1552**.

1545 24 Sept. 1830. George Morant Esq, 29 Norfolk Street, Park Lane, London.
[*Farnborough House*]: Recounts the missed appointment and the confusion over the referee's signature. Will correspond with Mr Hopper, as his name and connections will carry weight with London surveyors. Reports on work by Matthews and Harding's men at Farnborough.

1546 24 Sept. 1830.[1] H Percy Esq, architect, Sherborne, Dorset.
Suggests two dates for a meeting to enter the Dorsetshire business,[2] but if these are inconvenient proposes requesting that someone else be named, as he will not be able to meet until late in October.

1. MS *7 pm.*
2. Probably Ryme Intrinseca dilapidations. See **1572**.

1547 25 Sept. 1830. Benjamin Wingrove Esq, Trowbridge.
Expresses his condolences on the death of Wingrove's son [*Anthony Wingrove*], for whom he had the sincerest respect, but whose delicate health must in some measure have prepared Wingrove for this unfortunate result. Requests accounts and discusses the previous year's vouchers.

1548 25 Sept. 1830. Mr Fowler, Melksham.
Sends a cheque and asks for a stamped receipt.

1549 25 Sept. 1830. Mr Strong, Pewsey.
Sends a cheque and asks for a stamped receipt.

1550 26 Sept. 1830. Lieut Pitt, Malmesbury Troop, directed to Joseph Pitt Esq, MP, Eastcourt, Malmesbury.
Encloses a list of the accustomed parade movements of the regiment, and discusses details. Has applied to Mr Pettit relative to Pitt's letter. He has had no communication with the troop since Mr Hanks' application for appointment, for which he had given directions.[1]

1. Peniston signs as *Lieut and Assistant Adj.*

1551 25 Sept. 1830. The Commissioners of the Sarum and Eling (*Ealing*) Turnpikes.
Has surveyed the tollhouse being erected at Totton, reports that it is very fairly executed, and recommends the contractor be advanced £80.

1552 27 Sept. 1830. Thomas Hopper Esq, 1 Sovereign Street, Connaught Terrace [*London*].
Recounts the events which have delayed determination of the Farnborough business, and describes in detail how he and Mr Alason[1] had been asked to survey the work. The builder's gross bill, including measured work, a day bill, and a bill for freightage and sundries, totalled £6188. Peniston's valuation would not allow more than £3794, and his opinion was that the frightful difference derived from fraudulent intention in making up the accounts. Wishes to throw the entire accounts overboard and rely on the referee measuring the work; or if this fails to throw the whole into day work. Requests a meeting at Farnborough with Hopper professionally, so that he can explain these matters and so that Hopper can see the nature of the works executed.

1. Probably Thomas Allason, a London architect and surveyor: P. See also **1431**.

1553 27 Sept. 1830. Rt Hon Lord Arundell, Wardour Castle.
Understands from Mr Beare that Lord Arundell intends to stay at the White Hart, and invites him instead to stay at his house, where there will be room for his valet also. Asks for a frank for the enclosed letter to Hopper [**1552**]. Hopes to join the campaign although some rheumatism remains.

1554 27 Sept. 1830. G Morant Esq, 29 Norfolk Street, Park Lane, London.
[*Farnborough House*]: Is pleased that his arrangements with Harding and Stewart are acceptable. Has received a letter from Mr Hopperton asking him to try to procure from Mr Morant a cheque for whatever Peniston considers due to Mr Thornton. Believe that this attempt is partly to get some money, but also to elucidate the extent and nature of his opposition. Encloses a copy of his reply [**1555**], and suggests that Morant acquaints Messrs Smith and Bayley.

1555 27 Sept. 1830. W Hopperton Esq, 23 Ranelagh Street, Pimlico.
Has forwarded to Mr Morant with his own observations Hopperton's request on the part of Mr Thornton, but does not anticipate acquiescence, the final discussion of the business being so near at hand.

1556 27 Sept. 1830. Secretary of the committee appointed to conduct a ball and supper, Post Office, Devizes.
Apologizes for his long delay in accepting the invitation to attend the ball and supper at Devizes. Mrs Peniston cannot attend.[1]

1. Peniston signs as *Lieut WYC*, so this function was presumably connected with the regimental assembly.

1557 28 Sept. 1830. Mr Hagger, Court House, Cannington, Bridgwater.
Is aware that the expenses at Cannington will exceed the estimate, and for that reason requires the bills, so that the ladies might be fully aware of their expenditure. Does not wish to find fault, but the ladies must be aware of the likely expense before work begins. Proposes a visit with J M Peniston, but not until late Oct.

1558 29 Sept. 1830. Sils[1] Gibbons Esq, 36 ?Osnaburgh[2] Street, Regents Park.
Informs him of a circumstance relating to their Trust[3] which has come to light. Has learnt that Mrs Harrington has been drawing unauthorized sums of money from London bankers. Is more anxious, therefore, to wind up the concern as proposed at the ensuing Christmas. Will probably be away on business at Hartford Bridge when Gibbons visits, but could meet him there.[4]

1. The spelling is confirmed by references in WRO 451/393.
2. Name poorly written.
3. See **850** note 1.
4. This ends a book. MS note *210 since 12 May 1830 JMP*. Next book begins with a note, *210 brought from last book, numbers from May 11 1830 to Sept 29 1830.*

1559 30 Sept. 1830. H Percy Esq, Sherborne.
Taking advantage of a frank, confirms a meeting at Sherborne.

1560 1 Oct. 1830. Mrs M C Knight, Court House, Cannington.
Acknowledges with considerable pain her letter. Discusses unauthorized expenses incurred on the work at Cannington, for which Hagger is much to blame [*see* **1557**]. Disagrees with Mr Padden's prices for plasterwork, and if Padden is to undertake the work Peniston wishes to decline having any more to do with the business, considering him incompetent. Cannot visit Cannington until late October. Meanwhile work can continue if she wishes, but she has the power to stop it at any time and discharge the workmen. Expresses regret if he is not to have the power to serve her, and wishes his successors better fortune. Regrets it the more as he has had the gratification of seeing Spetisbury Chapel completed.

1561 1 Oct. 1830. Mr Hagger.
Reports on the letter which he has received from the mother prioress complaining of the amount of the bills. The complaint is reasonable as the ladies should have been informed of the additional expenses. Regrets that the reverend mother wishes Padden to execute the plastering, and if she is determined will decline any further direction of the business. Hopes that Hagger will do nothing further to shake the ladies' confidence.

1562 1 Oct. 1830. Messrs Smith and Bayley, Basinghall Street, London.
[*Farnborough House*]: Encloses copies of the letter to Hopper[1] and his reply, from which it appears Peniston must rely on the integrity and independence of the umpire. Assumes that the meeting on 8th Oct. will take place.

1. MS note *see last letter book*, i.e. **1552**.

1563 1 Oct. 1830. William Hopperton Esq, 23 Ranelagh Street, London.
[*Farnborough House*]: Queries whether their meeting for 8 Oct. stands, and requests immediate reply. Has not heard back from Mr Morant about Hopperton's letter referred to him.

1564 1 Oct. 1830. Mr Moore, Upton House, near Poole.
Wishes to hear by return if he is able to travel from Upton to Clarendon, where the fittings should now be finished. Should bring his accounts with him.

1565 1 Oct. 1830. Messrs Grieve, Grellier and Morgan, Belvedere Road, Waterloo Bridge.
Orders three casks of coarse plaster by Southampton.

1566 5 Oct. 1830. G Morant Esq, 29 Norfolk Street, Park Lane, London.
[*Farnborough House*]: At Smith and Bayley's wish encloses copies of the letter to Mr Hopper and his reply.[1] Assumes that the meeting still stands.

1. MS notes, *see last letter book Sept. 27; see the letter for Sept. 30, 1830*, i.e. **1552**.

1567 8 Oct. 1830. Mr Trapp, bricklayer, Warminster.
'What madness could induce you to extend your drain at Codford 100 yards instead of 100 feet as directed? You were present and assisted to measure it when Col A'Court and Mr Biggs directed where it should begin and where end. Mr Bennett of Codford told you you were wrong and that you had no business to go further than the county road extended, and begged you not to do it - yet you persisted and would do it. The county certainly will not pay you for more than 100 feet and I think it most likely the commissioners of the road will compel you to take up the drain that is on their part of the road, and leave the ditch as you found it. Indeed I think it is the best thing you can do, and endeavour to sell the bricks, as you must be accountable to Mr Daniell for those that are not used for the county road.'

1568 8 Oct. 1830. George Morant Esq, 29 Norfolk Street, Park Lane, London.
[*Farnborough House*]: Reports that the umpire has fixed a meeting at the Swan Inn, Blackwater, for the investigation of Mr Thornton's accounts. Solicitors are not to be present, but it is desirable that Morant be in the neighbourhood of Farnborough in case any communication with him proves necessary.

1569 8 Oct. 1830. Messrs Bramah, Pimlico, London.
Requests a meeting with someone from the firm on the day after the referee's meeting at Farnborough. Recalls earlier discussion about heating the green house, and now wishes an opinion on heating the entrance hall.

1570 9 Oct. 1830. Mr Strong, Pewsey.
Requests a stamped receipt for the cheque before the ensuing sessions.[1]

1. Written by M P Harris, on uncle's behalf.

1571 9 Oct. 1830. Mr Marsh, mason, Tisbury.
Requests accounts, including that for Fonthill Bridge if it is finished, in time for the sessions.[1]

1. Written by J M Peniston, on father's behalf.

1572 9 Oct. 1830. H Percy Esq, architect, Sherborne.
Sends account of dilapidations at Ryme Intrinseca, totalling £58 16s 3d., and discusses a legal point concerning drains on glebe land.[1]

1. See also **1578**.

1573 9 Oct. 1830. Mr Carnell.
Enquires about the state of the work on Rangebourne Bridge. If complete J M Peniston will survey it so that the bill can be passed at the sessions.

1574 9 Oct. 1830.[1] Mr Flooks, Wilton.
Submits a statement relative to the Grimstead quit rents, addressed to T Baker at Michaelmas 1830.

1. MS *Saturday evening*, undated.

1575 9 Oct. 1830. Charles Marett Esq, Southampton.
Returns drawings and papers relative to the alteration of St Michael's church, Southampton, with his account including expenses for examining them [*see* **1027**].

1576 13 Oct. 1830. Messrs Smith and Bayley.[1]
Reports on progress over the Farnborough business. Monday was wasted as Mr Hopperton and others had to be sworn. On Tuesday Thornton showed his accounts and made a very strong case. Peniston recounted his involvement, and the mode of his valuation, and suggested that the same mode should be adopted again. The umpire was unwilling to do this. Peniston detailed items in the accounts which indicated fraud, and then proposed the concession that Thornton be allowed his time and materials and reasonable profits. Mr Adams regarded this as honourable and liberal, but did not please Thornton, who, however, could hardly refuse.[2]

1. Addressed from Hartford Bridge.
2. A marginal note, headed *6 pm.*, reports further progress, and notes reckless expense incurred in the carriage of materials.

1577 15 Oct. 1830. Messrs Smith and Bayley, Basinghall Street, London.
Reports on the Farnborough enquiry. The parties worked late on Wednesday and continued on Thursday. The business was not quite finished, but insufficient remained to detain them another day, and Peniston returned home in order to attend sessions. The umpire's conduct is very satisfactory, and he is aware of the improvident expenditure incurred. He approves of Peniston's mode of settling the account, and is at a loss to ascertain how, from a survey of the building, the money claimed could have been expended. Peniston should hear from Mr Adams before he makes his final award.

1578 15 Oct. 1830. H Percy Esq, architect, Sherborne, Dorset.
The chancel was overlooked when they surveyed Ryme Intrinseca. Requests Percy to
cover any deficiencies in this respect, expressing perfect confidence in his judgement.

1579 15 Oct. 1830. William Garbett Esq, architect, Winchester.
Could not meet in Salisbury as had to obey an order to attend the city sessions.
Suggests a date to meet on their long protracted enquiry[1] after the county sessions.

1. Perhaps in connection with Miss Wyndham's premises. See **1605**.

1580 15 Oct. 1830. W Heald Ludlow Esq, House of Correction, Devizes.
Forwards the present year's county accounts, and apologizes for not attending in
person. His son should be able to explain anything not apparent from the books
themselves.

1581 18 Oct. 1830. Mr Carnell, builder, Devizes.
Agrees that the planking may be carried over the beams, instead of being notched
into them.[1]

1. Apparently written by J M Peniston on his father's behalf. The work may be Rangebourne
Bridge. See **1573**.

1582 21 Oct. 1830. Messrs Smith and Bayley, Basinghall Street, London.
[*Farnborough House*]: Copies a letter from Mr Adams, and his answer to Adams's
queries [**1583**].

1583 21 Oct. 1830. Charles Adams Esq, Queens Elms, Chelsea.
[*Farnborough House*]: Replies to queries. The total paid by Mr Morant to Mr Thornton
is £3,525 10s. The value of some old iron may be set against this. Draws attention to
apparently excessive wages paid at Farnborough. Mr Morant's butler, Busby, and the
builder, Mr Matthews, are both sworn, and will be truthful in giving information,
although the latter's observations may be thought to be coloured a little too high.
Discusses Peniston's own expenses for four or five days at the enquiry. 'PS My son
requests me to thank you for your kind remembrances, and to apologize for the
abrupt way in which he took his departure. He had a fair[1] excuse to offer for his
forgetfullness.'

1. MS *fair*, underlined.

1584 21 Oct. 1830. G Morant Esq, 29 Norfolk Street, Park Lane.
Copies the letter from Mr Adams, and his answer [**1583**]. Surprised not to have heard
from Messrs Harding and Stewart. Has written from time to time to Messrs Smith
and Bayley, and is now awaiting with no trifling anxiety the result of the Farnborough
business.

1585 22 Oct. 1830. Mr H P Burt, Devizes.
Encloses dimensions of balcony at Clarendon House. George Peniston is sending to Burt a tool chest by way of Bristol, for which he has paid freightage and expenses.[1]

1. Written by J M Peniston.

1586 22 Oct. 1830. Robert Gordon Esq, MP, Weymouth.
Accepts commission to inspect and report on new buildings at Dorset Lunatic Asylum. Asks for the name of any person able to supply local information to be sent to him by return, or else to the Antelope Inn, Dorchester.

1587 22 Oct. 1830. Most Noble Marquis of Bath, Longleat, Warminster.
Has examined and completed the paylist returns, and hopes that the accounts may pass without further comment.

1588 23 Oct. 1830. C Adams Esq.
[*Farnborough House*]: Reports that Messrs Smith and Bayley considered the lawyers' cost not worth addressing, but describes further expenses in connection with the enquiry which Peniston incurred, involving a journey to London and a wasted journey to Farnborough. Another minor expense was for Matthews to attend at Farnborough as a witness for Mr Morant.

1589 23 Oct. 1830. Messrs Smith and Bayley, Basinghall Street, London.
[*Farnborough House*]: Cannot give any good reason why he omitted to copy part of his letter to Mr Adams referring to his expenses [*see* **1582**]. Recounts his other expenses as detailed to Mr Adams [**1588**].

1590 29 Oct. 1830. J T Tyrell Esq, MP, Boreham House, Chelmsford, Essex.
Acknowledges a handsome pecuniary compliment, but values infinitely more the kind opinions expressed about him. Wellesley's intention of petitioning against Tyrell's return is news to him, and surely must be deemed frivolous and vexatious. Is truly sorry to hear of the death of the Duke of Athol, which will also doubtless be much regretted by Mr Hopper. Has had a hasty correspondence with Mr H, but has not yet had an opportunity of expressing personal congratulations on their success in Essex. Sends good wishes to Sir John, and remembrances to those who fought the good fight.[1]

1. See **1515**.

1591 30 Oct. 1830. Cobb.[1]
Encloses requested accounts, and John will send a statement and valuation of the works at Figheldean. Also encloses a cheque for £9, 'being I believe the amount returned to render me independent'. The sum of 2s., however, his coach hire when he gave evidence before Cobb's immaculate bench, must be returned.

1. No addressee, but letter begins, 'Dear Cobb'. James Cobb was a Salisbury attorney: P. The circumstances of the letter are obscure, but may in part be related to the Grimstead estate. See **1620**.

1592 30 Oct. 1830. G Morant Esq, London.
Mr Stewart called at the house while Peniston was away. He declines to estimate for the works at Farnborough, but will undertake them subject to Peniston's valuation. Does Morant wish to employ him before the final adjustment with Thornton? Expresses anxiety about the expected decision of Mr Adams.

1593 30 Oct. 1830. Charles Millett Esq, Hindon.
Must discuss with Mr Payne the increased prices which he has allowed before consenting to his valuation. Will arrange a meeting, but this cannot be before Millett's visit to Lord Calthorpe.

1594 30 Oct. 1830. - Woolaston Esq, Dorchester.
Forwards the lunatic asylum survey [*see* **1586**] and will be pleased to answer any queries. Has omitted this concluding paragraph from the report, and inserted it in this letter, leaving it to Woolaston's judgement whether or not to refer to it. 'In conclusion I think it my duty to observe that while I cannot but be of opinion that the architect has erred in judgement by introducing this species of arch without the necessary ties or abutments, he appears to have taken great pains in the selection of his materials and in the general execution of the different works.'

1595 30 Oct. 1830. Mr Pittman, plumber, Stalbridge, Dorset.
Expresses surprise at some items in his account,[1] including a copper pump put up in the brewhouse, and some apparently erroneous prices for which Pittman has himself only to blame.

1. Perhaps for work at Thornhill House. See **1436**.

1596 30 Oct. 1830. Robert Gordon Esq, MP, Burton Street, London.
Has forwarded the report and survey to Mr Woolaston, with a copy to Mr Gordon in London, hoping that it may meet his approval. Copies also the observation made in his letter to Woolaston [**1594**].

1597 30 Oct. 1830.[1] J L Alford Esq.
Answers points in his note. Will arrange to attend the case of the Bishop of Salisbury and Sloper. Trusts that Mrs Harrington will have time to prepare an account and explanation honourable to herself and satisfactory to the trustees. Cannot reply to her offer of £1,000 for the lease, but will co-operate with Mr Gibbons to give her preference in the disposal of the business. Has Mr Gibbons approved the sale of the wines by auction? Doubts the propriety of such a measure, about which he should have been consulted. If it is being done without Mr Gibbons' knowledge and consent then Peniston forbids it. How is Peniston's private claim to be disposed of?

1. MS *Saturday evening*, undated.

1598 31 Oct. 1830. Mr Hagger, Court House, Cannington, Bridgwater.
Intends to visit briefly, and requests that all enquiries and observations be listed for his attention, and all accounts prepared for examination.

1599 1 Nov. 1830. B Wingrove Esq, Trowbridge.
Sends money and requests a receipt for the £10 spent on Road Bridge.

1600 2 Nov. 1830. Mr Hulbert, surveyor to the Lacock Trust, Corsham.
Encloses a cheque for repairs to the roads over the three bridges at Lacock, and requests a stamped receipt. Foot Bridge is somewhat rutted and should be attended to.

1601 8 Nov. 1830. Messrs Carson and Miller.
Encloses the amount of their bill for Codford Bridge, less a deduction for bricks, and requests a stamped receipt.

1602 8 Nov. 1830. Mr George Golding, carpenter, Upton House, near Poole.
Must come to Clarendon to put the roof on, leaving the work at Upton until it is finished.[1]

1. Written by J M Peniston, on father's behalf.

1603 9 Nov. 1830. Messrs Bramah, Pimlico.
Encloses directions for commencing the greenhouse at Farnborough, and will write to Mr T Bramah in a few days on the subject.[1]

1. Written by J M Peniston on his father's behalf.

1604   10 Nov. 1830. Mr J W D Wickham, Frome.
Will give directions for the repair of the Wiltshire portion of the roads at Maiden Bradley bridges, assuming that they are the 'Woodlands Bridges' referred to by Wickham.

1605   11 Nov. 1830.[1] Richard Attwood Esq.
Will survey Witt's work as soon as a measuring account with Mr Garbett at Miss Wyndham's is settled, probably today. The Pensworth accounts are all but ready.

1. MS *Thursday morn Nov 11 1830.*

1606   11 Nov. 1830. Mr Haywood, House of Correction, Devizes.
Of the timber yards in Bath is best pleased with timber in store at Mr John Lester's, near Norfolk Crescent and close to the river. Requests that Mr Young should calculate on the scantlings, and order from Lester in Peniston's name, to be sent by Mr Shaw's barge. Has made arrangements for lead, which Mr Bishop will lay, and needs an estimate of the weight required for the guttering and flashings. Will make further enquiries about slate. Asks about progress, and how the air drain proceeds.

1607   11 Nov. 1830. Benjamin Wingrove Esq, Trowbridge.
Reiterates the need for a stamped receipt.

1608   11 Nov. 1830. Rev Christopher Fawcett, Whitchurch, Hants.[1]
Has surveyed the dilapidations at Boscombe, but has not yet completed the valuation. Will send a copy to Mr Down of Shaftesbury as requested.

1. See **1615**.

1609   11 Nov. 1830. Charles Marett Esq, Southampton.
Acknowledges with thanks a note enclosing £6 17s. 6d [*see* **1575**].

1610   11 Nov. 1830. Timothy Bramah Esq, Pimlico.
Has sent Mr Morant's directions respecting the conservatory and water closet for Farnborough, so that work may proceed. Regrets that Bramah has been troubled by that rascally fellow at Tidworth, and offers to render any service there or elsewhere [*see* **1618**]. 'Bill requests I will ask permission for him to spend some time at home at the ensuing Christmas.'[1]

1. William, Peniston's youngest son, had been working for Bramah since May 1830. See **1351, 1358**.

1611 11 Nov. 1830. H Percy Esq, architect, Sherborne.
Rev Mr Blennerhassett has written forgoing any claim for draining the glebe land, and in view of this liberality Peniston hopes that Percy will allow him the trifling sum for scouring the ditches. Asks to know the additional amount for repairing the chancel, so that the business can be closed. Peniston will then prepare a stamped valuation for Percy's signature. Expresses his pleasure at meeting Percy, but regrets that the distance involved will create an expense to his employer disproportionate to the sum he will have to receive.[1]

1. Ryme Intrinseca dilapidations. See **1572**.

1612 12 Nov. 1830. Messrs Stewart and Harding, builders, Farnham, Surrey.
Arranges to meet at Farnborough to discuss the conservatory.

1613 13 Nov. 1830. Mr Hagger, Cannington.
Encloses a drawing for Porter respecting the division of the modillions. Discusses architectural details.

1614 15 Nov. 1830. Robert Dugdale Esq, Wareham.
Encloses a cheque for £1 17s. 6d, with apologies for the delay in payment. The money had in fact been taken to Swanage by a friend to pay him, but had been brought back. Peniston had then intended to visit on his way to Upton House, but was prevented.

1615 16 Nov. 1830. Rev Christopher Fawcett, Whitchurch, Dorset.
Explains that he had replied to the previous letter [**1608**], but had misread the postmark as Andover instead of Blandford, and had therefore sent the reply to Whitchurch in Hampshire. Hopes to forward the valuation in a few days.

1616 16 Nov. 1830. J L Alford Esq.
Bishop of Salisbury v. Sloper. Requests details of the time, place, and nature of the evidence required of him.
Re Harrington estate.[1] Mr Ings had told him confidentially that Mrs Harrington's bill for £380 would become due but that he could not take it up. Peniston had suggested a meeting, but does not know the outcome, and is anxious not to communicate on the business more than absolutely necessary. Asks Alford to correspond with Mr Gibbons about it, and to use every professional exertion to close the business by the time appointed. Has not seen any advertisement for the disposal of the lease.

1. See **850, 1558**.

1617 16 Nov. 1830. Messrs Carson and Miller, Warminster.
Acknowledges letter and requests a stamped receipt for the bill, as settled at the last sessions. Disputes their claim for the price of bricks supplied by Sainsbury, and cannot allow an intermediate profit by a tradesman in a quite distinct branch of business. Asks whether the posts and rails at Fonthill Bridge have yet been erected.

1618 17 Nov. 1830. Timothy Bramah Esq, Pimlico.
'My dear Sir, As you wished me to report to you any observations I might hear relative to your operations at Mr Assheton Smith's, I this morning noted the following: Wednesday morning, ½ past nine, Novr. 17 1830. Mr Wolferstan the foreman of Mr Figes (who is an iron founder) has this minute informed me: that the plan for heating the house at Tidworth by Messrs Bramah was a complete failure; that they never could get the heat up to 60 degrees; and that Mr Northeast had told Mr Figes the above, who had repeated it to him. Mr Wolferstan also stated that some person whom he declined naming had detected the workman of Mr Bramah in the act of dipping the thermometer into hot water, for the purpose of deceiving those who were about to examine it to ascertain the heat of the apartment. I told Mr Wolferstan I should repeat the observations he had made, and he requested I would forbear doing so till he had spoken with Mr Figes. I immediately noted the conversation and on my return home (now 3 p.m.) I find a note of which the following is a copy:
    "Sir, On my return home I named the circumstance we were speakin [sic] of this morning to Mr Figes, when he again asserted, Mr Northeast told him on Sunday last Mr Bramah had failed in effectually heating Mr Assheton Smith's house, and that the thermometer could not be raised to 60 degrees. I am respectfully your obed't serv't, Thos. Wolferstan. Nov. 17 1830, To J Peniston Esq."
    I have been very[1] particular in noting these observations and trust it may be the means of exposing a villainous threat to injure you and yours. Again repeating, my dear Sir, my thorough readiness to serve you in any manner that circumstances may render desirable.'[2]

1. MS *very* inserted above the line.
2. A letter from Francis Bramah (Timothy's brother), dated 22 Nov. 1830, and a paper refuting the allegations, are WRO 451/60.

1619 18 Nov. 1830. Richard Attwood Esq.
Mr Crook has failed to convince him that his charge for work at Cowesfield Farm is correct. Has no objection to meeting a surveyor on Crook's part, if Attwood approves.

1620 18 Nov. 1830. Arthur Baker Esq, 5 Great George Street North, Dublin.
Sends balance sheet of receipts and payments to the present, and of sums due to the lords of the manor of Grimstead. Discusses the tenancies of Mr Joshua Tubb and Mr Wall. Has charged for negotiating with Mr Cobb relative to the claims of Mr Wynch's executors, and has also taken credit for a sum owed him by the lords of the manor of Dean. Seeks instructions over the case of Aaron Futcher, who resides in a cottage at

Grimstead and regards it as his own, refusing to pay rent. Has had many applications from the executors of the late Mr Wynch, but awaits directions from the lords of the manor.

1621 19 Nov. 1830. Mr G V Wing.
Expresses regret at Wing's indisposition when Peniston called on him. Regrets firstly that, Wing having agreed to the use of his name and put his shoulder to the wheel, he has now drawn back; and secondly that his decision will give their opponents a triumph, since it will be fatal to their intention of carrying the case to the courts above. Had Wing not withdrawn he would have been exonerated from all expense.

1622 19 Nov. 1830. Charles Adams Esq, Elm Cottage, near the new church, Chelsea. [*Farnborough House*]: Has received from Messrs Smith and Bayly copy correspondence between Mr Morant and Mr Adams. Has replied to them that a direct acknowledgement from Mr Morant of the correctness of Peniston's statement of monies paid is required. Mr Morant seems to be suggesting a meeting between Peniston and Adams. Peniston will be happy to wait on Adams in London, if he does not consider such a meeting an improper interference.

1623 19 Nov. 1830. Messrs Smith and Bayley, Basinghall Street [*London*].
It appears that Mr Adams requires a direct acknowledgement from Mr Morant of the correctness of Peniston's statement of monies paid. Will send a copy of Mr Morant's letter to Mr Adams, but fears that the only effect will be to induce him to lower the profits on the outlay of works ineffectually executed. Is becoming excessively fidgetty at the protraction of the business. Should Peniston arrange a meeting with Adams?

1624 19 Nov. 1830. Messrs Carson and Miller.
Has received more annoyance from asking them to procure materials and bricklayers for the work at Codford Bridge, than he has experienced altogether since employed for the county. Reiterates the arrangement, and offers to pay from his own pocket any reasonable expenses incurred thereby. But if they apply to the magistrates respecting their attempt to make a profit over the bricks, it would not redound very highly to their credit, and the magistrates would be apt to call the transaction by its proper name.[1] Gives notice that unless he receives a stamped receipt for the correct amount immediately, he will put the business in Mr Swayne's hands, and the magistrates can decide for themselves. Regarding Fonthill Bridge no extras expenses will be allowed, and the posts are to be covered properly and firmly with lead. This they did not do at Codford, and they must make good.

1. MS *proper name*, underlined.

1625 19 Nov. 1830.[1] Richard Webb Esq, Melchit.

'My dear Sir, I lose not a moment in[2] availing myself of the information you have kindly given me. Orders are already issued for the Salisbury Troop to hold themselves in readiness for immediate service and I trust we shall not be found wanting, if unfortunately our services are required.

'I am My dear Sir, very sincerely yours, J Peniston.'[3]

1. Letter is headed *Close, Friday Even'g 8 PM.*
2. *in* struck through.
3. The letter from Webb, reporting information from Broughton, to which this is the reply, is transcribed in Graham, vol.1, p.73-4, and Chambers, vol.1, p.22.

1626 19 Nov. 1830.[1] Rev'd R Parker.

'My dear Sir, Information has this even'g reached me that it is not improbable but that we may be visited by a body of the Mobility[2] in a short period. I know not whether my commandant L'd Arundell be at Wardour and therefore I address myself to you to request if he be not that you cause to be conveyed to Messrs Stringfellow and Jeffrey orders to hold themselves in readiness for active service at the shortest notice. It is rather a curious medium I have chosen of issuing military orders, but I trust you will not object to be one of the Church Militants on the present occasion.

'I am My dear Sir etc. etc., J Peniston.'

1. Letter is headed *Friday Ev'g 8 PM'.*
2. 'The mob, the lower classes': OED.

1627 19 Nov. 1830.[1] Capt'n Wyndham, Dinton House.

'Dear Sir, Information from most respectable authority has this ev'g reached me that a mob is to-morrow morn'g expected to assemble at Broughton for the purpose of riot and destruction. I have thought it necessary to issue orders to the Salisbury Troop to hold themselves in readiness for service at the shortest notice. I think it better to give you this information that you may exercise your judgment as to the propriety of giving your Troop similar orders.

'I am Dear Sir etc. etc., J Peniston Lieut ST WYC.'[2]

1. Letter is headed *Friday Ev'g 8 PM.*
2. i.e. Salisbury Troop, Wiltshire Yeomanry Cavalry.

1628 19 Nov. 1830.[1] To the Worshipful the Mayor of Salisbury.

'Dear Sir, I have this ev'g received from the most respectable authority information that a mob is expected to assemble tomorrow in Broughton for purposes of riot and destruction. I thought it proper in the absence of my Capt L'd Arundell to issue orders to the Salisbury Troop of W.Y.C. to hold themselves in readiness for service at the shortest notice. I think it my duty to convey this information to you as our first

Magistrate both as it may enable you to take any steps you may think proper and to account for such orders being issued.

'I am Dear Sir, etc. etc. etc., J Peniston.'

1. Letter is headed *Friday Ev'g*.

1629 19 Nov. 1830.[1] The Most Noble Colonel the Marquis of Bath, Longleat, Warminster.

'My Lord, I have this evening received information from the most respectable authority that a mob is expected to assemble at Broughton tomorrow morning – a place in Hampshire about 12 miles from Salisbury. In the absence of Lord Arundell I have directed the Salisbury Troop to hold themselves in readiness for service at the shortest notice. I have also directed a letter to Captain Wyndham to Dinton House giving him the information I have received, that he may exercise his judgment as to giving similar orders to the Hindon Troop. I think it my duty to convey the earliest information to your Lordship and respectfully suggest how far it may be desirable to draw the attention of officers commanding Troops to be on the alert at the present moment.

'I am my Lord, with the highest respect, your faithful and obedient servant, J Peniston Lieut WYC.'

1. Letter is headed *Close Salisbury Nov 19, 1830, 9 P.M.*

1630 20 Nov. 1830. David Winzar Esq.

Has surveyed the basement of his buildings in Endless Street [*Salisbury*], and is doubtful whether any means would be effective in preventing the rising of the water. Does not concur with the opinion of Mr Sleat and Mr Burch that the evil would not have happened if the stone floor had (*been*) laid down.

1631 20 Nov. 1830. Mr W Daniell, brick merchant, Warminster.

Encloses a cheque for bricks at Codford Bridge, and requests a stamped receipt.

1632 20 Nov. 1830. Mr Stewart, builder, Farnham, Surrey.

[*Farnborough House*]: Acknowledges letter and sketch [*see* **1612**]. Approves the back sheds but not the flower stand, and will write to Mr Morant [**1633**] for his decision.

1633 20 Nov. 1830. George Morant Esq, 29 New Norfolk Street, Park Lane, London.

[*Farnborough House*]: Mr Stewart has begun work on the conservatory, and has proposed plans for a potting shed and flower stand [*see* **1632**]. Encloses the sketch, and also an alternative of his own for the flower stand, whereby one looks down on the flowers instead of up at the flower pot. Requests a decision.

1634 21 Nov. 1830. The Most Noble Col. Marquess of Bath, Longleat, Warminster. 'My Lord, I am much pleased that the course I have pursued meets your Lordship's approval, and have also the gratification of informing your Lordship that our services have not been required. Indeed I think the great advantage of Yeomanry Corps is to prevent rather than cure the evils of commotion, as the knowledge that a body of men being in arms to suppress a riot is the best means to prevent it. I wrote in haste to your Lordship on Friday night. I now copy for your Lordship's information the letter I received from my friend Mr Webb[1] which induced me to take precautionary measures.

'I regret to say, Mr Pettit has not exactly followed your Lordships instructions relative to filling up the ordnance returns. He did not consult me and has partly filled them up in ink and in that erroneously; it will be impossible to correct them without scratching out the errors. Will your Lordship allow that to be done or will you apply for other blank returns?

'I have the honor to be, etc. etc. etc. etc. etc., J Peniston.'

1. See **1625** note 3.

1635 21 Nov. 1830. Charles Adams Esq, Elm Cottage, near the new church, Chelsea. [*Farnborough House*]: Does not wish to trouble him with a meeting unless it is specifically desired by Mr Morant. The wet coming into the servants hall is the result of a total want of framing to the roof.

1636 22 Nov. 1830.[1] Marquis of Bath.
'My Lord, I regret to say the peaceable appearances under which I addressed your Lordship last night have changed for other less pleasing. I was awoke between 12 and 1 o'clock by a person bearing the information that an express had arrived from a respectable farmer named Judd, requesting the aid of the Cavalry. Stating that himself and son had been beaten with bludgeons by a mob from adj'g parishes stimulating his own laborers to rise, that they had torn up the paling before his house and threatened to return and pull his house down. This person resides at Newtontoney, in this county about 10 miles from Salisbury.[2]

'I cannot but apprehend that from the success these parties have had in obliging their employers to raise their wages and inducing some of the magistrates to advance the scale of allowances, and which they were unwise enough to publish in our yesterday paper, it will run like wild fire through this and the adj'g counties holding out an inducement to the working classes to congregate for similar proposes[3]. And however desirable it may be that the wages of the laborer should be increased the medium by which this is now accomplishing is anything but desirable. Mr Wyndham our Member has been I understand informed of the foregoing circumstance, and has expressed a wish that some of the county magistrates might be sent for to meet early this morn'g at Salisbury to consider what course to pursue. I have in consequence sent an express to the Rev'd Mr Duke who resides about 7 or 8 miles from here[4] and Mr Cobb and their clerk of the division at 6 this morn'g to wait on Mr Fort who lives at about half the distance from us.[5]

'My son informs me that he saw a fire from one of the hills adj'g the town very distinctly last night about 11 o'clock. It appeared to be of magnitude and he supposed it to be about the neighbourhood of Amesbury.[6]

'If my Lord it should appear to you desirable under these or other circumstances to assemble the other Troops of the Regiment, I respectfully submit whether it may not be desirable for them to meet in divisions so as to cover the whole of the County. Thus the Swindon and Marlbro' Troops might be quartered at Marlbro'; the Salisbury and Hindon at Salisbury; the Devizes, Warminster, Melksham, Chippenham and Malmsbury in their respective towns. They would be thus at easy distances to support each other and the whole regiment might assemble at any given[7] in a short time, should circumstances render it necessary. The Salisbury and Hindon with the Marlbro' and Swindon would cover the whole of the south-eastern part of Wilts; the 2 former Troops with the Warminster on the S.W. and with the Devizes commanding the centre. The Warminster, Melksham and Chippenham Troops would keep Bradford and Trowbridge in check and the Devizes Troop would be well placed to co-operate with either. A constant chain of communication may be kept up either by orderlies or coaches. And your Lordship might receive daily information at Longleat and be enabled to issue orders from thence, unless you may think it may be desirable to establish your H'd Quarters at Devizes as the most central part of the county.

'I forgot to mention in my letter of last night that Capt Wyndham requires 6 pistols for the Hindon Troop, and our Q.M. informs me that we have 6 pistols unfit for service and wishes them to be exchanged. I shall endeavour to send this by an early coach for your Lordship[8] information. And am etc. etc., J Peniston.'

1. Letter is headed *Close, Salisbury ½ past 4 am, Nov 22, 1830.*
2. The letter, sent by James Judd to 'Mr Cobb' [presumably James Cobb of Salisbury], is in WRO 413/23, and is transcribed in Chambers, vol.1, p.26.
3. Recte *purposes.*
4. Rev Edward Duke, Lake House: P.
5. George Fort, Alderbury House. See RCH, Alderbury Hundred, p.86.
6. A fire was reported to have been started at Countess Farm, Amesbury, at about 10.30 p.m., 21 Nov. See Chambers, vol.1, p.25.
7. *place* omitted?
8. Recte *Lordship's.*

1637 22 Nov. 1830.[1] Capt'n Wyndham, Bramshaw.
'Dear Sir, between 12 and 1 o clock this morning I awoke[2] with information our services were requested at Newtontoney, where the mob had been amusing themselves on Sunday evening by beating Farmer Judd and his son and by pulling up[3] the paling as preparatory to pulling down[3] his house, which they threaten to do. As we cannot move but by an order of magistrates your name sake our Member as[4] requested an early assemblage of magistrates here this morning to consult and direct. I think it would be desirable for you to ride over here as early as you can this morning. You can then determine what is best to be done. I think our work is cut out for us, and the sooner the whole of the Regiment is on the alert the better. And I

have again written to our Col. which I purpose to send by an early coach this morning.

'I am with respect D'r Sir, your faithful servant, J Peniston.'

1. Letter is headed *5 AM, Nov 22, 1830*.
2. Written *awoken*, and corrected; recte *was awoken*?
3. MS *up* and *down*, underlined.
4. Recte *has*.

1638 22 Nov. 1830.[1] The Most Noble the Marquis of Lansdowne, Lord Lieut. of the County of Wilts, London.

'My Lord, I know not whether the circumstances which have recently transpired in this neighbourhood may yet have reached your Lordship, but I regret to say they have very riotous tendencies and appear to be spreading themselves but too rapidly.

'In consequence of information I received on Friday evening last of an expected riotous assemblage at Broughton, I felt it my duty in the absence of my Captain Lord Arundell to direct the Salisbury Troop to hold themselves in readiness for immediate service. And informed my Colonel the Marquis of Bath of the course I had pursued. He has been pleased to approve it. This storm however blew over and I wrote to his Lordship last night to apprise him of it but circumstances have since transpired that have induced me again to address. If your Lordship will do me the honor to peruse a copy of it which I send with this, it will explain what has taken place and what I have taken the liberty of recommending, should he think it desirable to order the other Troops of Wiltshire Yeomanry on service. My reasons for troubling your Lordship at this moment arises from an opinion that the Marquis of Bath would not assemble his Regiment without consulting your Lordship as Lord Lieutenant of the County. And if this assemblage should be considered desirable to prevent mischief no time is to be lost. And as I hope to be enabled to forward this so as that it may reach your Lordship this evening it would if it meet your approval enable Lord Bath to be in possession of your Lordship's sentiments by tomorrow's post. I will trust to your Lordship's kindness to excuse the liberty I take in thus addressing you, begging you will be assured that I have no other motive than an earnest wish to do my duty, and if possible to aid in preventing mischief, a service for which I think the Yeomanry are better calculated than in curing it.

'With the highest respect I have the honor to be, my Lord, Your Lordship's faithful and obedient servant, J Peniston, Lieut. Assisting Adjutant.'

1. Letter is headed *Close Salisbury 5 AM, Nov 22d 1830*.

1639 22 Nov. 1830. Lieut. Col. Baker.

'Sir, understanding from your servant that he is sending a parcel to you this evening, I take the opportunity of informing you that we are all in arms here. Riot, confusion and burning are the orders of the day as well as of the night in this once peaceful neighbourhood. From the information I received I felt it my duty to order the Salisbury Troop to be in readiness for immediate service since Friday night last.

This morning a meeting of the county magistrates was held, at which it was determined to request that the Hindon and Salisbury Troops would hold themselves in readiness to act under their orders, anticipating the probability of their services being required to-morrow. Enquiries were made for you which I was unable to answer, but stated my intention of writing to you this evening. I have been in correspondence with the Marquis of Bath, and I have this day written to the Marquis of Lansdowne recommending to the former to call out the Regiment and station them in divisions, so as to cover the whole face of the county, which is more in danger from insurrection than at any period within my knowledge. I recommend the Hindon and Salisbury Troops to be stationed in Salisbury; the Swindon and Marlbro' to be at Marlbro'; the Devizes, the Warminster, the Chippenham, Melksham and Malmsbury Troops to be quartered in their respective towns. By this arrangment I calculate the Marlbro' and Salisbury divisions will cover the S.E. part of Wilts. The latter with the Warminster the S.W., and with the Devizes the centre of the county. The Warminster, Melksham and Chippenham Troops will keep Bradford and Trowbridge in check. The Devizes will be well placed to co-operate with any other part of the county. An easy communication could be kept up with the respective Troops, and the whole might be if necessary concentrated in a very short time at any part of the county. The magistrates of this city and county are at this moment[1] busy in swearing in special constables for the peace of the city and its immediate neighbourhood. Mr H Everett is this afternoon returned from Biddesdon in the neighbourhood I believe of Ludgershall. He gives a frightful account of the proceedings there. I confess I cannot but feel anxious that you should be here at the present time, and hope we shall soon have the pleasure of seeing you.

'I am with sincere respect, dear Sir, your faithful and obed't serv't, J Peniston.

'PS. You will have the kindness to excuse haste. I was called up between 12 and 1 this morning. Up again at four writing till 8, in fact all day. I am now going to the Council House to assist in arranging the special constables.'

1. 3.30 p.m., according to Chambers, vol.1, p.33.

1640   25 Nov. 1830.[1]   Marquis of Bath.

'My Lord, our orders were yesterday so rapid in succession I had not time to close my letter.[2] You will have perceived, my Lord, the arrival of Lieut. Col. Baker, who was kind enough to add a few lines to my dispatch, I being at the time mounted. The Troop under command of L'd Arundell having received directions to proceed without loss of time to West Park, Mr Coote[3] its proprietor having been twice attacked by strong bodies of rioters, but he repelled them most gallantly, severely wounding several and taking 10 prisoners, who have since been committed. Lieut. Col. Baker marched with the Troop, who on their arrival found a strong civil and domestic force, so at to render it unnessary [sic] for the whole of the Troop to remain, but at the request of Mr Coot Lord Arundell left a detachment of 12 men under my command to stay the night. We had a good bivouac but it being the second night this portion of the Troop had been under arms, and their horses having been saddled the whole of the period, the duty has been somewhat severe. I have great pleasure in saying the duty has been met in the most cheerful and spirited manner by the Troop who turned out twice yesterday, each time in line and told off[4] within 7 minutes. Our Troop detachment returned to Quarters this morning at 9 am, making a detour of several villages in our way. Where we found all quiet and the villagers generally expressing great pleasure at our presence. Capt'n Wyndham with the Hindon Troop under the directions of L'd Radnor assisted in bringing in 12 prisoners from the neighbourhood of Alderbury last night, who are committed. The Hindon Troop are this day gone to Hindon and Mere, some factories in the latter place having been threatened. Lord Arundell expects Capt'n Wyndham's return tonight or to-morrow morning. Col. Myers is now here, having been sent by order of the Commander in Chief to ascertain the state of the country, and the disposable force to meet the exigencies of the times. He suggested it is most highly necessary that a constant communication should exist between the several stations in which Troops are placed, and that H'd Quarters sho'd be established from which general orders should emanate. At the suggestion of Col. Myers I send this by express, and shall be obliged by your Lordship's commands and opinion returned by the messenger.

'I am, my Lord, etc. etc. etc., J Peniston.

'I must plead somewhat of fatigue and confusion of ideas for the inaccuracies of this production.'

1. Letter is headed *Head Quarters, Nov. 25 1830, 5 pm.*
2. This letter appears not to have been copied into the letterbook.
3. Eyre Coote Esq, West Park, Rockbourne, near Fordingbridge: P.
4. *Tell off*, used of a troop of men, means to number themselves in succession (OED).

1641 25 Nov. 1830.[1] Mrs Harrington.[2]
'Madam, I am requested by L'd Arundell to beg you will provide a mess dinner for 6 o'clock tomorrow. His Lordship expects that, in addition to three officers of his own troop, there will be 2 of the Hindon Troop, 3 of the Lancers, Col. Myers and Col. Baker, in all ten. The numbers will be[3] of course depend upon the casualities of the services on which we are at present employed. I state for your information that our mess dinners at Devizes have been six shillings exclusive of waiters.

'I am, Madam, very faithfully, your obed't serv't, J Peniston, Lieut. Salisbury W.Y.C.'

1. Letter is headed *De Vaux Place, Thursday evening Nov. 25.*
2. Mary Harrington was landlady of the Black Horse Inn, Winchester Street, Salisbury (P), and her estate was the subject of a trust administered by Peniston. See **850** note 1.
3. Struck through.

1642 4 Dec. 1830. Mr Hagger, Court House, Cannington.
Sends a drawing for seats, the same as in Spetisbury chapel. Aplogizes for delay.

1643 5 Dec. 1830. Messrs Smith and Bayley.
[*Farnborough House*]: Acknowledges a copy of Mr Adams' award, which, 'though above my fears is still considerably below my hopes, for I had flattered myself the difference would have been nearer a thousand than five hundred pounds.' Discusses the account and expenses, believing that nevertheless Mr Morant took the correct course.

'I have been and am at the present moment so much engaged in military duties acting as adjt. to the WYC on service in this county for suppressing this riotous spirit now abroad that I have not time to refer to any particulars of the late enquiry. Should any farther information be required have the kindness to inform me. I hope soon to be at leisure to attend to my own business and that of my employer.'

1644 6 Dec. 1830. Mr Haywood, House of Correction, Devizes.
'Dear Sir, I must hope to be excused for not answering your letter before, but I can scarcely describe to you my multifarious engagements connected with military duties, but thank God we expect to be dismissed today. I have then to arrange the whole of the pay lists etc. etc. for the War Office.' Discusses the cheapest and best way of providing a slate roof for the house of correction.

1645 7 Dec. 1830. Messrs Stevens and Blackmore.
Orders cloth for uniforms, for the Marlborough, Swindon and Salisbury troops.

1646 7 Dec. 1830. C Millett Esq, Hindon, Wilts.
Arranges a meeting with Mr Payne to attend to Lord Calthorpe's accounts.[1]

1. By J M Peniston on his father's behalf.

1647 8 Dec. 1830. Charles Bowles Esq, Shaftesbury (*Shaston*).
The valuation for the Boscombe dilapidations is £113 11s. 9d.

1648 8 Dec. 1830. Rev Mr Fawcett, Whitchurch, Dorset.
Sends valuation of Boscombe dilapidations, and awaits to learn if any opposition is proposed.

1649 8 Dec. 1830. Mr Hagger.
Discusses architectural details for the Cannington work.[1]

1. By J M Peniston on his father's behalf.

1650 8 Dec. 1830. Messrs Hawkes and Moseley, army saddlers, Piccadilly.
Orders items of uniform and equipment for the Swindon troop.

1651 8 Dec. 1830. Mr Quartermaster Large, WYC., Swindon.
Has ordered part of the Swindon troop's wants. If, when the order arrives, the Swindon saddler can match prices and quality, Peniston will apply to the Marquis of Bath to allow the saddler to furnish the remainder.

1652 8 Dec. 1830. Lord Arundell.

'My Lord, I was honored by your Lordship's letter of yesterday, and its enclosure. I have great pleasure in reporting Sergt. Mackrell's progressive improvement. His medical attendants have now I understand great hopes of him, though they will not yet overture to pronounce him out of danger. I shall be truly grateful if it pleases God to spare his life.

'I regret to learn your opinion that all is not yet sound in your neighbourhood, and equally regret the causes.[1] I had hoped that your Lordship's benevolent example would have been followed, even though it had not been dictated by the same motives that operated in your conduct. For the time is now arrived when even policy is called upon to meet the exigency of the claim where humanity is wanting.

'I shall have great pleasure in accepting your Lordship's kind invitation to spend a day at Wardour, and will mention Sunday next for that purpose should it not be inconvenient to you. Your Lordship will be pleased to learn that, in answer to a letter from Col. Baker to Lord Bath, requesting his co-operation with himself and your Lordship in furtherance of my claim to the adjutancy, he answers most satisfactorily and kindly, stating his early attentions[2] of commencing the attack with Lord Lansdowne.

'I am with sincere respect, your Lordship's faithful and devoted servant, J Peniston.

'All seems perfectly quiet here.'

1. Presumably this, and the following comments, refer to the conduct of Lord Arundell's neighbour, John Bennet, M.P., and the battle at Pyt House between rioters and the Hindon Troop on 25 Nov. 1830.
2. Recte, *intentions*?

1653 9 Dec. 1830. Messrs Firman, buttonmakers, 153 Strand, London.

Orders buttons to be sent to Messrs Brown of Marlborough, and to the Swindon troop. Expects to place a further order for the other troops.

1. Wording almost identical to **1654**.

1654 9 Dec. 1830. Messrs Silvers, lacemakers, 25 Bedford Street, Covent Garden, London.

Orders lace to be sent to Messrs Brown of Marlborough, and to the Swindon troop. Expects to place a further order for the other troops.[1]

1. Wording almost identical to **1653**.

1655 11 Dec. 1830. Mr Perry, trumpeter, Devizes Troop WYC.

Asks for copies of all orders issued while Devizes was Lt Col Baker's headquarters, and for details of any new recruits.

1656   11 Dec. 1830.   Capt. Starkie WYC, or officer commanding the Melksham Troop, Melksham.
Requests order of service and return lists signed by the officers.

1657   11 Dec. 1830.   Cor't. Codrington, or officer commanding the Marlborough Troop, WYC, Wroughton or Marlborough (*Marlbro*).
The order of service was incomplete and may be objected to. The quartermaster has not yet sent his book, which is the only one outstanding. Discusses other forms.

1658   11 Dec. 1830.   R Payne Esq, architect, Gillingham, Dorset.
A severe fit of illness has confined him to his room for several days, and he asks to divert their meeting from Hindon to Salisbury. Requests that Payne examine the work at Hindon, especially the plastering.[1]

1. Written by J M Peniston on his father's behalf.

1659   11 Dec. 1830.   Messrs Stevens and Blackmore.
Orders uniforms for the Devizes troop.

1660   11 Dec. 1830.   Messrs Hawkes and Moseley, army saddlers, Piccadilly, London.
Orders uniforms and equipment for the Devizes troop. Draws attention to a weakness in the chacos previously supplied.

1661   [*undated*].   Messrs Silvers, lacemakers, 25 Bedford Street, Covent Garden, London.
Orders lace for the Devizes troop.

1662   11 Dec. 1830.[1]   Messrs Stevens and Blackmore.
Has already ordered lace and buttons for Captain Locke.[2] Any such items already held by them, procured by the desire of Mr Pettit, will be ordered next time, but cannot commit himself to ordering these articles from them in future without the Marquis of Bath's consent.

1. MS *Sat even'g*, undated.
2. Devizes Troop. See **1659**.

1663   11 Dec. 1830.   Lord Arundell, Wardour Castle.
Cannot visit because of indisposition, which he believes is the result of suppressing the gout. Is now suffering from the rupture of a vessel on the chest, but is recovering. Mackrell continues to improve and may be out of danger.

1664 [*undated*]. Messrs Firman, buttonmakers, 153 Strand, London. Orders buttons for the Devizes troop.

1665 12 Dec. 1830. E Berkeley Portman Esq MP, Bryanston House, Blandford.
'Sir, I shall have great pleasure if I can render you any assistance in your very praiseworthy attempt to restore the yeomanry caps in Dorsetshire. In answer to your queries: the expence of outfit of officer and private see inclosed statement. I know not whether government will make you any allowance beyond arms at starting. The allowance afterwards (to us) is £3 per man per annum by half-yearly payments in advance. By an arrangement in our regiment this sum is equally divided between the Col. and Captns. of the Troops. The Col. furnishing the different troops with new cloathing at stated periods and supplying what new appointments may be required from time to time. The Captns. paying from their moiety repairs of arms, appts. etc., a salary to a trumpeter and allowance for a drill serjt., and any other contingency that may present itself. I think I may venture to say these allowances have been found ample for the supply of our wants. When on permanent duty the officers receive the pay of their respective ranks, the non-commissiond officers and privates 7s. a day each to cover all expenses.

'Our staff consists of one Lieut. Col. Commandant the Marquis of Bath; Lieut. Col. Edw'd Baker; Major Benett; and our present Adjt. Mr Pettit being incapacitated by age and infirmity from acting, I have for some years past volunteered his duty for him. Our regiment originally consisted of 10 troops, now 9, but late events will I think restore us to our original number. The strength of the existing troops is rapidly increasing.

'I believe these are the extent of your queries. If you will present any others to me as they may arise, I shall be happy to answer them. I would offer to attend your meeting, but am at present confined by indisposition arising, I believe, from rather strong measures I took in repressing a gouty attack during our last service. Should you go on it will give me great pleasure on a future day to offer you any personal or other assistance in my power. I will take the liberty of suggesting to you it may be desirable to fix the minimum of your standard for horses at 14½ hands; to have at least one young subaltern officer to each troop; to be careful in the selection of your non-commissioned officers; let them be young, active, riding their own horses, and living as nearly together as circumstances will allow. The esprit-de-corps produced by these means may be of the greatest consequence to your future well-being. Experience has taught me the advantages arising from such a combination. If you can find officers I should not be anxious to have very large troops. In the first instance from 30 to 40 men could make a very good troop, and more easily put together than in greater numbers. I will again repeat if any farther advice or assistance should appear necessary do not hesitate to ask it. I shall be pleased to answer.'
'An officer's equipment:

chaco	4. 14. 6
sabre	4. 4. 0
tailor	23. 0. 0 ad libitum
sadlery etc.	18. 0. 0. about
brace of pistols	6. 0. 0. not necessary

'An estimate of the amount of equipment for a private in a yeomanry corps.

regimental jacket with gold lace and buttons complete	3. 3. 0.	very good
grey trowsers	1.10. 0.	
chaco (22s. 10½d.), plume (1s. 9d.), socket (4½d.)	1. 5. 0.	very good
cloak	1.14. 0.	
sword belt (7s.), knot (1s. 6d.)	8. 6.	
cartouche box	5. 6.	
cross belt	4. 6.	
bridle	18. 0.	
halter	5. 0.	
breast plate	2. 6.	
holsters (14s.) flounces (7s.)	1. 1. 0.	
girth and surcingle	7. 6.	
stirrups and leathers	10. 6.	
saddle bag and pad	13. 0.	
crupper	2. 0.	
spurs	3. 0.	
straps (cloak, saddle bag and holsters)	4. 9.	

	12.17. 9.
sword	10. 6.
pistol	14. 6.
	14. 2. 9.

1666 13 Dec. 1830. Lieut Ward, WYC, Englefield Green, Surrey.
Discusses some small mistakes and discrepancies in filling in claim forms. Suggests on balance that the returns should stand as they are, and any balance due to the War Office should be to their benefit at some future period of service. Hopes that Ward is approaching convalescence; Peniston is better, having spent the tedium of his confinement on military accounts. Complains that Potter[1] will not send his book.

1. Probably Daniel Potter, Quartermaster of the Marlborough Troop; Lieut Thomas R. Ward of Englefield Green also belonged to this troop: Chambers, vol.1, p.304.

1667 14 Dec. 1830. Captn Long, Chalcot House, Westbury.
Anxious to receive pay lists in order to send them to the War Office.

1668 14 Dec. 1830. Messrs Hawkes and Co, army saddlers, Piccadilly, London.
Orders uniform and equipment for the Marlborough troops, and reiterates the complaint about faulty chacos.

1669 15 Dec. 1830. Rev Mr Watkins.

'I have been ill since the harassing military duties of the late ... [*illegible*]. The above I hope will be satisfactory to all parties. Mr Burgess may throw off what he pleases for the love of God; he will plead travelling expenses which I do not allow. The plasterer must wait 'till I am able to come to South'ton.'

1670 15 Dec. 1830. George Morant Esq, 2 Upper Brook Street, London.

Discusses at length the outcome of the Farnborough enquiry, and defends the way in which they decided to conduct the affair. Agrees that the work was done in a wasteful and extravagant manner, and believes that he could have employed tradesmen who would have executed it much better for £2,000 less than the amount of Mr Adams' adjudication. Offers to put this assertion to the test by seeking the opinion of three respectable country surveyors. Offers Morant the opportunity to discharge him and entrust the completion of the works to another person. Messrs Bramah have promised to lose no time over the greenhouse apparatus, and the water closets are prepared.

1671 16 Dec. 1830. Mr Haywood, House of Correction, Devizes.

Asks about the roof. Explains that his illness has prevented a visit to Devizes.

1672 16 Dec. 1830. Mr Perry, Devizes Green, Devizes.

Requests urgently details of recruits and appointments, and the half-yearly accounts.[1]

1. Thomas Perry of Devizes Green was a private in the Devizes Troop, to which this letter presumably refers: Chambers, vol.1, p.306.

1673 17 Dec. 1830. Dr Thomas.

Agrees to proposals for roof repairs and colouring the front of a house, but is restricted because he is not the owner. Advises that the bricklayer's observations be regarded with caution, as he had neglected orders.

1674 17 Dec. 1830. Lieut Col Baker.

'I have at last received the last of the returns via Captn Long, the others being in Monday last. The orders of service I also forward. They are not quite regular, but I trust they will pass muster at the War Office. You will I know be pleased to learn that I am much better, but as a measure of prudence and precaution I have not yet ventured out, and starving has been the order of the day. If I long continue the present system I shall undoubtedly again become a light horseman. Dr Fowler has been very kind; he has not allowed a day to pass without calling.

'I believe we are all very quiet. I have heard nothing from our own neighbourhood to induce me to believe otherwise. I had a letter from Mr Portman in the early part of the week stating a meeting was about to be held at his house for the purpose of arranging the formation of a yeomanry corps in Dorsetshire, asking information on sundry points. I understand also Mr Coote is manufacturing a troop in his vicinity, and Mr Brodie is raising a corps bourgeois in Salisbury.'

1675 17 Dec. 1830. Most Noble Col Marquis of Bath, Longleat, Warminster.
Has sent paylist returns and orders of service to Lt Col Baker [**1674**]. Discusses the completion of other returns.

1676 18 Dec. 1830. Charles Millett Esq, Hindon.
Has only just received Payne's reply to a proposed meeting about the Hindon accounts. Submits and discusses tradesmen's accounts.

1677 18 Dec. 1830. Messrs Stewart and Harding, builders, Farnham, Surrey.
Messrs Bramah's men have been refused admission to fit up the heating apparatus in the conservatory at Farnborough House. They are to be given every assistance, since they are acting under Peniston's direction.

1678 18 Dec. 1830. Mr Busby, or person having the care of Farnborough (*Farnbro'*) House, Frimley, Surrey.
Messrs Bramah's men are to be allowed to proceed with their work at the conservatory, and Mr Stewart has been instructed to offer them assistance [**1677**].

1679 18 Dec. 1830. Rt Hon Sir William Freemantle, Stanhope Street, London.
Admits that there have been delays at Clarendon, as reported by Sir Frederick Bathurst, caused partly by illness and absence. Discusses details. Acknowledges flattering observations about the services rendered by the yeomanry, and hopes that a consequence may be the general re-establishment of local forces. Notes that he has served 35 of his 52 years in the service, and has never known so enthusiastic attachment as now prevails.

1680 18 Dec. 1830. Mr A Deltome, Messrs Bramah, Pimlico.
Surprised that his men were refused admission at Farnborough, and has written to the parties involved [**1677-8**]. Takes the liberty of addressing his son William under Mr Deltome's cover.

1681 22 Dec. 1830. Messrs Stevens, Blackmore and Sons.
Orders materials for uniforms, for the Salisbury troop.

1682 22 Dec. 1830. Lieut Col Baker.
Acknowledges a kind note. Has heard from Lord Bath that the high sheriff has ordered the yeomanry to hold themselves in readiness for immediate service in their respective districts. Lord Bath has circulated this order to captains of troops. The Salisbury Troop is ordered to assemble for the purpose of escorting prisoners, or other duties. Lord Arundell accepts an invitation.

1683 20 Dec. 1830.[1] Captain Lord Arundell.
Supplies details of expenditure and uniform of a Wiltshire yeoman, for the information of Lord Arundell's correspondent.[2]

1. MS *Monday evening*, undated.
2. In similar terms to, but more briefly than, the letter to Mr Portman above.

1684 23 Dec. 1830. George Morant Esq, 2 Upper Brook Street, London.
[*Farnborough House*]: Will direct Stewart to proceed in conformity with Morant's wishes. Discusses architectural details.

1685 25 Dec. 1830. Most Noble Marquis of Bath.
Confirms that the troop will assemble the following Monday, although he understands that the commission,[1] having opened on Monday, will adjourn until Thursday. Discusses half-yearly returns.

1. The Commission for the Special Assizes for Wiltshire opened in Salisbury on Monday 27 Dec., and adjourned until Friday 31 Dec. See Chambers, vol.1, pp.94-5.

1686 25 Dec. 1830. Rt Hon Lord Arundell.
Has not received orders from Devizes postponing the assembly until Thursday. Lord Bath has informed him that the Devizes and Marlborough troops will also be on duty. Asks that Lady Arundell be informed that Mr Osmund will give a character reference on Aubrey's behalf.

1687 24 Dec. 1830. [*no addressee stated*].
Reports satisfactory work by Brookman, builder, for the Sarum and Eling Turnpike Trust on the toll house at Totton [*see* **1551**].

1688 26 Dec. 1830. Mr Haywood, House of Correction.
Mr Figes, a most respectable ironmonger, will visit to assist in a valuation.

1689 31 Dec. 1830. Messrs Stevens and Blackmore.
Orders material for uniforms for the Malmesbury troop.

1690 [*undated*[1]]. Captn Earl Bruce; Captns. Lord Andover; Locke; Long; Goddard; Starky; Phipps.
'I am requested by Col the Marquis of Bath to forward you the annexed vote of thanks from the Mayor and Corporation of the Borough of Shaftesbury. His Lordship wishes you to direct its insertion in the orderly book of your troop.

1. It is clear from **1691** that Earl Bruce's copy of this letter was sent on 31 Dec.

1691 31 Dec. 1830. Lieut Ward, Marlborough Troop, WYC.
The troop is dismissed, on the high sheriff's orders, but must hold themsleves in
readiness at the shortest notice. Requests and discusses various returns.[1]

1. MS heading *In Earl Bruce's was written.*

1692 [*undated*]. Capt. Locke.
Discusses extra uniforms, and returns. Locke's troop is allowed to dismiss, on the high
sheriff's order, once the last detachment of prisoners has been brought up.[1]

1. MS headed *In Capt Locke's.*

1693 31 Dec. 1830. Hawkes and Moseley.
Orders uniforms and equipment for the Malmesbury troop.

1694 31 Dec. 1830. Messrs Silvers and Co., lace makers.
Orders lace for the Malmesbury troop.[1]

1. MS note at end of this letter: *The same written to Firman and Co ordering 40 doz of buttons for
the same.*

1695 31 Dec. 1830. Messrs Stevens, Blackmore and Co.
Orders cloth for uniforms, for the Devizes troop.[1]

1. The letters from **1559-1695** are numbered consecutively from 1-137.

INDEX OF PERSONS AND PLACES

Places are in Wiltshire unless otherwise stated. Places elsewhere are cross-referenced by county. All places, if not themselves parishes, are cross-referenced by ancient parish. The sub-heading 'as address' is used under frequently occurring places to distinguish letters which are addressed to but not directly concerned with that place. Homonymous persons are distinguished where possible. Forenames or initials, where not given in the letters, have been supplied from Pigot's directories or other appropriate sources wherever identifications are likely, and enclosed within square brackets if doubtful. Composite company names are cross-referenced under each surname. Apart from introductory page numbers (romans), index references are to letters numbers, not pages.

INDEX OF SUBJECTS

This index includes architectural features; buildings and rooms within them; building materials and equipment; trades and professions; military and religious affairs; conveyances and other travel and postage matters. Some subjects which fall outside these categories, including illnesses, abnormal weather, food and drink, and (selectively) financial and administrative matters, have also been indexed. Principal subjects discussed in the introduction are indexed, by roman page number; all other index references are to letter numbers, not pages.

WILTSHIRE RECORD SOCIETY
(As at December 1995)

President: PROF. C.R. ELRINGTON, F.S.A.
General Editor: DR JOHN CHANDLER
Honorary Treasurer: MICHAEL J. LANSDOWN
Honorary Secretary: JOHN N. D'ARCY

Committee:
MRS J.A. COLE
DR D.A. CROWLEY
S.D. HOBBS
P.M.A. NOKES
I. M. SLOCOMBE
K.H. ROGERS, F.S.A., representing the Wiltshire Archaeological and Natural History Society

---

Honorary Auditor: J.D. FOY
Correspondent for the U.S.A.: CHARLES P. GOULD

PRIVATE MEMBERS

ANDERSON, MR D M, 1 St Margaret's Hill, Bradford on Avon BA15 1DP

APPLEGATE, MISS J M, 55 Holbrook Lane, Trowbridge BA14 0PS

ASAJI, MR K, 1-2-401 gakuen-higahi, Nishi, Kobe, 651-21, Japan

AVERY, MRS S, c/o 4 Shady Bower Close, Salisbury SP1 2RQ

BADENI, COUNTESS, Norton Manor, Norton, Malmesbury SN16 0JN

BAINES, MRS B M, 32 Tybenham Road, Merton Park, London SW19 3LA

BAINES, MR R T, The Woodhouse, 52 St Mary Street, Chippenham SN15 3JW

BALL, MR S T, 19 The Mall, Swindon SN1 4JA

BATHE, MR G, Byeley in Densome, Woodgreen, Fordingbridge, Hants, SP6 2QU

BAYLIFFE, MR B G, 3 Green Street, Brockworth, Gloucester GL3 4LT

BEARD, MRS P S, The Anchorage, Port-e-Vullen, Maughold, Isle of Man

BERRETT, MR A M, 10 Primrose Hill Road, London NW3 3AD

BERRY, MR C, 9 Haven Road, Crackington Haven, Bude, Cornwall EX23 0PD

BLAKE, MR P A, 18 Rosevine Road, London SW20 8RB

BLAKE, MR T N, Glebe Farm, Tilshead, Salisbury SP3 4RZ

BOX, MR S D, 73 Silverdale Road, Earley, Reading RG6 2NF

BRADBY, MR E L, 13 Hansford Square, Combe Down, Bath BA2 5LH

BRAND, DR, P A, 55 Kennington Road, London SE11 6SF

BROOKE-LITTLE, MR J P, College of Arms, Queen Victoria Street, London EC4V 4BT

BRYANT, MRS D, 1 St John's Court, Devizes SN10 1BU

BUCKERIDGE, MR J M, 147 Herrick Road, Loughborough, Leics, LE11 2BS

BURGESS, MR I D, 29 Brackley Avenue, Fair Oak, Eastleigh, Hants, SO50 7FL

BURGESS, MR J M, Tolcarne, Wartha Mill, Porkellis, Helston, Cornwall TR13 0HX

BURNETT-BROWN, MISS J M, Lacock Abbey, Lacock, Chippenham SN15 2LG

CALLEY, SIR HENRY, Overtown House, Wroughton, Swindon SN4 0SH

CARDIGAN, RT HON EARL OF, Savernake Estate Office, Marlborough SN8 1PA

CAREW HUNT, MISS P H, Cowleaze, Edington, Westbury BA13 4PJ

CARR, PROF D R, Dept. of History, 140 Seventh Avenue South, St Petersburg, Florida 33701 USA

CARTER, DR B J, 28 Okus Road, Swindon SN1 4JQ

CAWTHORNE, MRS N, Dawn, 47 London Road, Camberley, Surrey GU15 3UG

CHANDLER, DR J H, Jupe's School, The Street, East Knoyle, Salisbury SP3 6AJ

CHAVE, MR R A, 39 Church Street, Westbury BA13 3BZ

CHURCH, MR T S, Mannering House, Bethersden, Ashford, Kent TN26 3DJ

CHURN, MR R H, 5 Veritys, Hatfield, Herts, AL10 8HH

CLARK, MR G A, Highlands, 51a Brook Drive, Corsham SN13 9AX

CLARK, MRS V, 29 The Green, Marlborough SN8 1AW

COLE, MRS J A, 113 Groundwell Road, Swindon SN1 2NA

COLEMAN, MISS J, 16 Den Road, Bromley BR2 0NH

COLLINS, MR A T, 11 Lemon Grove, Whitehill, Bordon, Hants, GU35 9BD

CONGLETON, LORD, West End Farm, Ebbesbourne Wake, Salisbury SP5 5JW

COOMBES-LEWIS, MR R J, 45 Oakwood Park Road, Southgate, London N14 6QD

CORAM, MRS J E, London House, 51 The Street, Hullavington, Chippenham SN14 6DP

COULSTOCK, MISS P H, 15 Pennington Crescent, West Moors, Ferndown, Dorset BH22 0JH

COVEY, MR R V, Lower Hunts Mill, Wootton Bassett, Swindon SN4 7QL

COWAN, COL M, 24 Lower Street, Harnham, Salisbury SP2 8EY

CRITTALL, MISS E, 3 Freshwell Gardens, Saffron Walden, Essex CB10 1BZ

CROWLEY, DR D A, 2 Manor Court, Greater Lane, Edington, Westbury BA13 4QP

D'ARCY, MR J N, The Old Vicarage, Edington, Westbury

DIBBEN, MR A A, 18 Clare Road, Lewes, East Sussex BN7 1PN

EDE, DR M E, 12 Springfield Place, Lansdown, Bath BA1 5RA

EDWARDS, MR P C, 33 Longcroft Road, Devizes SN10 3AT

ELKINS, MR T W, 42 Brookhouse Road, Cove, Farnborough, Hants, GU14 0BS

ELRINGTON, PROF C R, 34 Lloyd Baker Street, London WC1X 9AB

FASSNIDGE, MR H, 8 St Margaret's Hill, Bradford on Avon BA15 1DP

FAY, MRS M, 29 Denison Rise, Bishopsdown, Salisbury SP1 3EW

FLOWER-ELLIS, DR J G, Swedish University of Agricultural Sciences, PO Box 7072, S-750 07 Uppsala, Sweden

FORBES, MISS K G, Bury House, Codford, Warminster BA12 0NY

FOSTER, MR R E, The New House, St Giles Close, Great Maplestead, Halstead, Essex CO9 2RW

FOY, MR J D, 28 Penn Lea Road, Bath BA1 3RA

FREEMAN, DR J, Inst of Historical Research, Senate House, London WC1E 7HU

FROST, MR B C, Red Tiles, Cadley, Collingbourne Ducis, Marlborough SN8 3EA

FULLER, MRS B, 65 New Park Street, Devizes SN10 1DR

FULLER, MAJOR SIR JOHN, Neston Park, Corsham SN13 9TG

GHEY, MR J G, 18 Bassett Row, Bassett, Southampton SO1 7FS

GIBBS, MRS E, Sheldon Manor, Chippenham SN14 0RG

GODDARD, MRS M J, The Boot, Scholards Lane, Ramsbury, Marlborough SN8 2PL

GOODBODY, MR E A, 12 Clifton Road, Chesham Bois, Amersham, Bucks, HP6 5PU

GOUGH, MISS P M, 39 Whitford Road, Bromsgrove, Worcs, B61 7ED

GOULD, MR C P, 1200 Old Mill Road, San Marino, California, 91108, USA

GOULD, MR L K, 263 Rosemount, Pasadena, California, 91103, USA

GRIFFITHS, MR T J, 29 Saxon Street, Chippenham

GUNSTONE, MR L, 47 St Michaels Road, Bath BA2 1PZ

HALLWORTH, MR F, Northcote, Westbury Road, Bratton, Westbury BA13 4TB

HAMILTON, CAPTAIN R, West Dean, Salisbury SP5 1JL

HARE, DR J N, 7 Owens Road, Winchester, Hants, SO22 6RU

HARTCHER, REV DR G N, St Francis Xavier Seminary, Rostrevor, SA, 5073, Australia

HATCHWELL, MR R C, The Old Rectory, Little Somerford, Chippenham SN15 5JW

HAWKINS, MR M J, 121 High Street, Lewes, East Sussex BN7 1XJ

HAYWARD, MISS J E, Pleasant Cottage, Crockerton, Warminster BA12 8AJ

HELMHOLZ, PROF R W, Law School, 1111 East 60th Street, Chicago, Illinois, 60637, USA

HENLEY, MR R G, 33 West View Crescent, Devizes SN10 5HE

HENLY, MR H R, 99 Moredon Road, Swindon SN2 3JG

HICKMAN, MR M R, 184 Surrenden Road, Brighton BN1 6NN

HILLMAN, MR R B, 18 Carnarvon Close, Chippenham SN14 0PN

HOBBS, MR S D, 63 West End, Westbury BA13 3JQ

HORNBY, MISS E, 41 Silverwood Drive, Laverstock, Salisbury SP1 1SH

HORTON, MR P R G, Hedge End, West Grimstead, Salisbury SP5 3RF

HUGHES, PROF C J, Old House, Tisbury, Salisbury SP3 6PS

HUGHES, MR R G, 60 Hurst Park Road, Twyford, Reading RG10 0EY

HUMPHRIES, MR A G, Rustics, Blacksmith's Lane, Harmston, Lincoln LN5 9SW

INGRAM, DR M J, Brasenose College, Oxford OX1 4AJ

JAMES, MR J F, 3 Sylvan Close, Hordle, Lymington, Hants, SO41 0HJ

JEACOCK, MR D, 16 Church Street, Wootton Bassett, Swindon SN4 7BQ

JELLICOE, RT HON EARL, Tidcombe Manor, Tidcombe, Marlborough SN8 3SL

JOHNSTON, MRS J M, Greystone House, 3 Trowbridge Road, Bradford on Avon BA15 1EE

KAY, MR A H, 15 Napier Crescent, Laverstock, Salisbury SP1 1PJ

KENT, MR T A, Rose Cottage, Isington, Alton, Hants GU34 4PN

KIRBY, MR J L, 209 Covington Way, Streatham, London SW16 3BY

KNEEBONE, MR W J R, 20 Blind Lane, Southwick, Trowbridge BA14 9PG

KOMATSU, PROF Y, Institute of European Economic History, Waseda University, Tokyo, Japan

KUNIKATA, MR K, Dept of Economics, 1-4-12 Kojirakawa-machi, Yamagata-shi 990, Japan

LAMPARD, MRS M L, The School House, Crockerton, Warminster BA12 8AD

LANSDOWN, MR M J, 53 Clarendon Road, Trowbridge BA14 7BS

LAURENCE, MISS A, c/o Arts Faculty, Open University, Milton Keynes MK7 6AA

LAURENCE, MR G F, St Cuthberts, 20 Church Street, Bathford, Bath BA1 7TU

LODGE, MR O R W, Southridge House, Hindon, Salisbury SP3 6ER

LONDON, MISS V C M, 55 Churchill Road, Church Stretton, Salop, SY6 6EP

LONG, MR S H, 12 Goulton Close, Yarm, Stockton on Tees, Cleveland TS15 9RY

LUSH, DR G J, 5 Braeside Court, West Moors, Ferndown, Dorset BH22 0JS

MARSH, REV R, Peterhouse, 128 Ifield Road, West Green, Crawley, West Sussex RH11 7BW

MARSHMAN, MR M J, 13 Regents Place, Bradford on Avon BA15 1ED

MARTIN, MS J, 21 Ashfield Road, Chippenham SN15 1QQ

MATHEWS, MR R, P O Box R72, Royal Exchange, NSW, 2000, Australia

MATTHEWS, CANON W A, Holy Trinity Vicarage, 18a Woolley Street, Bradford on Avon BA15 1ED

MERRYWEATHER, MR A, 60 Trafalgar Road, Cirencester, Glos, GL7 2EL

MOLES, MRS M I, 40 Wyke Road, Trowbridge BA14 7NP

MONTAGUE, MR M D, 15 Ryrie Street, Mosman, NSW, 2088, Australia

MOODY, MR R F, Harptree House, East Harptree, Bristol BS18 6AA

MORIOKA, PROF K, 3-12, 4-chome Sanno, Ota-ku, Tokyo, Japan

MORLAND, MR T E, 47 Shaftesbury Road, Wilton, Salisbury SP2 0DU

MORRIS, MISS B, 9 Cleveland Gardens, Trowbridge BA14 7LX

MORRISON, MRS J, Priory Cottage, Bratton, Westbury

MOULTON, DR A E, The Hall, Bradford on Avon BA15 1AB

NEWBURY, MR C COLES, 6 Leighton Green, Westbury BA13 3PN

NEWMAN, MRS R, Tanglewood, Laverstock Park, Salisbury SP1 1QJ

NOKES, MR P M A, Wards Farm, Ditcheat, Shepton Mallet, Som, BA4 6PR

O'DONNELL, MS S J, c/o Dept. English Local History, Marc Fitch House, 5 Salisbury Road, Leicester LE1 7QR

OGBOURNE, MR J M V, 14 Earnshaw Way, Beaumont Park, Whitley Bay, Tyne and Wear, NE25 9UN

OSBORNE, COL R, Unwins House, 15 Waterbeach Road, Landbeach, Cambridge CB4 4EA

PAFFORD, DR J H P, Hillside, Allington Park, Bridport, Dorset DT6 5DD

PARKER, DR P F, 45 Chitterne Road, Codford St Mary, Warminster BA12 0PG

PATRICK, DR S, The Thatchings, Charlton All Saints, Salisbury SP5 4HQ

PAVELEY, MR A W, 135 Lower Camden, Chislehurst, Kent BR7 5JD

PERRY, MR S H, Priory Cottage, Broad Street, Bampton, Oxon

PLATT, MR A J, Daubeneys, Colerne, Chippenham SN14 8DB

POWELL, MRS N, 4 Verwood Drive, Bitton, Bristol BS15 6JP

RADNOR, EARL OF, Longford Castle, Salisbury SP5 4EF

RAMSAY, MRS R, 15 Chalbury Road, Oxford OX2 6UT

RATHBONE, MR M G, Craigleith, 368 Snarlton Lane, Melksham SN12 7QW

RAYBOULD, MISS F, 20 Radnor Road, Salisbury SP1 3PL

REEVES, DR M E, 38 Norham Road, Oxford OX2 6SQ

ROGERS, MR K H, Silverthorne House, East Town, West Ashton, Trowbridge BA14 6BG

ROOKE, MISS S F, The Old Rectory, Little Langford, Salisbury SP3 4NU

SAWYER, MR L F T, 51 Sandridge Road, Melksham SN12 7BJ

SHEDDAN, MISS J A, 8 Sefton Avenue, Auckland 2, New Zealand

SHELBURNE, EARL OF, Bowood House, Calne SN11 0LZ

SHELDRAKE, MR B, 28 Belgrave Street, Swindon SN1 3HR

SHEWRING, MR P, 73 Woodland Road, Beddau, Pontypridd, Mid-Glamorgan CF38 2SE

SHORE, MR B W, The Breck, 25 Westerham Road, Oxted, Surrey RH8 0EP

SIMS-NEIGHBOUR, MR A K, 2 Hesketh Crescent, Swindon SN3 1RY

SLOCOMBE, MR I M, 11 Belcombe Place, Bradford on Avon BA15 1NA

SOPP, MR G A, 23952 Nomar Street, Woodland Hills, California, 91367, USA

SPAETH, DR D A, 1 University Gardens, University of Glasgow, Glasgow G12 8QQ

STEELE, MRS N D, 4 Shady Bower Close, Salisbury SP1 2RQ

STERRY, MS K, 8 Watercrook Mews, Westlea, Swindon SN5 7AS

STEVENAGE, MR M R, 49 Centre Drive, Epping, Essex CM16 4JF

STEVENS, MISS M L E, 11 Kingshill Close, Malvern, Worcs, WR14 2BP

STEVENSON, MISS J H, Inst of Historical Research, Senate House, London WC1E 7HU

STEWARD, DR H J, Graduate School of Geography, Clark University, 950 Main Street, Worcester, Massachusetts, 01610-1477, USA

STEWART, MISS K P, 6 Beatrice Road, Salisbury SP1 3PN

STRATTON, MR J M, Manor Farm, Stockton, Warminster BA12 0SQ

SYKES, MR B H C, Conock Manor, Devizes SN10 3QQ

SYLVESTER, MR D G H, Almondsbury Field, Tockington Lane, Almondsbury, Bristol BS12 4EB

TAYLOR, DR A J, Rose Cottage, Lincolns Hill, Chiddingfold, Surrey GU8 4UN

TAYLOR, MR C C, 13 West End, Whittlesford, Cambridge CB2 4LR

THOMPSON, MRS A M, 18 Burnaston Road, Hall Green, Birmingham B28 8DJ

THOMPSON, MR & MRS J B, 1 Bedwyn Common, Great Bedwyn, Marlborough SN8 3HZ

THOMSON, MRS S M, Shirley House, High Street, Codford, Warminster BA12 0NB

TIGHE, MR M F, Strath Colin, Pettridge Lane, Mere, Warminster BA12 6DG

TOMLINSON, MRS M, Hill Cottage, Little Easton, Dunmow, Essex CM6 2JE

TSUSHIMA, MRS J, Malmaison, Church Street, Great Bedwyn, Marlborough SN8 3PE

TURNER, MR I D, Warrendene, 222 Nottingham Road, Mansfield, Notts, NG18 4AB

VERNON, MISS T E, Summerhouse Cottage, 86 Coxwell Court, Cirencester, Glos, GL7 2BQ

VINCENT, MS M A, 28 Rochester Road, Lodge Moor, Sheffield S10 4JQ

WAITE, MR R E, 18a Lower Road, Chinnor, Oxford OX9 4DT

WALKER, MR J K, 82 Wainsford Road, Everton, Lymington, Hants, SO41 0UD

WALL, MRS A D, 31 Edith Road, Oxford OX1 4QB

WARNEFORD, MR F E, New Inn Farm, West End Lane, Henfield, West Sussex BN5 9RF

WARREN, MR P, 6 The Meadows, Milford Hill Road, Salisbury SP1 2RT

WEINSTOCK, BARON, Bowden Park, Lacock, Chippenham

WELLER, MR R B, 9a Bower Gardens, Salisbury SP1 2RL

WHORLEY, MR E E, 190 Stockbridge Road, Winchester, Hants, SO22 6RW

WORDSWORTH, MRS G, Quince Cottage, Longbridge Deverill, Warminster BA12 7DS

WRIGHT, MR D P, Haileybury, Hertford SG13 7NU

YOUNG, MRS D L, 25 Staveley Road, Chiswick, London W4 3HU

YOUNGER, MR C, 8 Ailesbury Way, Burbage, Marlborough SN8 3TD

UNITED KINGDOM INSTITUTIONS

Aberystwyth
 National Library of Wales
 University College of Wales
Bath. Reference Library
Birmingham
 Central Library
 University Library
Brighton. University of Sussex Library
Bristol
 Avon Central Library
 University Library
Cambridge. University Library
Chippenham. Technical College
Coventry. University of Warwick Library
Devizes. Wiltshire Archaeological and
 Natural History Society
Dorchester. Dorset County Library
Durham. University Library
Edinburgh
 National Library of Scotland
 University Library
Exeter. University Library

Glasgow. University Library
Gloucester. Bristol and Gloucestershire
 Archaeological Society
Leeds. University Library
Leicester. University Library
Liverpool. University Library
London
 British Library
 College of Arms
 Guildhall Library
 Inner Temple Library
 Institute of Historical Research
 London Library
 Public Record Office
 Royal Historical Society
 Society of Antiquaries
 Society of Genealogists
 University of London Library
Manchester. John Rylands Library
Marlborough. Memorial Library,
 Marlborough College
Norwich. University of East Anglia Library

Nottingham. University Library
Oxford
  Bodleian Library
  Exeter College Library
  New College Library
Reading
  Central Library
  University Library
St Andrews. University Library
Salisbury
  Bourne Valley Historical Society
  Cathedral Library
  Salisbury and South Wilts Museum
Sheffield. University Library
Southampton. University Library

Swansea. University College Library
Swindon
  Royal Commission on the Historical
    Monuments of England
  Thamesdown Borough Council
  Wiltshire Family History Society
Taunton. Somerset Archaeological and
  Natural History Society
Trowbridge
  Wiltshire County Council, Library and
    Museum Service
  Wiltshire Record Office
Wetherby. British Library Document Supply
  Centre
York. University Library

INSTITUTIONS OVERSEAS

AUSTRALIA

Adelaide. Barr Smith Library, Adelaide
  University
Canberra. National Library of Australia
Kensington. Law Library, University of New
  South Wales
Melbourne
  Baillieu Library, University of
    Melbourne
  Victoria State Library
Nedlands. Reid Library, University of
  Western Australia
Sydney. Fisher Library, University of Sydney

CANADA

Halifax, Nova Scotia. Dalhousie University
  Library
London, Ont. D.B. Weldon Library,
  University of Western Ontario
Montreal, Que. Sir George Williams
  University
Ottawa, Ont. Carleton University Library
St John's, Newf. Memorial University of
  Newfoundland Library
Toronto, Ont
  Pontifical Inst of Medieval Studies
  University of Toronto Library
Victoria, B.C. McPherson Library,
  University of Victoria

DENMARK

Copenhagen. Royal Library

EIRE

Dublin. Trinity College Library

GERMANY

Gottingen. University Library

JAPAN

Osaka. Institute of Economic History, Kansai
  University
Sendai. Institute of Economic History,
  Tohoku University

NEW ZEALAND

Wellington. National Library of New
  Zealand

SWEDEN

Uppsala. Royal University Library

UNITED STATES OF AMERICA

Ann Arbor, Mich. Hatcher Library,
  University of Michigan
Athens, Ga. University of Georgia Libraries
Atlanta, Ga. The Robert W Woodruff
  Library, Emory University
Baltimore, Md. George Peabody Library,
  Johns Hopkins University
Binghamton, NY. State University of New
  York
Bloomington, Ind. Indiana University
  Library
Boston, Mass.
  Boston Public Library

New England Historic and Genealogical
    Society
Boulder, Colo. University of Colorado
    Library
Cambridge, Mass.
    Harvard College Library
    Harvard Law School Library
Charlottesville, Va. Alderman Library,
    University of Virginia
Chicago.
    Newberry Library
    University of Chicago Library
Dallas, Texas. Public Library
Davis, Calif. University Library
East Lansing, Mich. Michigan State
    University Library
Eugene, Ore. University of Oregon Library
Evanston, Ill. United Libraries,
    Garrett/Evangelical, Seabury
Fort Wayne, Ind. Allen County Public
    Library
Haverford, Pa. Magill Library, Haverford
    College
Houston, Texas. M.D. Anderson Library,
    University of Houston
Iowa City, Iowa. University of Iowa Libraries
Ithaca, NY. Cornell University Library
Las Cruces, N.M. New Mexico State
    University Library

Los Angeles.
    Public Library
    University Research Library, University
      of California
Minneapolis, Minn. Wilson Library,
    University of Minnesota
New Haven, Conn. Yale University Library
New York.
    Columbia University of the City of New
      York
    Public Library
Notre Dame, Ind. Memorial Library,
    University of Notre Dame
Piscataway, N.J. Rutgers University Libraries
Princeton, N.J. Princeton University
    Libraries
Salt Lake City, Utah. Family History Library
San Marino, Calif. Henry E. Huntington
    Library
Santa Barbara, Calif. University of California
    Library
South Hadley, Mass. Williston Memorial
    Library, Mount Holyoke College
Stanford, Calif. Green Library, Stanford
    University
Urbana, Ill. University of Illinois Library
Washington. The Folger Shakespeare Library
Winston-Salem, N.C. Z. Smith Reynolds
    Library, Wake Forest University

LIST OF PUBLICATIONS

The Wiltshire Record Society was founded in 1937, as the Records Branch of the Wiltshire Archaeological and Natural History Society, to promote the publication of the documentary sources for the history of Wiltshire. The annual subscription is £15 for private and institutional members. In return, a member receives a volume each year. Prospective members should apply to the Hon. Secretary, c/o Wiltshire Record Office, County Hall, Trowbridge, Wilts BA14 8JG. Many more members are needed.

The following volumes have been published. Price to members £15, and to non-members £20, postage extra. Available from the Hon. Treasurer, Mr M.J. Lansdown, 53 Clarendon Road, Trowbridge, Wilts BA14 7BS.

1. *Abstracts of feet of fines relating to Wiltshire for the reigns of Edward I and Edward II*, edited by R.B. Pugh, 1939
2. *Accounts of the parliamentary garrisons of Great Chalfield and Malmesbury, 1645-1646*, edited by J.H.P. Pafford, 1940
3. *Calendar of Antrobus deeds before 1625*, edited by R.B. Pugh, 1947
4. *Wiltshire county records: minutes of proceedings in sessions, 1563 and 1574 to 1592*, edited by H.C. Johnson, 1949
5. *List of Wiltshire boroughs records earlier in date than 1836*, edited by M.G. Rathbone, 1951
6. *The Trowbridge woollen industry as illustrated by the stock books of John and Thomas Clark, 1804-1824*, edited by R.P. Beckinsale, 1951
7. *Guild stewards' book of the borough of Calne, 1561-1688*, edited by A.W. Mabbs, 1953
8. *Andrews' and Dury's map of Wiltshire, 1773: a reduced facsimile*, edited by Elizabeth Crittall, 1952
9. *Surveys of the manors of Philip, earl of Pembroke and Montgomery, 1631-2*, edited by E. Kerridge, 1953
10. *Two sixteenth century taxations lists, 1545 and 1576*, edited by G.D. Ramsay, 1954
11. *Wiltshire quarter sessions and assizes, 1736*, edited by J.P.M. Fowle, 1955
12. *Collectanea*, edited by N.J. Williams, 1956
13. *Progress notes of Warden Woodward for the Wiltshire estates of New College, Oxford, 1659-1675*, edited by R.L. Rickard, 1957
14. *Accounts and surveys of the Wiltshire lands of Adam de Stratton*, edited by M.W. Farr, 1959
15. *Tradesmen in early-Stuart Wiltshire: a miscellany*, edited by N.J. Williams, 1960
16. *Crown pleas of the Wiltshire eyre, 1249*, edited by C.A.F. Meekings, 1961
17. *Wiltshire apprentices and their masters, 1710-1760*, edited by Christabel Dale, 1961
18. *Hemingby's register*, edited by Helena M. Chew, 1963
19. *Documents illustrating the Wiltshire textile trades in the eighteenth century*, edited by Julia de L. Mann, 1964
20. *The diary of Thomas Naish*, edited by Doreen Slatter, 1965
21-2. *The rolls of Highworth hundred, 1275-1287*, 2 parts, edited by Brenda Farr, 1966, 1968
23. *The earl of Hertford's lieutenancy papers, 1603-1612*, edited by W.P.D. Murphy, 1969
24. *Court rolls of the Wiltshire manors of Adam de Stratton*, edited by R.B. Pugh, 1970
25. *Abstracts of Wiltshire inclosure awards and agreements*, edited by R.E. Sandell, 1971
26. *Civil pleas of the Wiltshire eyre, 1249*, edited by M.T. Clanchy, 1971
27. *Wiltshire returns to the bishop's visitation queries, 1783*, edited by Mary Ransome, 1972
28. *Wiltshire extents for debts, Edward I - Elizabeth I*, edited by Angela Conyers, 1973

29. *Abstracts of feet of fines relating to Wiltshire for the reign of Edward III*, edited by C.R. Elrington, 1974
30. *Abstracts of Wiltshire tithe apportionments*, edited by R.E. Sandell, 1975
31. *Poverty in early-Stuart Salisbury*, edited by Paul Slack, 1975
32. *The subscription book of Bishops Tounson and Davenant, 1620-40*, edited by B. Williams, 1977
33. *Wiltshire gaol delivery and trailbaston trials, 1275-1306*, edited by R.B. Pugh, 1978
34. *Lacock abbey charters*, edited by K.H. Rogers, 1979
35. *The cartulary of Bradenstoke priory*, edited by Vera C.M. London, 1979
36. *Wiltshire coroners' bills, 1752-1796*, edited by R.F. Hunnisett, 1981
37. *The justicing notebook of William Hunt, 1744-1749*, edited by Elizabeth Crittall, 1982
38. *Two Elizabethan women: correspondence of Joan and Maria Thynne, 1575-1611*, edited by Alison D. Wall, 1983
39. *The register of John Chandler, dean of Salisbury, 1404-17*, edited by T.C.B. Timmins, 1984
40. *Wiltshire dissenters' meeting house certificates and registrations, 1689-1852*, edited by J.H. Chandler, 1985
41. *Abstracts of feet of fines relating to Wiltshire, 1377-1509*, edited by J.L. Kirby, 1986
42. *The Edington cartulary*, edited by Janet H. Stevenson, 1987
43. *The commonplace book of Sir Edward Bayntun of Bromham*, edited by Jane Freeman, 1988
44. *The diaries of Jeffery Whitaker, schoolmaster of Bratton, 1739-1741*, edited by Marjorie Reeves and Jean Morrison, 1989
45. *The Wiltshire tax list of 1332*, edited by D.A. Crowley, 1989
46. *Calendar of Bradford-on-Avon settlement examinations and removal orders, 1725-98*, edited by Phyllis Hembry, 1990
47. *Early trade directories of Wiltshire*, edited by K.H. Rogers and indexed by J.H. Chandler, 1992
48. *Star chamber suits of John and Thomas Warneford*, edited by F.E. Warneford, 1993
49. *The Hungerford cartulary: a calendar of the earl of Radnor's cartulary of the Hungerford family*, edited by J.L. Kirby, 1994

VOLUMES IN PREPARATION

Wiltshire Society minute books of apprentices, 1819-1922, edited by H.R. Henly; *Wiltshire papist returns and estate enrolments, 1705-87*, edited by J.A. Williams; *Crown pleas of the Wiltshire eyre, 1268*, edited by Brenda Farr; *Salisbury city ledger A*, edited by D.R. Carr; *Wiltshire visitation returns, 1864*, edited by D.A. Crowley and Jane Freeman; *Wiltshire glebe terriers*, edited by S.D. Hobbs and Susan Avery; *The Hungerford cartulary, vol.2: the Hobhouse cartulary*, edited by J.L. Kirby. The volumes will not necessarily appear in this order.

A leaflet giving full details may be obtained from the Hon. Secretary, c/o Wiltshire Record Office, County Hall, Trowbridge, Wilts. BA14 8JG.